"Some seem to think of the Natural [Law ...] sky." Others treat it as an abstract and perhaps antiquated theory about the nature of law that one finds only in dusty old law books—something of merely historical interest. But for Hadley Arkes the Natural Law is not only the glue that holds human life together but also the blood pulsing through its veins. With the penetrating insight of an Aristotle or a James Wilson, the moral fervor of a Daniel Webster, and the wit of a G. K. Chesteron, Arkes demonstrates that laws, policies, and judicial decisions always embody some understanding of moral principle and so are never morally neutral, even if policymakers and judges today often pretend that they are. Neither we nor elected officials nor judges can avoid making moral judgments in matters of policy and law. When it comes to excavating the grounds of those judgments—whether in matters moral, or law and jurisprudence, or the American Founding—there is no better guide for the expedition than the inimitable Hadley Arkes."

—**Paul DeHart,** professor of political science at Texas State University

"A learned and deeply felt appeal for the restoration of traditional moral principles to a place in the working jurisprudence of American law. The author's treatment and condemnation of the practice of abortion provides his most trenchant example of the Natural Law's place in this effort."

—**R. H. Helmholz,** Ruth Wyatt Rosenson Professor of Law at the University of Chicago

"With the grace, wit, and clarity of C. S. Lewis in his influential book *Mere Christianity*, Professor Hadley Arkes has laid out the path of moral reasoning that is inherent in any true understanding of law. Though recognized by the founding generation and the first few that followed, that understanding is largely rejected by the legal academy, lawyers, and judges of our day. Cutting through the esoteric theories and self-refuting nihilism that blind so many of those 'burdened with a legal education,'

Professor Arkes elucidates in the style of Lewis, but with greater rigor and detail, the fundamental axioms and principles of reason from which the moral truths that comprise the Natural Law are drawn. *Mere Natural Law* is an important book for anyone concerned about the role of the courts in shaping the culture."

—**William C. Griesbach,** United States district judge for the
Eastern District of Wisconsin

"Natural Law is today subject to contortions from both its supporters and critics that often render it opaque to jurists and legislators, and unrecognizable to citizens. Its critics contrive ever more sophisticated ways to conceal their positivist nihilism, and many of its supporters concede too much ground to modern philosophical obfuscations, using unnatural language and concepts. Thus the great virtue of Hadley Arkes's *Mere Natural Law* is how it cuts through the self-imposed confusions and reacquaints us with the commonsense first principles of Natural Law. Common sense is ironically uncommon today, and to the extent that nature as the ground of law was something that had to be discovered, *Mere Natural Law* could be said to be a rediscovery. Its lively prose and compelling line of arguments can be compared to a stately clipper ship emerging from a becalming fog with a fresh wind to fill its sails."

—**Steven F. Hayward,** lecturer at Berkeley Law

"This book will start you down the path to recovering the meaning of everything."

—**Larry P. Arnn,** president of Hillsdale College

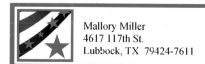

Mallory Miller
4617 117th St.
Lubbock, TX 79424-7611

Praise for

MERE NATURAL LAW

"In a legal environment where the long-standing reference to 'princi-ples of moral law' was dropped from the Model Rules of Professional Conduct in the 1960s, *Mere Natural Law* dares to assert that our legal system is based on certain 'anchoring moral truths' that are accessible to reason and that legal actors ignore at our peril. With wit, wisdom, and vivid examples, Hadley Arkes challenges the pervasive moral relativism of today's mainstream legal thought."

—**Mary Ann Glendon,** Learned Hand Professor of Law emerita at Harvard University and author of *A Nation under Lawyers*

"Hadley Arkes wants the moral judgments that all of us make rou-tinely in everyday life, and that have been central to many great acts of statesmanship, to resume their place in the judgments of courts in matters great and routine. His *Mere Natural Law* is perfectly timed—the Supreme Court's quest for a morally agnostic Constitution may have run its course, and many are seeking a way forward. Like Arkes's previous apologetics for Natural Law, this one is learned, lucid, and emphatic, and will be vigorously debated by veteran adherents and opponents. But it is also addressed to the merely perplexed—down-to-earth, conversational, even chatty. Those who fear Natural Law is too theoretical for our practi-cal world, do not fear to enter here."

—**Christopher DeMuth,** distinguished fellow at the Hudson Institute

"Hadley Arkes offers progressives, positivists, and originalists alike this superb practical text on 'mere Natural Law.' Without the 'anchoring prin-ciples' found in everyday reason and our innate sense of right and wrong, legal judgments express only 'feelings' or crude exertions of power. Arkes demonstrates through examples, logic, and humor how 'mere Natural Law' works as the bedrock of our legal system."

—**Edith Hollan Jones,** judge on the U.S. Court of Appeals for the Fifth Circuit

"With his characteristic learning, wit, and insight, Hadley Arkes encourages us all to become naïve again, to trust the moral judgments available through common sense, reflection, and lived experience. In doing so, he recovers the anchoring truths that are the moral ground of the American political and constitutional order. His is a deeper originalism since it refuses to bury the moral truths that the Founders themselves upheld but could largely afford to take for granted. Arkes brilliantly shows that Natural Law is the furthest thing from a theoretical abstraction. It is, instead, rooted in the logic of morals: 'that the good is higher, more desirable than the bad.' Drawing on the wisdom of Aristotle, Aquinas, Thomas Reid, and Abraham Lincoln, Arkes recovers 'mere Natural Law' and along the way makes a truly impressive case for the 'moral turn in jurisprudence.'"

—**Daniel J. Mahoney,** senior fellow at the Claremont Institute and author of *The Statesman as Thinker*

"*Mere Natural Law* will invite stylistic comparison with C. S. Lewis, pursuant to which, it turns out, Hadley Arkes's well-established literary reputation does not suffer in the least."

—**R. George Wright,** Michael McCormick II Professor of Law at Indiana University

"Does anyone write about Natural Law with greater humanity, philosophical acumen, and humor than Hadley Arkes? No one comes to mind. *Mere Natural Law* deserves to be set alongside C. S. Lewis's *Mere Christianity* in its profundity and gimlet-eyed appreciation of the manifold depredations of our relativistic culture, hankering everywhere after false gods. Arkes is a natural teacher, and his deep appreciation of the Natural Law roots of the American Founding make this book an indispensable Baedeker for our amnesiac times."

—**Roger Kimball,** editor of the *New Criterion*

MERE NATURAL LAW

Mere Natural Law

*Originalism and the Anchoring Truths
of the Constitution*

HADLEY ARKES

REGNERY GATEWAY
Washington, D.C.

The foreword by Michael M. Uhlmann, adapted from his essay "The Need for Natural Law," appears here courtesy of *Claremont Review of Books*, in whose fall 2011 issue it was originally published.

Regnery Gateway™ is a trademark of Salem Communications Holding Corporation
Regnery® is a registered trademark and its colophon is a trademark of Salem Communications Holding Corporation

Cataloging-in-Publication data on file with the Library of Congress
ISBN: 978-1-68451-301-7
eISBN: 978-1-68451-326-0

Published in the United States by
Regnery Gateway, an Imprint of
Regnery Publishing
A Division of Salem Media Group
Washington, D.C.
www.Regnery.com

Manufactured in the United States of America

10 9 8 7 6 5 4 3 2 1

Books are available in quantity for promotional or premium use. For information on discounts and terms, please visit our website: www.Regnery.com.

In memory of Judy Frances Sonn Arkes
March 4, 1941–November 13, 2014
And for our granddaughter, Elena Haya Arkes

Particular intelligent beings may have laws of their own making, but they have some likewise which they have never made. . . . Before laws were made, there were relations of possible justice. To say that there is nothing just or unjust but what is commanded by the positive laws, is the same as saying that before the describing of a circle all the radii were not equal.

—Montesquieu, *The Spirit of the Laws*

For this command which I am giving you today is not too wondrous or remote for you. It is not in the heavens, that you should say, "Who will go up to the heavens to get it for us and tell us of it, that we may do it?" Nor is it across the sea, that you should say, "Who will cross the sea to get it for us and tell us of it, that we may do it?" No, it is something very near to you, in your mouth and in your heart, to do it.

—Deuteronomy 30:11–14

Contents

Michael M. Uhlmann on
Hadley Arkes and the Natural Law

I begin with the observation that lawyers in general are an anti-philosophical race. They like their philosophy in small, easily digestible doses and tend to disdain anything that smacks of metaphysics. This disposition is partly a consequence of their day-to-day experience, which seems to be filled with infinite contingency, relieved only by the certitudes of positive law. But this feature of the legal trade has been exacerbated in every respect by a century or more of legal realism, which has trained lawyers and judges to think of law and morals as two categorically discrete subjects that must forever be kept separate. The good news is that lawyers are good at reasoning by analogy and can be taught to think syllogistically.

Here is the entry point for the kind of reasoning about law that Hadley Arkes has devoted his life to explaining. Better than almost anyone else I know, he makes explicit the syllogistic structure of moral reasoning of a sort that lawyers (and for that matter, everyone else) employ all the time—the skeleton, so to speak, of their thought. Give him a couple of Aristotelian propositions (the law of non-contradiction, for example) and a sprinkling of Kant, and the next thing you know people who have, as it were, never thought about thinking are thinking quite explicitly like the rational moral beings they are and have always been.

The best way to instruct lawyers and judges about higher things, I think, is to stick with specific cases and hypothetical examples drawn from their actual experience. In his voluminous writings over the years, Arkes has repeatedly demonstrated an unusual, indeed brilliant, knack for doing just that. He has done it again in his recent works, where he takes well-worn and familiar topics such as *ex post facto* laws, liberty of contract, and freedom of the press and shows how the positive law in each instance presupposes a certain kind of moral logic that one ignores only at one's peril. Presented with concrete examples of this sort—and the list is almost infinite—lawyers and judges (whether they agree or disagree with particular policy conclusions) will feel a reassuring *terra firma* under their feet; they will, in short, feel at home, which is where you want them to be if you seek to energize their moral imagination. In a word, you cannot expect lawyers and judges to become moral philosophers—God forbid!—but you can teach them how to reason morally and, perhaps, to become confident when doing so.

Beyond real and hypothetical cases, it might be instructive as well to draw out the moral suppositions that lie beneath many maxims of the common law—those dealing with the foundational principles of tort and contract, for example, or more generally the injunction that a party seeking justice must come into court "with clean hands." More general historical inquiry has a role to play here as well: Why not seek to instruct lawyers and judges about the nature of positive-law reasoning before Oliver Wendell Holmes Jr. and the legal realists got hold of legal education? Along this line, the eighteenth and nineteenth centuries open a gold mine of opportunities. It would be instructive, for example, to walk lawyers and judges through parts of Blackstone's or Chancellor Kent's commentaries on the common law.

On constitutional matters, what about taking a look at John Adams's *Defence of the Constitutions of Government of the United States of America* or Justice Joseph Story's treatises? And later, there is Thomas Cooley's *Constitutional Limitations*, which was the treatise par excellence of legal practitioners and judges in the late nineteenth century and the first decades of the twentieth.

Such inquiries would go beyond mere historical interest. The point, rather, would be to show present-day law students, lawyers, and judges how their predecessors reasoned about the positive law and its dependence on moral reasoning. Toward the same end, it might be useful to consider some of the nineteenth-century state supreme court reports, which not only summarized the briefs but excerpted lengthy parts of the oral arguments. Modern lawyers might find it instructive, I think, to see how comfortably the language of law and morals intersected in an earlier era.

There was a time when Natural Law thinking was much closer to the surface of positive law than modern teachers and students of law—and judges as well—typically imagine or are even capable of imagining.

—Adapted from Michael M. Uhlmann, "The Need for Natural Law," *Claremont Review of Books*, fall 2011

Acknowledgments

R eaders and listeners have noticed that my late dear friend
Daniel Robinson has made a series of cameo appearances in
my lectures and essays, as he does in this book. He will not
appear as often as James Wilson, John Marshall, and Abraham
Lincoln; but the brief mentions hardly catch the depth of what I
learned from him—or what we managed to teach each other—over
fifty years, in late nights in Amherst and long walks through
Georgetown. But many other friends have affected my understanding
in ways that will surely be reflected in these pages, even though this
book is not meant to be thick in citations and endnotes. It becomes
harder, in this season of my own life, to recall every strand I've drawn
from dear friends, but I'm sure that these friends, living and gone,
have made their influence in these chapters even when they were not
named: Michael Uhlmann, Harry Jaffa, Michael Novak, Ralph
McInerney, Gerard Bradley, Robert George, J. Budziszewski, John
Noonan, John Finnis, David Forte, Michael Pakaluk, James Stoner,
Paul DeHart, Father James Schall, and Russell Hittinger.

I have not sought to mark off the space for this book by showing
where it may stand within the vineyard containing different strands

of teaching in Natural Law. That exercise contains its own importance and fascination, and I've done a bit of it in other writings. But I've decided to forgo it here for the sake of getting more quickly to the point. I will not be dealing with "theories" of Natural Law. I will be moving rather to those primary truths that any ordinary man needs to grasp before he starts dealing with that array of theories, sure to come at him, as he tries to get on with the business of life.

I am grateful to R. R. (Rusty) Reno, the editor of that remarkable journal *First Things*, for the permission to draw upon three lengthy essays I published in that journal, as I wove them into the arguments in this book: "Recasting Religious Freedom" (June/July 2014), "The Moral Turn," (May 2017), and "On Overruling Roe" (March 2022). *First Things* not only remains the premier journal on religion and politics but also bears the echo of another work on first principles that will always claim a special place in my heart (and my royalties).

This book might not have been written if I had not been encouraged by Thomas Klingenstein to launch a new center that would continue and extend my own teaching on Natural Law. With that offer of backing, I phased out of the Ney Chair at Amherst College, calling a gentle end after fifty years. The sponsorship and support of the project would later shift to my dear former student, Doug Neff, joined by others among my favorite students, most notably Kevin Conway and Michael Petrino. The project was then renamed the James Wilson Institute in honor of one of the premier minds among the American Founders, a man who has not drawn the appreciation and celebration he deserves. His writings have long threaded through my own work, as they do in these pages. It was Doug Neff's genius to discover another one of my former students, Garrett Snedeker, to act as my deputy. Garrett, with his unremitting energy and imagination—and with his outreach to prospective allies of all ages—is the one who has really shaped this institute as a thriving entity. Thanks in large part to his exertions, we are told now that the institute has come to mark a distinct place in the landscape, with a distinct perspective on the law. The project has drawn the interest of judges and lawyers, along with businessmen and citizens who have not been burdened with a legal education. Garrett's late father, William, had also been my student at Amherst, and so the connections to Amherst run deep. No one could have shown more devotion than Garrett or accomplished so much in these ten years. And he has helped sustain the momentum of writing that would bring forth…one more book.

I've been blessed over the years with editors who have been content to leave me, as they say, with "light" and diffident editing. But I've been blessed now to have, in Elizabeth Kantor, an editor who was willing to keep me busy and nearly dazed, shifting from one screen to another as I tried to respond to her many suggestions and track down every missing note, as she would have it, in the most exacting way, including the best translation we could find for Cicero. She was tempted of course to suggest at times changes, in a prose not exactly mine. And at times too rare, perhaps, I gave in. But she was with me at every step, seasoned in her vocation, savvy and sound in her judgments—and enduring in her devotion. And so, not the least point of satisfaction in completing this book was to complete it with Liz.

The last word is for Judy. This is the first book I've written since my beloved wife, Judy, died eight years ago. I dedicated my first book to her exactly fifty years ago, and it has become clearer to me ever since that everything we have done, in our work as well as with our family, has sprung from the marriage. Ours was a story become rarer these days: We married early, in our senior year in college. And so there were two young people wrapping their lives around each other, finishing their schooling, taking the first steps into the world of professional work together. In a way, we were growing up together, finding our footing in the world, and then beginning a family by bringing forth our own two sons, Peter and Jeremy. Our lives were so wound around each other that I remembered scenes and people in Judy's life whom she had forgotten, and she could snatch back in turn the memories that had fled from me. We became the custodians, then, of each other's biographies. And so a large part of one of us would be lost when the other one of us died. She worked for three years in publishing in Chicago, our native ground. She joined the University of Chicago in furnishing support for us while I was doing graduate work in the greatest department of political science in the world. She later gave up a scholarship at the University of Chicago to do a master's degree in teaching (MAT) for the sake of following me to Washington for a fellowship at the Brookings Institution. But a committee came together quickly to give her the same scholarship at George Washington University. We later went on to Amherst, Massachusetts, where we launched the new phase in our lives. Judy would come to nurse two sons and a husband working through his first stumbling days as a professor. Ten years later we were back in Washington. I was at the Woodrow Wilson Center working on a book, and Judy was returning to George Washington University for the job most beautifully suited to her, the director of academic publications. Everything printed under the auspices of the university had to come under her hand. That would encompass the courses offered in the catalogue and the abstracts written for doctoral dissertations. It was said that some Ph.D. candidates could not give a clear account of what their dissertation was about until Judy helped them rewrite their abstracts. And in reviewing the courses proposed for the catalogue, she became a force for the coherence of the offerings. She would raise questions about the cloudy substance of what certain professors were affecting to teach. In one notable case she raised a challenge as to whether there was a sufficient body of writing on the subject to justify a new Ph.D. program. And so, in one of many notes I saved, she decided to take a reluctant leap into the "curricular wars." "Would we not be suggesting," she remarked, "that the somewhat thin body of work in Asian-American lit is analogous to the several centuries and endeavor that span *Beowulf* and the works of Chaucer, Spenser, Shakespeare, Marlowe, Bacon, Webster, Jonson, Milton, Donne, Dryden et al.?" These were all writers she had studied intensively herself. But if the university were open to grand new fields so narrow, she had another suggestion: "Let's open it up really wide and add a field in the works of Viennese expatriates who lived within a mile of the University of Chicago, 1945–55."

One afternoon she stopped in to the office of an academic department and noticed on the shelf a photo of Winston Churchill. She remarked that it was an especially fine photo. The young woman behind the desk, a very recent graduate, reported that other visitors had expressed the same appreciation for the photo, but confessed that she did not know who the figure in the photo was. Judy explained who Winston Churchill was. But then she told the young woman that she, Judy, had been in the Battle of Britain "in utero." Her parents were being interned in England after her father had been interrogated by the Gestapo and they had fled from a Vienna occupied by the Nazis. The young woman, still candid on her innocence of these things, acknowledged that she had never heard of the Battle of Britain. Judy then explained that it had been the moment of high danger when Germany was bombing England. To which the young woman said, "Why were they [the Germans] doing that?!"

In a time when people were keenly aware of why they were doing that, Judy's parents made a perilous trip by boat across the Atlantic (with Judy "in utero"). They landed in New York early in 1941, and Judy was born in the Bronx on March 4. The date was particularly interesting because that was the date on which presidential inaugurations were held until 1937. I remarked to Judy that we knew many people in their eighties (and I am eighty-two as I set down these words now). Did she realize that anyone who shared her birthday and turned eighty on the day she was born was born on the day of Lincoln's first inaugural? I found that charming; she did not.

But it was a reminder: we were both born at the beginning of this massive war, when civilization truly hung in the balance. Had it not been for Churchill—and then for FDR, projecting American power into the world—neither one of us would probably be alive. We had both come into the world when everything was at stake—everything touching the terms of principle on which a people lived, the way we governed ourselves, and the moral codes by which we would try to live our lives together. Judy recalled Lincoln's saying that we were involved in a real "experiment" on whether a free people could govern itself. With no trace of fluffy sentiment, she thought that the answer was now coming in, and that the "experiment" was failing. With the wave of moral relativism flowing on, few people in the circles of the urbane wished to be seen as gauche enough to take seriously that "truth" of the Declaration on the rightful and wrongful governance of human beings. Among the "educated," that "truth" has come to be regarded as no more than a grand sentiment, popular at the time—as Barack Obama observed, the "rejection of absolute truth" is "implicit in the very idea of ordered liberty."[1] And yet that is precisely, and literally, what James Madison and Abraham Lincoln understood the principles asserted by the Declaration of Independence to be: an "absolute" truth about the way human beings deserve to be governed. But if it has become conventional to doubt in this way the moral ground of the American regime—its goodness or rightness—why should it be a surprise that in our own time reverence for the Founders and the regime they made would recede? Nay, more than that: we find a new passion to tear down monuments even to George Washington and Abraham Lincoln, and to regard the government they shaped as irredeemably racist. It is not hyperbole, but a sober report on the real state of things, to say that students in schools public and private are now being taught to hate their country.

Judy and her family found refuge in this country only because those institutions put in place by the Founders were still standing. For people like them, and for those of us who still remember why the English stood fast in the bombing of their cities, this new turn of affairs in our country is not only scary but incomprehensible. And so here we are, trying to find a way of explaining again to a new generation—or even to remind an older generation—of the moral ground on which the American regime was founded. Judy had no beamish optimism, but she knew well the remarkable powers of creation and conversion that spring from our natures. And so, whether the odds were good or bad, she was tenacious enough never to give in—never to stop making the argument.

I am dedicating this book to the memory of my dearest Judy and to the future of our beloved granddaughter, Elena.

Hadley Arkes

August 2022

CHAPTER 1

The Natural Law Challenge

I n story or song, there are few caricatures of the moral skeptic sharper than the figure drawn by Tom Stoppard, with his usual dash, in his play *Jumpers*. The temper of the skeptic was caught in Stoppard's description of the man who is reluctant to concede that the train for Bristol has left Paddington Station unless he himself has been there to see it leave—for after all, that piece of intelligence might be "a malicious report or a collective trick of memory." And even then he would credit that report only under the proviso that "all the observable phenomena associated with the train leaving Paddington could equally be accounted for by Paddington leaving the train."[1] What was a caricature in 1972 quickly became real, for that character walks among us. He votes, he runs for office, and he raises children. He does these things without a second thought, even when he disclaims any grounds for knowing what constitutes the "good" in the men and women he forms through his parenting.

But even the savvy and clever Tom Stoppard, writing in 1972, could not have imagined just how far the passion for relativism would unfurl—to the point where people with advanced degrees forcefully insist that we cannot tell the difference between a male and a female.

1

That difference now is regarded in some quarters as merely "assigned" at birth. And so we are required by the courts to affirm that a man may pronounce himself a woman—or a woman, a man—solely on the strength of an earnest report on his (or her) feelings. The people around them in their offices or businesses will be compelled to respect that judgment, in word as well as deed—or else put themselves and their employers in legal peril.

No one who has spent some time in the academy over the last fifty to seventy years could have failed to see this movement revving up for a long while. But no one who has lived through it all, and paid attention, could be anything less than staggered by the way in which these doctrines of relativism have spread out from the colleges and universities to the broader public, upending many churches and finding aggressive support now in the boardrooms of the leading corporations.

In the face of these trends, even many people who count themselves as "liberals" have had the experience of feeling, as the saying goes, disoriented. As they recoil from this long march to liberation—from what they see as "a bridge too far"—they find themselves reaching longingly back. But reaching back for what? For one thing, they may want to recover the simple willingness to recognize what is there, before our eyes. It's the old "what is" question: What is a chair? What is a man? What is a woman? It may soon kick in on them that they are really asking for a willingness to respect the "truth" about what is before them and the way the world moves—though if they have come through an American college, they may be shy of speaking that loaded word "truth." And if they are concerned with questions of right and wrong, at a time when children are lured away from parents for surgeries, they may realize that they had always taken for granted that, among the things we may really know as truths, some of them must have been moral truths.

But if they find themselves moving along this path, looking for some ground of confidence in speaking seriously of moral truths, then they are on a path that, in one way or another, will lead back to ... the Natural Law. We might be tempted to say that they are engaged in a "recovery" of the Natural Law, except for one cardinal point: the Natural Law has never been missing. It has always been with us. It has been blocked from view at times, in part because it is so deeply planted in our assumptions and language that we may hardly be aware of it. But it has been further blocked from view as people have been more and more drawn to a world of theories bold and novel, and so removed from the language of ordinary folk that only people schooled at the most expensive colleges can understand them. What has been lost, without much notice, is that commonsense understanding of ordinary people, in which the Natural Law finds its ground.

Cicero, reaching for the heights in his *Republic*, gave us the most stirring description and the loftiest hopes for the Natural Law: that "there will not be different laws at Rome and at Athens, or different laws now and in the future, but one eternal and unchangeable law will be valid for all nations and all times."[2]

Those are summoning lines, but for many people they may sound like airy sentiments flying high above, without meaning in our lives as lived every day. But ordinary people, without the least awareness of the terms used by philosophers, will often have the sense of what philosophers mean, without being able, quite yet, to explain it. And so ordinary folk will have the sense that taking an alcoholic drink is not always harmful; that the harm will depend on the circumstances and on matters of degree, of excess or moderation. But the same people are not likely to turn around and say that "genocide, taken in moderation, may be harmless or inoffensive." While the ordinary man is not likely to give us an account of the properties that make these judgments differ, he will recognize that there are certain wrongs whose wrongness will not be effaced by degree or circumstance. Without quite having the vocabulary at hand, the ordinary man or woman will have the sense of harms that are "contingent" on matters of degree or circumstance, as opposed to wrongs that are "categorical"—wrong in all instances, in all times and places, wrongs that can never really be explained away or justified by the claim that they bring benefits to some other people and leave them, indeed, serenely better off.

That same ordinary man is likely to grasp immediately the sense of a practical ranking, or ordering, of "rights" that has been understood since the days of Cicero. And so he is likely to understand, without trouble, the unfolding of this scene:

A plane lands in New York with passengers coming from Britain and other countries. One of the passengers happens to be mugged or assaulted when he reaches the streets of New York. We assume that we don't have to look at his passport before the police dash to his aid. His claim to the protection of the law against a lawless assault would not seem to depend on his citizenship.

But the same man may not take himself over to the City College of New York and expect to be enrolled, especially with that subsidized tuition that the people of New York have generously made available to the citizens of New York—to people who live and work there and have some attachment to the place. In the nineteenth century, it was common to hear "the rights that arise from membership in certain communities" (such as "the right to use the squash courts at Amherst College") as opposed to "rights that arise from nature, rights that will hold for all people in all places."

That is a distinction, I think, that any ordinary person will readily grasp even if he doesn't have a college degree. But when he does grasp it, he may not realize that he touches the core of the gravest argument that has ever arisen in our politics, in our crisis of "the house divided." That was the argument engaged in the classic debates between Abraham Lincoln and Stephen Douglas, an argument that ran to the moral root of the American regime. For the heart of the question was whether those "unalienable rights" mentioned in the Declaration of Independence were rights grounded in *nature* or if they were simply rights that could be created or withdrawn by the authorities in any place—as in the right to use the squash courts. The chief conclusion emerging from the logic of natural rights was that the only rightful government over human beings is based on "the consent of the governed." Or, to put it in the way it was understood in the years of the American Founding, no man is by nature the ruler of other men in the way that men are by nature the rulers of dogs and horses. To think otherwise is, in Jefferson's words, to assume that "the mass of mankind" are "born...with saddles on their backs," while a privileged few are born "booted and spurred, ready to ride them legitimately."[3]

If there was a right of human beings to be governed only with their consent, where would those rights hold? The answer was this: everywhere in the world where human nature was the same and human beings were distinguishable from horses and dogs. Hence the notion of rights grounded in nature, or *natural rights*. As Lincoln would say, the framers had the wit to incorporate, in a revolutionary document, "an abstract truth applicable to all times and places."

For Lincoln, the core of the matter was that "no man is good enough to govern another man, without that other's consent. I say this is the leading principle—the sheet anchor of American republicanism." He went on, in his famous speech at Peoria, to appeal to the Declaration of Independence and remind his listeners

> that according to our ancient faith, the just powers of governments are derived from the consent of the governed. Now the relation of masters and slaves is, PRO TANTO, a total violation of this principle. The master not only governs the slave without his consent; but he governs him by a set of rules altogether different from those

which he prescribes for himself. Allow ALL the governed
an equal voice in the government, and that, and that only
is self government.[4]

But Stephen Douglas, as the leader of the Democratic Party, with
its stronghold in the South, was compelled to defend the legitimacy
of slavery. And in defending slavery, he was compelled to put himself
at odds with that deep principle of human freedom and natural
rights. For Douglas, the rightness or wrongness of slavery was not
grounded in nature, in the enduring things that separate men from
animals. It depended solely on the rights created by the people who
had the power to rule, whether they were monarchs or a ruling
majority in a popular election. Returning for a moment to that ranking of rights I mentioned earlier, the full force of Douglas's position
becomes brutally clear: *All* of our rights would fall into that last category, of rights created or rejected in different enclaves. Our right
not to be enslaved would stand on the same plane as our right to use
the squash courts or to receive a subsidized education. It would be a
right dependent entirely on the sufferance of the ruling majority in
any given time and place, a right that might be expanded or withdrawn as it suits the interests of those who rule.

James Wilson, a Scotch émigré who became one of the premier
figures of the American Founding, saw the same slide into the denial
of natural rights on the part of learned men who were not attentive
enough to what they were saying. He found that telling slip when
William Blackstone, that famous English commentator on the law,
wrote of "civil liberties" as though they were "civil privileges, provided
by society, in lieu of natural liberties." Wilson's warning was that the
term "civil liberties," still with us today, feeds the notion that our rights
"flow from human establishment, and can be traced to no higher
source." He drew then the inference that would later be brought out

in our gravest crisis by Lincoln. Wilson put it with a ringing force that will resonate, I hope, in the pages to come:

> [If we were to credit Blackstone,] the connection between man and his natural rights is intercepted by the institution of civil society.... If this view be a just view of things, then, under civil society, man is not only made *for*, but made *by* the government: he is nothing but what the society frames; he can claim nothing but what the society provides.[5]

But what were those rights "grounded in nature," and how do we know them? On that subject I will have more to say in these pages that follow—though I confess that, on this matter, I have already had more than my share to say. Those compelling questions have been my concern, as the Bible would say, "going out and coming in." I never planned it that way, but my books led there as I followed the train of questions from *The Philosopher in the City* (1981) to *First Things* (1986). I had the chance in those books to give a fuller account of the reasoning that explained the moral truths that, as Lincoln said, are "applicable to all men and all times." Or at least to explain them with as much deftness as I could summon as a young professor in his early forties. I might have offered some slight improvements and illuminations in my book *Natural Rights and the Right to Choose* (2002), and I sought to bring everything together, at the root, with an account contained in one chapter, "The Natural Law—Again, Ever," in *Constitutional Illusions and Anchoring Truths: The Touchstone of the Natural Law* (2010). I mention these previous writings in part to alert readers to the many things I've said about Natural Law that I will not be troubling my readers by repeating in this new book, which has been shaped to a different purpose. Nor will I take the time in this work to offer a historical survey of the theories of Natural Law,

plausible or implausible, that have flirted with the credulity or drawn
the attachment of serious people over the years. One singular advantage is that I will not trouble to review here, for my readers, all the
nonsense spoken on this subject by estimable writers who should
have known better.

Spinoza, for example, identified Natural Law with the laws of nature
that govern the ways of each individual thing. "Fishes are determined
by nature to swim, and the greater to devour the less by sovereign natural right."[6] I have referred to this as the Kern and Hammerstein theory
of Natural Law: "Fish gotta swim / Birds gotta fly."[7] But we can count
on the fact that the fish are not likely to be litigious in defending such
a "right." As the venerable Samuel Pufendorf observed, it was a profound mistake to confuse these two meanings of Natural Law, to con-
found the laws of determinism with "laws" and "rights" in their moral
significance. Over a hundred years earlier (in 1539) Francisco de Vitoria
had rejected a comparable argument to the effect that the stars had a
natural right to shine and the sun to emit light. By that reasoning, as
Vitoria pointed out, we would be doing "an injustice to the sun by closing the blinds" and blocking the light.[8]

For the past ten years I have been making the case anew for
Natural Law to audiences of lawyers, judges, businessmen—and citizens who are not burdened with a degree in law. That has been the
work of my James Wilson Institute on Natural Rights and the
American Founding. It is a curious mark of our time that a defense
of the American Founding and its grounding in Natural Law should
be taken as "conservative" in our politics. The American Revolution
was seen, for good reason, as one of the most liberating events in the
sweep of history. For the Americans at the time did not seek to vindicate merely their rights as Englishmen, but rights that could be
claimed by human beings wherever they were to be found. One
would think that for the left, even today, the Founding should be the

lodestar for any politics that would call itself "progressive." But the difficulty for the left today springs from the fact that the Natural Law supplied for the Founding an anchoring *moral truth* about the rightful and wrongful governance of human beings.

With that governing moral sense, every moment of liberty pointed to the question of whether our freedom was being directed to ends that were good or bad, rightful or wrongful. People of the Founding era seemed commonly alert to the point that every instance of freedom carries the possibility of "license," or the abuse of freedom for wrongful ends. But that stance has put the Natural Law and the American Founding at war with a passion of the progressives in our own day, who seek a liberation unbounded, a liberation not to be stifled or cabined by cramped moral restraints. And the deepest liberation of all has been from any moral or legal restraints on sexuality. With the *Bostock* case in 2020, "transgender" people were anointed as a protected class under the Constitution—that is to say, it would not be legitimate for the law to cast an adverse judgment on those who are transgender any more than it could cast any longer a critical or adverse judgment on anyone on the basis of race. And with that move, the trend of nihilism may have reached its terminus. Unless, of course, the ethic of liberation truly has no bounds, and it will push on further even as it devours itself.

Natural Law, as the bearer of moral truths, must be marked now as anathema to the left in our own time. For liberal jurisprudence today, the "right to abortion" is taken truly as the anchor of personal freedom, far more than the freedoms of religion and speech. That gradual but decisive shift may also explain why the passion to promote abortion and to compel its acceptance in settings both public and private has risen over the willingness to respect religious aversions to abortion. Or to indulge even a liberal tolerance for speech that calls abortion into question. And after all, it stands to reason that the most *natural* question to ask about "natural rights" is this: When do they begin? The elementary answer, tendered by James Wilson, came in his classic lecture on natural rights. Those rights begin *as soon as we begin to be*: "In the contemplation of the law, life begins when the infant is first able to stir in the womb. By the law, life is protected not only from immediate destruction, but from every degree of actual violence, and, in some cases, from every degree of danger."[9]

This commonsense understanding will always mark the Natural Law in our own time as the deep opposition to the advanced agenda of the left. Along with the Catholic Church, the Natural Law may be branded as the enemy of all things just and rightful in our own day, or simply derided with the confidence that it will no longer be taken seriously. The role of enmity to the Natural Law has been taken on directly by the left; the derision has been left to the conservatives.

A deep irony of our time is that the Natural Law has become anathema to the left, and yet it has become every bit as much scorned by "conservative jurisprudence." Over the last forty to fifty years, conservative jurisprudence has been shaped by the recoil from the radical remaking of the Constitution by the Warren and Burger courts—a remaking that was at best slowed by the Rehnquist and Roberts courts that followed. Despite the succession of these Republican chief justices, and a Court amply filled by Republican appointees, the Court managed to unfold, in a long series of cases, a culture of radical "autonomy" detached from any moral principles that could mark the limits of that autonomy. And so the Court moved in a train of decisions from contraception and abortion to same-sex marriage and transgenderism. With each step, conservatives recoiled from the moral substance of what was done, but they took care to say almost nothing about the moral substance of the cases. For they had quite absorbed the notion that moral judgments ran beyond the proper sphere of judges and the boundaries of jurisprudence itself.

My own late friend Justice Antonin Scalia made the focus of his moral passion the fact that the defenders of marriage were deprived of "the peace that comes from a fair defeat."[10]

What he carefully omitted from his dissents was a *substantive defense of marriage* as it had been sustained in the laws: the union of one man and one woman with a commitment made binding in the law. On the moral rightness of that position, I do not think he ever suffered a flicker of doubt. But in his understanding of his office, or his official duty, Justice Scalia did not think that his legal judgment here should be governed by his moral judgment. As he put it in his dissent in *Obergefell v. Hodges*, "It is not of special importance to me what the law says about marriage. It is of overwhelming importance, however, who it is that rules me. Today's decree says that my Ruler, and the Ruler of 320 million Americans coast-to-coast, is a majority of the nine lawyers on the Supreme Court."[11] And this much must be said on his behalf: with a political elite more and more inclined to take the gravest decisions in our law out of the hands of ordinary people and voters, Scalia, joined frequently by Justices Thomas and Alito, offered the main resistance.

In the style of the celebrated Justice Oliver Wendell Holmes, the conservatives seemed to cling to a science of law rendered ever purer as "law" by the fact that it was radically detached from the moral sentiments and convictions of judges. To take the most striking case, the conservative critique did not touch the wrongness of taking innocent human life in abortion. The most damning indictment conservatives could muster was that the Constitution said nothing about the subject of abortion and that judges therefore had no grounds for declaring any right to abortion emanating from the Constitution. Of course, the Constitution itself had said nothing about marriage when the Supreme Court in 1967 struck down the laws that barred interracial marriage and declared a new constitutional right to marriage.

And yet, no conservative luminary declared that decision to have been a flexing of "raw judicial power" by taking the issue of interracial marriage out of the hands of voters in the separate states. No conservative figure asked where "marriage" was found in the text of the Constitution.

For conservatives, the major fault in this long train of decisions remaking the law and our culture was not with the specious moral reasoning employed by the other side but with the fact that moral reasoning had been used at all. The cardinal vice, for the conservatives, was that liberal judges kept moving outside the text of the Constitution to invent new rights with reasoning ever more ingenious. For the deep certainty of the conservatives was that any move beyond the text of the Constitution, any appeal to principles that had existed before the text, was simply a move into the world of arbitrary, subjective judgment, where nothing more could be found than the personal feelings of the judges themselves. There, stripped down, was the story that told all: not just the liberals but even mainline Republican judges had come to regard the claim to know moral truths as a lovely relic, to be treated with bemusement but not taken seriously by the urbane. The more conservative judges, Democrat and Republican, respected the conventional lines about moral truths as a matter of lingering piety. But in their heart of hearts they had lost their conviction that there really were genuine moral truths accessible to reason. Antonin Scalia would insist on the authority of local legislatures, or the ruling majority in any place, to prohibit entertainments that were *contra bonos mores*, for the purpose of encouraging, rather, good morals, shaping the character of the community and its people. But when it came to the content of the legislation, he was convinced that the local community was simply exercising the right to make a "value judgment" on the things it regarded as decent and fitting. "Value judgment," though, is a term that came into play with Nietzsche and Max Weber. The phrase came into use when people found their surety fading when speaking of "moral truths." Things were simply endowed with the standing of "goods" for the people who "valued" them; they could not claim the adherence of people who did not "value" the same things.

Scalia himself did not have the slightest doubt about the existence of enduring moral truths. Still, he was adamantly averse to making an appeal to the moral truths of the Natural Law because, as he said, those truths could not command a "consensus." His friends would gently ask whether he had taken a survey and found a "consensus" on *that* proposition: that the presence of disagreement marked the absence of truth. We would protest that we had never been asked for our own opinion or given a ballot, and if we had been polled, we would have deprived the world of a "consensus" on that point. He was well aware, of course, that even the plainest truths could never command a consensus, for there would always be people who would not see them or who would flatly deny them. But he had seen more than his share of judges, soaring with moral passion, proclaiming grand new rights anchored in neither the laws of reason nor the Constitution. His pessimism was about bringing moral truths *into the law* when they inspired wide disagreement. He was simply not confident that he could expect anyone to share or honor moral truths on the ground of reason alone. That left it to others to try to make the case that there are indeed moral truths accessible to reason—and not merely airy, high-sounding sentiments, but axioms that guide and govern our most practical judgments. No one thinks of testing to see if those principles command a "consensus," for no one ever has reason to wonder whether they are true. But over the years, the conservatives had lost their conviction about any such anchoring truths grounded in the canons of reason, and along with that loss of conviction came a posture of mirthless derision of the Natural Law.

To adapt a line then from Henry James, it might be said that when it comes to the question of Natural Law the liberals and conservatives among our lawyers and judges have come to be merely "chapters in the same book." To restore an understanding of Natural Law in our own time is not, then, to bring forth another version of "conservative jurisprudence." For that jurisprudence of Natural Law would be neither liberal nor conservative. It would be simply anchored in the laws of reason, much as the American Founders understood the principles of law they were drawing upon in shaping the regime and the Constitution they brought forth.

But the case for Natural Law comes to us with a new sharpness following the defection of Justice Neil Gorsuch from the bloc of conservatives in the cases on transgenderism in 2020 (*Bostock v. Clayton County* and *Harris Funeral Homes v. EEOC*). Through the alchemy of "textualism," Justice Gorsuch sought to show that the Civil Rights Act of 1964 banned discrimination based not only on sex but also on "sexual orientation" and on the various ways that people could conceive anew their own "gender identities." Gorsuch was the highly celebrated successor to Justice Antonin Scalia. He was vetted and heralded as an "originalist" and "textualist" by the reigning conservative authorities. He was endorsed and vouched for as representing the best that "conservative jurisprudence" could produce. With *Bostock* the conservative legal movement felt the shock of embarrassment running deep. That embarrassment was hardly attenuated, but rather amplified, when one young professor critical of the decision nevertheless pronounced it a proud moment for conservative jurisprudence: "One can agree on method," he cheerily said, "and still disagree in particular cases. That all of the opinions were textualist is a huge victory in and of itself!" If the justices had decided to take out pen and quill and write the opinions in longhand, that professor could have pronounced this a grand day for penmanship. The professor had given us the latest ringing affirmation of Justice Holmes. For what he celebrated is a style of jurisprudence so serene in its detachment from moral judgment that it is proud to have nothing to say, as a system of jurisprudence, on the things that are right or wrong, just or unjust.

As Justice Alito pointed out in his dissenting opinion to the *Bostock* case, virtually no one in 1964 could have dreamed that the Civil Rights Act banned discrimination against homosexuals or transgender people.[12] But in a piece written before the decision, I had warned that it just would not do for the conservatives to cite the dictionaries on the meaning of sex in 1964. Liberals would be free to play the trump card of Lyman Trumbull. Senator Trumbull of Illinois had steered the Fourteenth Amendment to passage in the Senate, and he had had to assure his colleagues up and down that there was nothing in the Equal Protection Clause that barred interracial marriage. But today we have a fuller, clearer sense of why the Fourteenth Amendment would indeed forbid laws against miscegenation. In the same way, judges could easily argue now that we must bring to the Civil Rights Act a more amplified view of what "sex" has come to mean. The only way to counter that argument is to make the move that conservative judges have been so averse to making: the move beyond the text of the statute to those objective truths, confirmed in nature, on the differences that must ever separate males from females.

The most telling criticism of the decision in *Bostock,* truly penetrating to the core, was the one offered by David Crawford, Michael Hanby, and Margaret Harper McCarthy of the John Paul II Institute in Washington, D.C. They were focused on the companion case to *Bostock*, the case of *Harris Funeral Homes v. EEOC.* They had argued in an elegant brief for the case that the main issue was not the freedom of Anthony Stephens to dress and present himself as a female. For the Court to come down on the side of Stephens was to do nothing less than confirm Stephens's understanding of his gender—and *compel everyone around him to affirm that understanding.* If they did not, they could be accused of sustaining a "hostile work environment" and put themselves and their employers at legal risk.[13]

In the aftermath of the decision, the three writers sharpened their critique, saying that the Court had legislated, in their judgment, a new "metaphysic": the judges had struck at the very root of the law in denying the necessary way that human beings by nature must be constituted. And in doing so, they said, the Court had given us, as C. S. Lewis put it, "the abolition of man"—and woman.[14] For a child moving into adolescence it could raise the most serious confusion on what it is that truly distinguishes his father from his mother. Or himself from his brothers and sisters.

And yet, as conservative critics offered their most serious critique of the decision rendered by Gorsuch and his colleagues in *Harris* and *Bostock*, they typically focused on errors in the reading of precedents and statutes; confusions in the meaning of "discrimination on the basis of" as opposed to "because of"; errors in the true methods of "textualism"; and the confounding of "sex" with "sexual orientation." As conservative critics took stock of the depth of mistakes in this opinion, what was missing was any recognition that this decision struck at the very meaning of "the human person" as we are constituted by nature as males and females. If that anchoring truth about "the human person" were taken as what it is, that would alter the lens with which "conservative jurisprudence" looks out on the landscape of the law. And once it was altered, how many other matters would be seen in a different light through this lens of the Natural Law?

But ignoring this truth about the nature of the human person has not been counted by conservatives as the deepest wrong in this decision. In fact, it has hardly even registered as one of the faults in this judgment as a *legal* judgment. For conservatives, this is not the kind of subject that comes into sight when their minds turn to "law" and "jurisprudence." What was revealed in the conservative reaction to

Bostock—and revealed in a jarring way—is that the appeal to the anchoring moral truths of the law has been, by and large, ruled out by what counts now, in our own day, as "conservative jurisprudence."

For those of us who have been part of a project to recover the teaching of the Natural Law, the shock of this crisis presented a moment of breakthrough: conservative lawyers and judges, caught up short in disbelief, were finally suspecting that something had gone awry. And so I am writing at a time when people seem to be open, as they have rarely been open, to the simple and compelling things that can be said in introducing them anew to the Natural Law. I say introduce them anew, though some are hearing it for the first time. But in the style of Plato's *Meno*, they discover that the truths of Natural Law are simply locked away in their own souls. Once the right questions are posed, the answers spring forth unforced, and the real surprise of the Natural Law is that people have the sense that they have known these things all their lives.

Justice Elena Kagan grandly announced, at her confirmation hearings to the Supreme Court, that "we are all originalists" now.[15] But I must count myself, for the record, as an original originalist. For many years, I had the privilege of teaching on the American Founding, with the sublime task of reading closely the writings of those remarkable men who shaped this American regime and the Constitution. Men such as John Marshall and Alexander Hamilton had a knack of tracing their judgments back to those anchoring truths that were there before the Constitution, truths that would be there even if there were no Constitution. Jonathan Gienapp has made a beguiling case that the sources feeding the Revolution and the Constitution were much wider and deeper than the things relayed into print:

> [W]hile writing constitutions down fueled several trans-
> formations, doing so did not immediately or necessarily

oblige Revolutionary-era Americans to imagine their constitutions as [John Marshall and other jurists] later would.
Nothing about the sheer act of reducing constitutions to
paper either signaled a clear break from prior constitutional assumptions or automatically clarified anything
about those new constitutions' basic attributes. Thus, when
the federal Constitution first appeared, the simple fact that
it was written offered only preliminary guidance....

By unavoidable necessity, the Constitution's meaning
was radically underdetermined. Only experience, medi-
ated by the presence of discussion and adjudication, could
settle it.[16]

As we came to see in our work at the James Wilson Institute, there
were many principles so long understood in the law that James
Wilson and Oliver Ellsworth regarded it as an embarrassment that
they should be written down. The two were averse, for example, to
putting anything in the Constitution on the wrong of *ex post facto*
laws. As Ellsworth said, "There was no lawyer, no civilian who would
not say that *ex post facto* laws were void in themselves. It cannot be
necessary to prohibit them."[17] And Alexander Hamilton and John
Marshall would offer elegant examples, in essays and judicial opinions, of when it was necessary to move beyond the text of the
Constitution. They would reach back to those principles that were
before the text for the sake of explaining how the Constitution bore
sensibly on the cases before them. In *Beyond the Constitution*, I
sought to add to that record the notable example of some judges in
our own time who have seen themselves compelled to move along
the same line.[18] The Founders took for granted those anchoring axioms of the Natural Law as the moral ground of the Constitution they
were seeking to put in place. But those anchoring truths were so

grounded in common sense that, in a trick of the eye, lawyers in our own time had stopped noticing them. I would hold then to an originalism that contains the moral ground of the law as that Founding generation understood it.

I have been drawn then ever more to that common sense of Natural Law as a teaching that is accessible to us ordinary human beings. But more than that: readily—and instantly—understood. It cannot involve things that are esoteric, or the mastery of "theories" that can be unlocked only with advanced degrees. As Aquinas said, the divine law we know through revelation, but the Natural Law is the law that is accessible to human beings as human beings.[19] We might almost say, *natural* to human beings. In the 1970s my late beloved friend Daniel Robinson rediscovered the work of the remarkable Scotsman Thomas Reid, from the late eighteenth and early nineteenth century. Reid's work threads through those wondrous lectures on law that were given by the Scot émigré James Wilson, who was one of the leading minds among the American Founders. Robinson expounded on the "common sense realism" of Thomas Reid in his own luminous lectures at Oxford, which can be seen and heard with delight today on YouTube. The work of Reid and Wilson connects the teaching of the American Founders with those understandings of "common sense," accessible to all functional persons, the things that anyone would have to understand *before* he starts contending with "theories." As Robinson put it, these things involve those matters so foundational that we absorb them often without the least awareness that we know them. They are things, as he said, that we are just "compelled to take for granted every day" as we get on with the business of living.

I thought the time had come, then, to offer a book that opened the question of Natural Law by beginning with those anchoring truths of the Natural Law that are understood by virtually everyone. And I don't mean those fuzzy aspirations often thrown out as a gesture to the high-minded, lines such as: "Try to be generous and understanding," "Try to be kind," or "Try not to be so quick to find fault." All fine sentiments. But ordinary people can grasp principles of common sense that are far more precise, with a practical import. And it can be shown how those truths thread themselves through our cases in law on the gravest subjects. Contrary to the caricatures so often offered, there is nothing the least foggy or cloudy about those anchoring truths. They can be concrete and precise in the way they bear on cases. The moment seemed right, then, for a book that looked plainer and more accessible to readers. Without diminishing in any way the writers who have illuminated the problem for us in the past, I thought the matter could be addressed in a style closer to that of C. S. Lewis. That accomplished teacher of the classics and literature had a touch for conveying deeper truths in a simpler way. Hence the title of this book, mirroring one of his most famous, one that reached a wide circle of readers, beyond the professoriate: *Mere Christianity*. Lewis appealed, in that book and elsewhere, to those principles that are accessible even to children. This trait was picked up by a character in another of Tom Stoppard's plays, *Professional Foul*: Chetwyn, a young professor of classics whose interests center on Aristotle. Chetwyn remarks to a colleague that, even with serious questions of right and wrong, "a good rule, I find, is to try them out on men much less clever than us. I often ask my son what *he* thinks."

"Your son?" asks his colleague.

"Yes," says Chetwyn, "He's eight."

Once or twice in this book, I have made the same move, hoping to touch in the same way those anchoring truths that virtually anyone can grasp at once. And that, once grasped, come with the sense that we have known them all the time.

Mere Natural Law.

CHAPTER 2

The Path of Vignettes

I t must surely be one of the most venerable truths, though still widely unnoticed, that comedians are in the same business as philosophers. Comedians make their living by playing off the shades of logic contained in our language. One thinks here of Groucho Marx, leaving a party late in the evening and stopping on his way to offer a word to the hostess. "I've had," he says, "a lovely evening.... This wasn't it."

And there was Henny Youngman's advice as to how one keeps a marriage going, preserving the romantic spirit for forty years and more. "Twice a week," he said, "we go to an intimate dinner with candlelight and wine. Twice a week we go—she goes on Tuesdays, I go on Thursdays."

At times a joke touches an idea that people take as one of the anchoring principles in their lives. One thinks here of Bertrand Russell's joke about Mrs. Christine Ladd-Franklin, who claimed to be a "solipsist." She earnestly professed to believe that she could not know for sure that there was anyone in the world apart from herself, but at the same time she was deeply disappointed that she could not find other solipsists who might come to a meeting of solipsists.

Now if our ears were properly trained, the following proposition, which has become one of the most widely travelled fallacies in our public discourse, would induce the same urbane giggling: *If there were indeed moral truths that held their truth in all places and times, those truths would be recognized and affirmed in all places. But the very fact that moral questions inspire such widespread disagreement is prima facie evidence that those truths do not exist.*

As the philosophers would point out, this argument reduces to this proposition: The very presence of disagreement on any matter of consequence must mark the absence of truth. But I would be compelled to register my own disagreement with that proposition, and by its very terms that should be enough to establish its falsity. It is what the philosophers would call a self-refuting proposition. It dissolves as soon as it is pierced with the right question. And yet Justice Harry Blackmun was willing to establish a new branch of our jurisprudence on the basis of a proposition of this kind, which collapses on itself in six seconds. In the hands of Blackmun, it read in this way: "When those involved in the respective disciplines of medicine, philosophy, and theology are unable to arrive at any consensus [on the question of when life begins], the judiciary, at this point in the development of man's knowledge, is not in a position to speculate as to the answer."[1]

Blackmun was wrong

The mistake now runs through our political life, across the spectrum. As I have noted, Justice Scalia cited the widespread disagreement on moral matters as the ground for doubting that the Natural Law had any serious truths to propound, and so as a matter of high prudence he set himself against an appeal to Natural Law in the course of deciding cases in our law. He thought that it would be easier to appeal to the historical record, to establish just what principles of right had been planted and accepted in our history. The justice never seemed jarred when his own "historical" account of, say, the right to bear arms would simply elicit a rival and contentious reading of the historical record by his liberal colleagues. The fact that disagreements on the history ran deep did not dislodge him from his confidence that, even in the presence of disagreement, there were truths for his theory of jurisprudence to unearth. Justice Neil Gorsuch, years later, would acknowledge that the tenets of "originalism" and "textualism" favored by Scalia could bring forth answers widely divergent. But for Gorsuch, as for Scalia, those doctrines did not lose their plausibility or truth because they failed to inspire widespread agreement.[2]

The self-refuting proposition above collapses in seconds because it falls into self-contradiction—which is to say it runs afoul of the proposition that anchors the "Laws of Reason," namely the Law of Contradiction, that two contradictory propositions cannot both be true. It would be news to many lawyers and writers these days that the Natural Law finds its ground not in "theories" but in those anchoring or "necessary truths" that cannot be denied without falling into contradiction. A former president of Amherst College once remarked that I had "a theory of Natural Law." I remarked that when people say things of that sort they imply that they are standing back in wholesome detachment watching different "theories" whiz past. And that somehow they are able to make judgments about what fragments of those theories are plausible or implausible, true or false. I then asked, Can you take me back to the standards of judgment you were relying on here in determining the things you could know as true or false? But as he did, he was forced back to those axioms of reason that some of us have taken to be the very ground of the Natural Law. Those remarkable lawyers of the Founding generation—James Wilson, Alexander Hamilton, John Marshall—showed a remarkable gift in tracing their judgments back to those "axioms" or necessary truths that underlay their judgments. And it was precisely in taking the trouble to do that that they gave us some enduring lessons on how to recover the brand of Natural Law that they found so compelling.

My late dear friend Daniel Robinson used to say that he wanted as the epitaph on his gravestone, "He died without a theory." He had written eighteen books, and he ended his days lecturing on Kant at Oxford—he was no stranger to "theories." But he was drawing rather on the "common sense" school of philosophy, expounded so handsomely by Thomas Reid during the Scottish Enlightenment. As Reid appealed to "common sense" he was drawing his readers back to those things so simple, so evident to any functional person, that they are things we must be able to know before we start trafficking in theories. Before we move to the level of bantering with David Hume about the meaning of "causation," the ordinary man knows of his own active powers to cause his own acts to happen. As Robinson remarked, these are the kinds of things that, of necessity, we are compelled to take for granted.[3] What seems to come as surprising news, even to people seasoned in the vocation of law, is that we find the ground of Natural Law not in theories but in those axioms of reason that are readily grasped by ordinary folk. They are axioms so woven in common sense that we may hardly even be aware that we know them. But they come into sight when one poses simple questions to ordinary people. Thomas Reid caught the precise sense of this matter in his classic *Essays on the Active Powers of the Human Mind*: "[T]here are truths, both speculative and moral, which a man left to himself would never discover; yet when they are fairly laid before him, he owns and adopts them, not barely upon the authority of his teacher, but upon their own intrinsic evidence, and perhaps wonders that he could be so blind as to not see them before."[4]

As Daniel Robinson remarked, the man with amnesia may doubt just who he is, but he cannot be in doubt *that* he is.[5] Thomas Reid jestingly twitted Descartes for his curious obtuseness on this matter of personal identity. Descartes professed to escape from the quandary of proving his existence by offering the aphorism *Cogito ergo sum*—I think, therefore I am. But as Reid observed, it was "evident he was in his senses all the time, and never seriously doubted of his existence; for he takes it for granted in this argument, and proves nothing at all": "I am thinking, says he—therefore I am. And is it not as good reasoning to say, I am sleeping—therefore, I am? or, I am doing nothing—therefore, I am? If a body moves, it must exist, no doubt; but, if it is at rest, it must exist likewise."[6]

Who among us could possibly remember the morning we awakened as youngsters and realized that we were, today, the same persons we had been yesterday? That ball and those clothes we thought were ours, those parents we thought were ours, were presumed to be ours today as well. The existence of that personal identity is one of those anchoring points that cannot coherently be denied, and yet in our time it may produce vast, even lethal confusions. The child who awakened that morning, bearing the name he knew, was the same entity, the same being as the one who emerged from the womb on the day he was born, even before he was anointed with the name by which he would be known. Flash back to 2003: An accomplished biologist at Princeton was offering a lecture on the development of the offspring in the human womb, and at one moment she referred to the "pre-embryo." From the audience came the question: Was she suggesting that the "pre-embryo" was of a different kind, a different entity, from the one we would later call an "embryo"? Or did she assume that we were speaking of the same entity, bearing a relation of identity with the one later called an "embryo"? She readily confirmed that she was doing the latter; she did not mean to suggest that there was anything less than a relation of identity connecting these two phases of the life taking form in the womb. And yet if that is true, that small being would bear the same identity with the being who emerges at birth, recognized as a child, and soon endowed with a name. One would think it obvious, then, that anyone who destroyed the "cluster of cells" described as a "pre-embryo" would be removing, in a stroke, that same notable figure we would know later as the anchor on the evening news. The point is primary, rudimentary, and necessary, and yet it seems to have been curiously missed in our own time even by people with advanced degrees.

As we are drawn back persistently to these anchoring and necessary truths, we need to keep returning also to the proverbial Man on the Street, or to any ordinary person in our own time. How do we think he would react if he were asked, "Why is it, in this age of 'animal rights,' that we're still not signing labor contracts with our horses and cows? Or that we are not seeking the 'informed consent' of our dogs before we authorize surgery on them?" I think we would expect him to be baffled by the question, as something it never occurred to him to ponder. For it goes without saying—does it not?—that animals do not have the capacity to reason over the terms of a contract, make promises, and undertake obligations. There is only one kind of creature who is capable of reckoning his interests, making a "commitment," and honoring that commitment even when it no longer accords with his interests or inclinations. That is exactly the cardinal point taught by Aristotle in the *Politics*: there is only one kind of creature suited by nature for political life. Only a creature of reason is able to frame propositions that can command the credence and respect of others and take the standing of "law."

In these natural reactions, our proverbial Man on the Street would have grasped the very point of the "proposition," as Lincoln called it, that "all men are created equal." That was, as Lincoln said, "the father of all moral principle" among us. It does not mean that all human beings are equally intelligent and virtuous, that everyone deserves the same rewards or penalties. It means simply that human beings are not suited by nature to rule over other humans in the way that humans are compelled by nature to rule over horses and cows. Or to put it another way, beings who can give and understand reasons deserve to be ruled by a regime that elicits their consent. Hence the conclusion drawn in the Declaration of Independence: the only rightful government over human beings is one that draws "its just powers from the consent of the governed." That was the central "truth" of the Declaration, and where would that truth hold? Answer: in all times and places where that difference in nature between humans and other animals continues to hold. Hence the notion of "natural rights," rights that are grounded in nature and that remain the same everywhere and always.

In our own time, we find people with degrees in law who profess to find something mysterious about the notion of "natural rights," as though the matter were engulfed by a fog of abstraction. But there is nothing abstract about the matter as it has been understood in our politics and law. Lincoln observed that holding a human being as a slave was the clearest instance of governing a man without his consent. There was nothing abstract about this notion of "natural rights" in the understanding of those slaves who petitioned for their freedom in Massachusetts in 1774:

> We have in common with all other men a natural right to our freedoms without being deprived of them by our fellow men, as we are a freeborn people and have never forfeited this blessing by any compact or agreement whatever.... But we were unjustly dragged by the cruel hand of power from our dearest friends, and some of us stolen from the bosom of our tender parents.... We therefore beg...that we may obtain our natural right, our freedoms, and our children be set at liberty at the year of 21.[7]

To these men in slavery the notions of "nature" and "natural rights" were strikingly clear. And indeed my point here is that the Man on the Street, that ordinary man who thinks it obvious that we cannot make contracts with animals, has essentially grasped the core of the principle here. He understands why humans cannot be rightly ruled, or dealt with, in the way that humans are compelled to deal with animals. And in that way he has grasped what Lincoln understood as the "first principle" that marked the character of the American regime. He may not be able to name that principle, any more than he can name the Law of Contradiction even as he spots people telling him inconsistent stories. But it is part of his very nature to grasp the heart of the matter, and the rest can be drawn out simply by asking the questions that will unlock his understanding.

Anyone having commerce these days with "theories" will find himself dealing most often with generalizations that, at best, may claim to be true most of the time. But as we shall see, the anchoring ground for Natural Law is found in propositions that are not merely true most of the time, but true of necessity, true under all conditions. Thomas Reid warned against the tendency to extract "principles" from "inductive propositions" or generalizations drawn from experiments. For "experience informs us," he said, "only of what is, or has been, not of what must be": "Though it should be found by experience in a thousand cases, that the area of a plane triangle is equal to the rectangle under the altitude and half the base, this would not prove that it must be so in all cases and cannot be otherwise."[8]

If we couldn't grasp the principles that mark the character and properties of a triangle, we would have to measure each time we make use of a triangle and need to calculate the length of lines. It is a well-known truth that married men are likely to be healthier and lead longer lives. But as everyone knows, that is not *necessarily* true—it is not true in all cases. It is not true in the way it must indeed be true that it is wrong to hold people blameworthy or responsible for acts they were powerless to effect.[9] Thomas Reid and also Immanuel Kant, in his own way,[10] recognized that point as the very "first principle" of all moral and legal judgment.

Immanuel Kant put out an apt and pointed warning about writers who sought to deduce principles of moral judgment, and what might be called "a theory of human nature," by generalizing on "the particular natural characteristics of humanity" or the "particular constitution of human nature."[11] And in our own time, one of our most highly published jurists did not exactly enhance his distinction when he suggested that incest and infanticide may be in accord with Natural Law because they seemed to be an intractable part of the human record. They must, he thought, spring from something deeply planted in human nature. This eminent lawyer and judge had fallen precisely into the mistakes that Kant had warned of so tellingly: the tendency to work out a theory of human nature by simply generalizing upon the checkered record of our species. Killing has ever been a part of the human experience, and yet the Natural Law has always condemned the killing of the innocent. It has also made the clearest distinction between the higher and lower parts of human nature. The man who can respect a law beyond his appetites has enduringly been regarded as a far better man than one who recognizes no law beyond his own personal wants. Lincoln touched that sense of the matter when he appealed, in his first inaugural address, to "the better angels in our nature."

That understanding of things "higher or lower" is entailed, as we shall see, by the very logic of moral judgment—that the good is preferable, more desirable, higher, than the bad. That logic has little to do with the conventions or "culture" that prevail in one place or another. Even in a criminal band there is a ranking of "virtues"; those of unbroken loyalty who keep their word or preserve their silence at key moments are marked as the supremely "better" men, to be admired and emulated. But that brings us back again to the only creature who by nature has the capacity to respect a law or a moral code beyond his own appetites. As Aristotle taught us at the very beginning, in the *Politics*, the political order arises *by nature for only one kind of creature*, precisely that same creature who alone can respect a law that may not be of his own making. The defining mark of the *polis* is now, as it was with Aristotle, the presence of "law": the capacity to make decisions that are binding on everyone who comes within the boundaries of the community. And there is only one kind of creature who has the competence to frame the kinds of propositions that can rightly command the respect and assent of other creatures of reason. That sense of human nature is bound up with the rationale or justification of law, as it has been understood ever since there have been laws.

That sense of things has endured even after Justice Holmes led the modern movement to deny the connection between law and a distinctly human nature in the sweep of his contempt for Natural Law. What he also denied, with the same sweep, was that need to offer a justification for those measures imposed as laws.[12]

In the fetching early pages of *Mere Christianity*, C. S. Lewis appealed to the moral understanding that can be grasped, at its root, with the common sense of ordinary people. He conjured up some familiar lines, likely to be heard any day from "children as well as grownups," from "educated people as well as uneducated": "They may say things like this: 'How'd you like if anyone did the same to you?'— 'That's my seat, I was there first'—'Leave him alone, he isn't doing you any harm'—'Why should you shove in first?'—'Give me a bit of your orange, I gave you a bit of mine'—'Come on, you promised.' People say things like that every day...."[13]

"People" may say these things every day, and yet Lewis drew his examples mainly from the things said by, or to, children. And what is intriguing is that the children were not merely complaining about someone else's behavior. They were expressing more than their "likes" and "dislikes." As Lewis noted, the complainant, even as a child, "was appealing to some kind of standard of behavior which he expects the other [person] to know about." As they fall into an argument, "it looks, in fact, very much as if both parties had in mind some kind of Law or Rule of fair play or decent behavior or morality or whatever you want to call it, about which they really agreed." If they didn't have that awareness of a rule lurking somewhere, "they could not quarrel in the human sense of the word. Quarrelling means trying to show that the other man is in the wrong. And there would be no sense in trying to do that unless you and he had some sort of agreement as to what Right and Wrong were."[14] Or: without the silent surety that they had access to certain standards of reason or judgment in arriving at answers that were better or worse.

In their natural reactions, moving along this path, children show their grasp of the same foundational point made in a striking and witty way by that remarkable Scot Thomas Reid. Reid was read closely by the American Founders, and especially by Scottish émigré James Wilson, who managed to quote Reid in one of the earliest decisions of the Supreme Court. Reid was addressing the moral "skeptics" who insisted that moral judgments did not hinge on reasons, that they simply reflected the subjective judgment in any case on what gave people pain or pleasure. Reid put the problem in this way:

> Suppose that, in a case well known to both [my friend and me], my friend says, *Such and such a man did well and worthily; his action is highly approvable.* This speech... expresses my friend's judgment of the man's conduct....

Suppose again, that, in relation to the same case, my
friend says, *The man's conduct gave me a very agreeable
feeling.*

The speech, if approbation be nothing but an agreeable
feeling, must have the very same meaning with the first....
But this cannot be.... The first expresses plainly an opinion
or judgment of the conduct of the man, but says nothing
of the speaker; to wit, that he had such a feeling.[15]

In the second case, the man would be giving us a report on his
own sensation. His remark would convey no judgment of whether
the man was justified and worthy of approval—worthy of being
approved in the same way by other men. If our moral judgments were
reduced merely to personal feelings, then, as Reid wryly observed,
there would be no need for anyone to fulfill the function of a "judge":
"He ought to be called a feeler."[16] As G. E. Moore would point out,
about a hundred years ago, there could be no such thing then as a
"moral argument."[17] For what are we challenging? Whether the person arguing on the other side earnestly has strong feelings in favor
of his position? Two people may have different *feelings* in strongly
approving or condemning abortions. Neither party can refute the
other's claim to his own feelings. But in the meantime, they have
ceased to argue about the rightness or wrongness of abortion itself.

Lewis used the disarming example of children to teach another
lesson that Aristotle had taught in his *Politics*: that it is the distinct
nature of human beings to complain, show outrage or a sense of
grievance on matters high and low, and to be given to *argument*. As
Aristotle said, animals may emit sounds to indicate pleasure or pain,
but the speech of human beings is of a world apart. Human beings
can offer judgments on what is good or bad, just and unjust. They
can reason over matters of right and wrong.[18] Indeed, they have an

incorrigible tendency to give—and resist—reasons as they seek to *justify* their own judgments. What Lewis managed to show, in his homely example, was just how natural these reflexes are, so natural that they find expression even among children in complaints about "fairness."

My argument in this book is that the very ground of Natural Law—and the principles that govern our judgments in Natural Law—can be drawn from precisely the same common sense that is accessible to children and to ordinary folk. In that vein, I would submit that the child, with his natural understanding, grasps something that clearly runs beyond the judgment of Justice Holmes and his epigones.

Take, for example, the case of a seven-year-old who has been set upon by a band of roughnecks in school—he was beaten up and his pocket money stolen. Now what reaction seems more plausible to impute to that seven-year-old:

- That he feels set upon, hurt without warrant—that he has a sense of grievance, a sense of having been wronged? Or,
- That he has the sense that the kids who beat him up must have been right; that their very success in overpowering him must reveal that right was on their side?

My own reading is that the second response is quite implausible. The first response is, and will ever be, the most likely and sensible response. But if that's the case, we assume that the child understands, as part of his natural reactions, this cardinal point in political teaching: that power cannot be the source of its own justification, that the success of some people in overpowering others cannot itself establish the rightness of the act. But we would be saying then that the child would grasp at once the understanding that was put forth with a sharp, eloquent force by Jean-Jacques Rousseau:

> Strength is a physical attribute and I fail to see how any moral sanction can attach to its effects. To yield to the strong is an act of necessity, not of will. At most it is the result of a dictate of prudence. How, then, can it become a duty?... [T]o admit that Might makes Right is to reverse the process of effect and cause. The mighty man who defeats his rival becomes heir to his Right. So soon as we can disobey with impunity, disobedience becomes legitimate. And since the Mightiest is always right, it merely remains for us to become possessed of Might. But what validity can there be in a right which ceases to exist when Might changes hands?...
>
> If I am waylaid by a footpad at the corner of a wood, I am constrained by force to give him my purse. But if I can manage to keep it from him, is it my duty to hand it over? His pistol is also a symbol of Power. It must, then, be admitted that Might does not create Right, and that no man is under an obligation to obey any but the legitimate powers of the State.[19]

Rousseau managed to convey in the most dramatic and compelling way the question that has always attended the presence of political or legal power when it is seen clearly for what it is: The logic of the law is that it binds (*ligare*); it overrides personal choice and private freedom and replaces them with a uniform rule or policy imposed on all. People may be committed through the laws to policies or ends they regard as morally objectionable. And the question raised over the years by the leading writers in political philosophy is just how that state of affairs can be *justified*. How is it that some men, invested with the trappings of authority, may rightly expect to have their edicts treated with the force of law? On what ground do they expect people to obey, to acquiesce in the overriding of their personal interests and the closing down of their freedom to take a different path? But to ask whether this state of affairs can be "justified" is to put the moral question up front. For we are asking: What principle can we cite, what reasons can we give, to show that there is something rightful or just about this law, even when it seems to cut against the interests of some groups or to offend the sentiments of others?

Rousseau alerts us to the fact that from the very beginning of law, with the flexing of legal authority, we find ourselves in a binary situation. There are two options before us: We can insist that the imposing of laws on people is something that immanently calls out for justification (which is to say, an account of its moral rightness or justness). Or we can claim that power is indeed the source of its own justification, that the success of some men in seizing and holding power over other people is the surest sign of the rightness of their rule.

What needs to be understood at the very beginning is that when we reject the notion of brute power as the source of its own justification, when we insist that the exercise of power and the making of laws need to be *justified*, we have made a clear choice for the moral path. We have taken the "moral turn." And that choice, that path, *marks precisely the choice for the Natural Law.* There is no way of prettying up any longer the fact that this moral path was explicitly rejected and ridiculed by Justice Holmes as part of his sweeping rejection of Natural Law.

In his classic essay "The Path of the Law," Holmes famously—or infamously—registered his hope that "every word of moral significance could be banished from the law altogether."[20] When Holmes wrote in that way, he was expressing the voice of the Modern Project in law. He aspired to establish a science of law, purified by the removal of any terms of moral significance. That aspiration began well before Holmes, but Holmes was gifted with the aphorisms and the turns of phrase that linger. In any case, the scholar James Herget observed that "by the last quarter of the nineteenth century, the leading jurists had practically turned all responsibility for questions of morality over to the nonlawyers. Moralists were not interested in law, and lawyers were not interested in morality."[21] As Holmes condensed the matter, "Moral rights if there are any—These are for the philosopher." Not for the lawyer or judge.

This understanding came to be deeply absorbed by lawyers trained in the best schools. Nowhere was it expressed more sharply than in a line of Judge Jon Newman in Connecticut, which Justice Brennan lifted to the plane of a governing axiom in the 1970s in *Maher v. Roe*, a case on the public funding of abortion. As Judge Newman put it, "Abortion and childbirth, when stripped of the sensitive moral arguments surrounding the abortion controversy, are simply two alternative medical methods of dealing with pregnancy...."[22] One might as aptly say that, stripped of the moral differences, a fireplace and arson are just different ways of heating a house. To strip the moral significance from the two acts simply removes any ground for judgment that the acts may be justified or unjustified, rightful or wrongful. And why would one wish to do that in anything called the "administration of justice"?

Holmes could hold more fully to that purging of moral concerns precisely because he rejected, at the root, the very notion of moral truth. "All I mean by truth," he said, "is the path I have to travel." That is to say, something irreducibly personal and subjective. On one occasion Holmes defined truth as "that which I can't help believing"—or, for the ruling majority, the majority that enacts its passions into law, "the can't help believing of a majority." And correspondingly, a universal truth would mean, as he said, "the majority vote of that nation that could lick all others."[23] Holmes must have known that anyone half-literate would not need him to translate his conclusion into terms that used to shock decent people: that by morality he simply meant, as Rousseau saw it so accurately, the Rule of the Strong, or Might Makes Right. As Rousseau was the sharpest in explaining, anyone taking that line has rejected the moral path, the path of giving reasons or justifications for imposing laws on people.

I would throw myself again on the commonsense understanding grasped by the youngster, or by the ordinary man who is set upon unjustly. He is almost never struck with the insight that the thugs who beat him up must have been justified, that their success in mustering power over him must stand as proof that they *deserved* to win and impose their will on him. Virtually any ordinary person not burdened by tutelage in law school would instantly grasp what the overly educated Justice Holmes failed to understand and spent the years of his fame actively denying. That simple recognition may provide the point of entry for this book, and the guide through its pages. For my contention is that the Natural Law does not find its ground in "theories" but in those axioms of understanding that are readily accessible to ordinary people. But more than that, as Daniel Robinson argued, these understandings *precede* the grasp of theories, for they run back to those things we are simply compelled to take for granted as we get on with our lives.[24] And as I have suggested, we may be so accustomed to taking them for granted that we are serenely unaware of them—until that moment when someone poses a simple question and we suddenly become alert to what we have long known.

CHAPTER 3

The Ploughman and the Professor

I n a kind of throwaway line at the very end of his opinion for the
Court in *Gibbons v. Ogden*, that classic case on the Commerce
Clause, Chief Justice John Marshall apologized to his readers for
consuming so much time "in the attempt to demonstrate propositions which may have been thought axioms." In a charming, revealing way, he assumed that all of his literate readers understood that
certain anchoring axioms had to be in place before one could carry
out a demonstration. In a controlled experiment, we would need to
understand the difference between conditions A and non-A, which
is to say that we would have to know the Law of Contradiction. If we
don't grasp that principle, there would be no way to learn it in the
course of an experiment or demonstration. It is the kind of thing we
need to know *before* we can step into a "demonstration."

Part of the charm is that Marshall should worry that this exercise
might have struck his educated readers as "tedious," and yet he
thought it to be quite necessary nevertheless:

It is felt that the tediousness inseparable from the endeav-
our to prove that which is already clear, is imputable to a

39

considerable part of this opinion. But it was unavoidable. The conclusion to which we have come, depends on a chain of principles which it was necessary to preserve unbroken; and, although some of them were thought nearly self evident, the magnitude of the question, the weight of character belonging to those from whose judgment we dissent, and the argument at the bar, demanded that we should assume nothing.[1]

Marshall understood that these foundational cases early in the legal life of the new republic offered occasions for teaching. And what he taught on this occasion has a lingering relevance for the nature of jurisprudence and the vocation of judging. For what Marshall taught here could have been applied to any judgment rendered by an official body with the force of law: that it can never be out of season to take the time to trace one's judgment back to those anchoring truths or axioms on which a judgment ultimately rests. They may not be the points that decide the case at hand, but they are necessary for any judgment that would claim the force of reason.

Marshall was hardly alone among the Founders in his grasp of "axioms" and the logical properties of "propositions." Nowhere was that point confirmed with more elegance and economy than by Alexander Hamilton in the introduction he struck off for *Federalist* no. 31. The subject of that paper was taxation, and in the course of his essay Hamilton worked his way to a judgment that would hardly be different from judgments that might be reached in our own day by those two worthy managers in the Senate, Mitch McConnell and Chuck Schumer. But any disinterested reader, simply looking at the text, would notice at once some strikingly different furnishings of mind. For this is how Hamilton put matters in place:

In disquisitions of every kind there are certain primary truths, or first principles, upon which all subsequent reasonings must depend. These contain an internal evidence which, antecedent to all reflection or combination, command the assent of the mind.... Of this nature are the maxims in geometry that the whole is greater than its parts; that things equal to the same are equal to one another; that two straight lines cannot enclose a space; and that all right angles are equal to each other. Of the same nature are these other maxims in ethics and politics, that there cannot be an effect without a cause; that the means ought to be proportioned to the end; that every power ought to be commensurate with its object; that there ought to be no limitation of a power destined to effect a purpose which is itself incapable of limitation.[2]

Hamilton touched here on the understanding of things we may grasp, as the saying goes, as *per se nota*, or as true in themselves. The clearest example has been that anchoring axiom in the Laws of Reason that "two contradictory propositions both cannot be true." Any attempt to deny that proposition must fall into a contradiction that dissolves in gibberish. And that test of self-contradiction provides the touchstone for anything that offers itself to the world as a "truth," let alone a necessary truth. An earnest undergraduate proclaims his insight that "there is no truth," and the stock response of the philosopher is to ask, "What of that proposition—that there is no truth? Is that itself true?" When we encounter propositions that cannot be denied without falling into contradiction, that is a sign that we are running up against what Kant called an "apodictic" or "necessary" truth. The necessary truth here is that there is indeed "truth."

It may be elusive and cloudy in many domains, but on many matters in this vast world, in all of its fields and crevices, there are truths to be known.

As I remarked earlier, the proverbial Man on the Street may not have on his lips the word "axiom" or the Law of Contradiction, but he must be acutely aware of cases where he has been told things quite at odds with one another; and he certainly knows that he cannot be and not be at the same time. As Bertrand Russell remarked, we know that a tree cannot be a tree and not a tree at the same time, and when we assert something about that tree, we are not giving a report on the state of our mind or merely about what we ourselves perceive or grasp. We are giving, also, an account of the state of things in the real world.[3]

The first principles of the Natural Law may be grasped precisely in this way, by ordinary folk, before the brew of "theories" that entrances the minds of people dabbling in "higher education." Thomas Jefferson caught the sense of the matter quite aptly when he remarked in a letter to Peter Carr in August 1787 that one could "state a moral case to a ploughman and a professor. The former will decide it as well, and often better than the latter, because he has not been led astray by artificial rules."[4] Lawyers these days may not be as apt to see things through the commonsense moral reasoning of the Natural Law because they have been diverted, with their minds truly formed by theories—what Jefferson meant by those "artificial rules." And they don't see that the precepts of Natural Law are readily understood because they are bound up with the things that ordinary people readily know, the things they can grasp, as Hamilton said, as true *per se nota*, as true in themselves.

In my own experience there has been no clearer confirmation of that point, no clearer example of the reasoning of the Natural Law—and no example so readily and instantly understood—as that fragment that Lincoln wrote for himself, when he imagined himself engaged in a conversation with an owner of slaves. He was putting the question of how it could be justified to make a slave of a black man:

> You say A. is white, and B. is black. It is color, then: the lighter having the right to enslave the darker? Take care. By this rule, you are to be slave to the first man you meet, with a fairer skin than your own.
>
> You do not mean *color* exactly?—You mean the whites are *intellectually* the superiors of the blacks, and therefore have the right to enslave them? Take care again. By this rule, you are to be slave to the first man you meet, with an intellect superior to your own.
>
> But, say you, it is a question of interest; and, if you can make it your *interest*, you have the right to enslave another. Very well. And if he can make it his interest, he has the right to enslave you.[5]

The upshot was that there was nothing one could cite to remove black people from the circle of rights-bearing beings that could not be cited to justify the enslavement of whites as well. There was nothing esoteric here. What Lincoln offered was simply a model of principled reasoning. Once again, as Aquinas said, the divine law we know through revelation, but the Natural Law we know through reasoning that is accessible to human beings as human beings—the kind of reasoning that is "natural" to beings with the capacity to enter into arguments. Lincoln's argument could be understood across religious divisions—it could be understood by Presbyterians, Baptists, Catholics, and even atheists. And it could be understood by people who had not been burdened with a college education. That was what

Jefferson meant when he said that the ploughman could be as clear-headed as the professor in reasoning through a serious matter of right and wrong.

For many years, some of us have drawn on precisely the same mode of principled reasoning to show that the task of deliberating seriously about abortion would not involve an appeal to religious "belief." The question may be raised, in the style of Lincoln, in this way: Why is the offspring of *Homo sapiens* in the womb anything less than a human being? It doesn't speak? Neither do deaf mutes. It has yet no arms or legs? Well, other people lose arms or legs without losing their standing as human beings to receive the protections of the law. There is nothing one could cite to disqualify the child in the womb as a human being that would not apply to many people walking around, well outside the womb. Nowhere in this chain of reasoning is there an appeal to faith or revelation. In other words, one doesn't have to be Catholic to understand this argument—and that has been precisely the teaching of the Church, that this is not a matter of "faith" and "belief," but a matter to be weighed with the evidence from embryology and the principled reasoning of the Natural Law.

It has been fashionable, I know, even in conservative quarters, to think the principles of Natural Law must be rather hazy ideals hovering in the sky, sentiments rather than propositions that can be judged true or false. But putting aside the logical problems that afflict that view, we would find, if we looked closely, that there is not the slightest disagreement about the key precepts of the Natural Law. Indeed, they are so woven into our practical judgments *that we may hardly even be aware that we are using them.* For they involve, in J. Budziszewski's memorable line, those things "we can't not know."[6]

But what kinds of things, critical to our law, do ordinary people understand in that way? Well, as I have noted, even ordinary people readily grasp that anchoring axiom of the laws of reason, the Law of Contradiction. They know that they cannot be and not be at the same time. Even people without much formal education will often be quick to catch characters who tell them conflicting stories—and catch on without much awareness that they are grasping an anchoring truth called the Law of Contradiction. But as I've also noted, ordinary people grasp the anchoring "proposition," as Lincoln called it, "the father of all moral principle" in the American people: that no human being is by nature the ruler of other human beings in the way that men are by nature compelled to be the rulers of horses and dogs or in the way that God is by nature the ruler of men.[7] As James Wilson put it in his lectures on jurisprudence, the rule of a superior would be eminently warranted in the case of "Him who is Supreme." But of those sublunary beings somewhere between the angels and the beasts, there can be, he said, "neither superiority nor dependence."[8] The summary line is that "all men are created equal," that creatures of reason may be rightly governed only with the rendering of reasons, in a regime that elicits their consent to the terms on which they are governed. The ordinary man, as I said, grasps the core of the matter when he reacts with puzzlement to the question of why we are not, in this progressive age, signing labor contracts with horses and cows. He recognizes at once—as a matter to be grasped *per se nota*—that it makes no sense to speak of contracts with dogs or horses, for there is only one kind of creature who can understand what it means to make a promise and bear a commitment.

But apart from that anchoring point, I would move to two axioms that thread through our practical judgments in the law at every level, and that may supply the grounds of a large portion of the judgments we need to reach in the most controversial cases in our constitutional law. The first, to which I have alluded already, is the axiom that James

Wilson and Thomas Reid regarded as the first principle of our moral and legal judgment. And again we can approach the problem through a question we could put to that proverbial Man on the Street:

What do we guess he would say if he learned that Jones, accused of a serious crime, was in intensive care and recovering from surgery at the time the crime was committed? Or that Jones was heavily medicated at the time and had no firm control of himself? Or that Jones had not been born when the crime had taken place?

Does anyone doubt that the ordinary man, undistracted by theories, would quickly say that of course Jones could not have been guilty of the crime, that he should not be tried or convicted? That is to say, virtually everyone would back into the proposition that Thomas Reid and Kant, in different ways, took as *the first principle of moral judgment*: that we don't hold people blameworthy or responsible for acts they were powerless to effect. As Kant recognized, it makes sense to cast moral judgments of praise or blame on people only in the domain of freedom, where people have the active power to cause their own acts to happen. As Thomas Reid put it, "To call a person to account, to approve, or disapprove of his conduct, who had no power to do good or ill, is absurd. No axiom of Euclid appears more evident than this."[9]

That axiom forms the ground of the insanity defense, but it also explains the deep wrong in racial discrimination. For the reigning assumption there is a version of "determinism": in this instance, that we are "determined" or controlled in our conduct most critically by race. And so, if we know the race of any person, people may casually assume that they are in a position to draw moral inferences as to whether they are dealing with a good or bad person. We have seen judges writing in that vein about people being punished, in effect, for their race—for conditions they were powerless to control. The then justice Rehnquist observed once about resident aliens, barred from certain privileges before they became citizens, that they would be, in effect, "a minority group, like blacks or Orientals, [bearing an] identifiable...status over which the members are powerless."[10] But that same principle applies in many other situations where people, for various reasons, may not be in full control of themselves. Of course, there may be the most difficult factual questions as to whether Jones was so deeply under medication or hypnosis, or so incapacitated, that he could not have performed that burglary. All of these things are matters quite "contingent" on the circumstances, and maddeningly *variable* in their possibilities. But the decisive point is the one thing in this mix that is never variable, never contingent, never open to question: that if Jones really was powerless to effect the acts in question, he cannot be judged blameworthy and responsible for this wrong. *That principle will never cease to be true under any circumstance.* It will be the one thing remaining stable—and readily grasped—even while everything else may be in doubt.

How many such propositions do we have? More than people seem to realize. From Reid's anchoring first principle one can draw out a skein of implications with practical bearing on the law. I would offer here just one thread that can be drawn out, one whose import for our law may be recognized instantly. John Stuart Mill pointed out that we stop using the language of "like" and "dislike" and start using the language of "right" and "wrong" when we think that "a person ought to be punished in some way...."[11] But the corollary of that proposition is that we should visit punishment *only* on wrongdoers. If we begin by respecting that difference between innocence and guilt, we insist that the evidence for wrongdoing should be tested, in a demanding way, with the canons of reason, rather than extracting a confession by pummeling a suspect or having him run over hot coals. And as we follow that logic further down the line, we draw the inference that people accused of crimes should have access to the evidence and witnesses against them for the sake of rebutting them, and in rebutting them arrive at a verdict that is substantively accurate in distinguishing between innocence and guilt—between those who are deserving or undeserving of punishment. *By this moral logic*, a person does indeed have a right "to be informed of the nature and cause of the accusation; to be confronted with the witnesses against him"—he would have that right in principle *even if it had not been set down in the Sixth Amendment*. If it had not been set down, it is entirely possible that it would have been "discovered" by a judge who was drawing out the implications contained in the logic of the "due process of law"—and he would not have been wrong. But to put it even more sharply, if you follow me here, this right would be implicit in the very logic of the rule of law *even if there were no Constitution.*

Now we are quite aware that juries and judges make mistakes, and they may also be corrupted. We know that justice is not always done even when the rules in place are the right ones. And yet none of that dislodges our conviction that anything that calls itself the rule of law will have to be a system in which people accused of crime, in ordinary criminal trials, have access to the witnesses and evidence brought against them in order to have the chance to rebut them. But to say that is to say that our commitment to these principles is *categorical*, quite independent of whether we think that they produced the right or the wrong result in any particular case before us.

What I've been describing here is a discipline of judgment as simple as it is tight. We begin with things that are grasped *per se nota*, as necessary—as with the principle that we may not hold people blameworthy or responsible for acts they were powerless to effect. With short steps, we draw out the implications that arise simply, and with the same necessary force, from the very logic of law and moral judgment—and we arrive at such things as the right of the accused to see the evidence and witnesses posed against him.

One of my favorite jurists, Justice George Sutherland, worked in this way, with short steps all connected to that axiom of respecting the difference between innocence and guilt. In the classic case of *Patton v. United States* in 1930, the defendants had been accused of bribing a Prohibition agent. But during their trial, one juror, in a panel of twelve, had become ill. A mistrial might have been declared, but the defendants waived their interest in a jury of twelve and accepted a verdict by a jury of eleven. The judgment of that jury ran against the defendants, who soon appealed, claiming that they had been improvident in making their own waiver.

For Sutherland, the correct judgment in this case could be settled through a string of propositions that began with the right of a defendant to enter a plea on his own guilt or innocence. That right could be traced back to that moral logic underlying the law: We are justified in inflicting punishment only on the guilty, and the purpose of a trial is to use the canons of reason in the most strenuous way to test evidence and make accurate distinctions between the innocent and the guilty. But who is obliged to offer evidence that can save an innocent man from being punished unjustly? The answer, coming in a moral voice, is anyone and everyone. That same logic holds as well for the defendant accused of the crime. If there is a right on the part of the accused to plead his innocence, there must also be a right for him to plead guilty. If he does not speak the plain truth, he would become complicit in punishing an innocent person in his place. The right to plead guilty must entail then the right to waive his trial (by making the trial unnecessary). But if there is a right to waive a trial, that right must entail the right to waive a trial by jury. And if there is a right to waive all twelve members of a jury, then it must entail the right to waive just one juror on a panel of twelve. Patton may have guessed wrong in weighing his chances, but as Sutherland showed, the arrangements violated nothing in the Constitution or the principles of law.[12]

When judges work in this way, they take as their craft and their vocation the discipline of finding an anchoring ground of principle for their judgments in one of those axioms or necessary truths. From there, they can proceed, as Sutherland did in this case, by drawing out the implications that arise from those categorical truths. As James Wilson reminds us, any implication drawn accurately from a necessary truth must itself be a necessary truth. Sutherland, as a jurist, would look for that anchoring ground and the principles that could be drawn from those axioms. But nothing in those principles could possibly tell judges the "right price" for a pair of pants, the right number of divisions in breaking up AT&T, or the standards to govern wage-price controls. None of these conclusions arise as implications from the string of underlying first principles. The quick test for identifying principles is the question, "Is it necessarily true that...?" Is it necessarily true that real estate values will improve if Whole Foods moves into the neighborhood? In one case, our friend Judge Janice Rogers Brown had to deal with the question of whether it was the mark of some serious wrongdoing that the Hein Hettinga company was able to market milk at 20 cents less a gallon in Southern California. Was that really enough to constitute a "disorderly market condition" that the law has any justification in barring or even punishing?[13]

Judge Brown took the occasion to look back on the long run of cases, from the New Deal to our own day, that disparaged "economic liberty" as a freedom of lesser rank. That kind of freedom was readily overridden as judges sustained regulations that had at times only a fictive relation to any "good" that the government professed to seek. The *Hein Hettinga* case offered a fine opportunity to look back at the New Deal and the attempt to impose price controls in aid of farmers. In 2006 the U.S. secretary of agriculture put forth a rule that bore on the "producer-handlers" of milk. These handlers drew in milk from the farmers who produced it and then marketed the milk, perhaps in places quite distant from the producer. The new rule seemed to be aimed directly at the Hein Hettinga company. It required a producer-handler who produced over 3 million pounds of fluid milk per month within a certain marketing area to compensate the farmers if the milk went on to be marketed at a price notably higher than the price paid by the handlers to the producers!

Judge Brown brought back a classic case from the New Deal, *Nebbia v. New York*, in which the Court had sustained an outlandish policy of price controls on milk. The state had imposed a price of 9 cents for a quart of milk. Leo Nebbia had the effrontery to offer two quarts of milk for 18 cents, plus a loaf of bread![14] In the case of Hein Hettinga, Judge Brown brought back the common sense once grasped readily by judges experienced in the world: that there was no principle that could tell us the proper price in nature for a quart of milk. But the case also revealed, to Brown, a less than lovely truth about our politics: Controls of this sort are not easily challenged and displaced through the democratic process because the interests gathered around the business of farming will tend to be much more influential in local legislatures than the random discomforts of the public. Brown was moved to cite the irascible H. L. Mencken: "Government is a broker in pillage, and every election is a sort of advance auction sale of stolen goods." And with characteristic flair, she pronounced her own, muted anathema: "The Hettingas' collision with the [Milk Regulatory Act of 2005] reveals an ugly truth: America's cowboy capitalism was long ago disarmed by a democratic process increasingly dominated by powerful groups with economic interests antithetical to competitors and consumers. And the courts, from which the victims of burdensome regulation sought protection, have been negotiating the terms of surrender since the 1930s."[15]

Judge Brown was going back to the kind of elementary or foundational reasoning that Justice Sutherland had drawn on in a compelling way when he struck down the law for minimum wages for women in the classic *Adkins* case in 1923.[16] That case has been roundly condemned along with *Lochner v. New York*.[17] It was taken as an example of conservative judges defending cold natural rights against the earnest effort of liberal majorities to experiment in the cause of "social justice." But that fashionable interpretation has preserved a comfortable abstraction, quite detached from the persons suffering real injuries in these cases. What has gone unseen for years in the *Adkins* case is that Sutherland was going to the rescue of Ms. Willie Lyons, who was operating an elevator in the Congress Hotel in Washington, D.C. Ms. Lyons appreciated her job and wanted to keep it. She was earning $35 a month plus two meals a day. It was the best job, she said, that she was able to find, and her employers were quite willing to keep her in that job. But under the new laws, they could employ a woman in that job only for a wage of $72.50 per month. And yet the laws that sought to cast protections over women in this way cast no such protections over men. Men were free to take jobs at the going market rate, which turned out to be . . . $35 a month and two meals per day. In other words, a law passed out of tenderness for the protection of women would now work systematically to replace women with men.

My late friend Justice Scalia came to accept the consensus that took hold even among the conservative judges as they made their peace with the vast alterations of the law that came with the New Deal. And so, while he thought that the minimum wage was, as he said, a crazy idea, he found nothing unconstitutional in it. And yet with reasoning as primary—and as compelling—as the reasoning I've marked off here, Justice Sutherland made the powerful case that schemes of wage-price controls—and, by implication, rent controls—were indeed unconstitutional. He offered no judgments on whether these policies were likely to be salutary or destructive. He did not argue about whether the minimum wage would cut out jobs at the entry level. His argument simply showed what was wrong *in principle* with wage-price controls, even if one claimed on occasion that they happened to "work."

One way or another these policies would seriously abridge personal freedom—they were based on mere theories that were deeply untenable, propositions that simply could not be true of necessity. From the fact that a person is a woman, we have no way of determining what income she would need to preserve her morality and avoid falling into prostitution. We do not know whether she is a widow or a single mother trying to support a family; whether she is a teenager trying to earn some spending money and get experience in a job or whether she is an heiress who does not need the money. And from the fact that a man falls into the class of an *employer*, whether in a small family business or a corporation, we have no basis for saying that he is capable of paying any wage stipulated by central authorities for any job. As Sutherland put it: "The law is not confined to the great and powerful employers but embraces those whose bargaining power may be as weak as that of the employee. It takes no account of periods of stress and business depression, of crippling losses, which may leave the employer himself without adequate means of livelihood."[18]

Nor should anyone leap to the conclusion that no menial job, offering experience and spending money, should be offered by an employer unless he can pay enough to sustain a whole family. In the case typically made for the minimum wage, the employer is cast as a skinflint or exploiter who could deliver any of his workers from financial straits if he would only summon compassion enough. But as Sutherland put it, "Certainly the employer by paying a fair equivalent for the service rendered, though not sufficient to support the employee, has neither caused nor contributed to her poverty. On the contrary, to the extent of what he pays he has relieved it."[19]

But on that central claim for the law, on the matter of guarding the morality of the working woman, Sutherland observed that "the relation between earnings and morals is not capable of standardization. It cannot be shown that well-paid women safeguard their morals more carefully than those who are poorly paid. Morality rests upon other considerations than wages."

Here Sutherland was making the same point that would be decisive in the ruling made two decades later by Justice Jimmy Byrnes and his colleagues in *Edwards v. California* (1941). In that case California had sought to bar the migration of indigent persons into the state during the Depression. Byrnes remarked that "poverty and immorality are not synonymous." In his concurrence, Justice Jackson put precisely the same point in another way when he said that "California had no right to make the condition of Duncan's purse" the basis of moral inferences about him, barring him from the state—and "punishing one who extended him aid":

> We should say now, and in no uncertain terms, that a man's mere property status, without more, cannot be used by a state to test, qualify, or limit his rights as a citizen of the United States. 'Indigence,' in itself, is neither a source of rights nor a basis for denying them. The mere state of being without funds is a neutral fact—constitutionally an irrelevance, like race, creed, or color.[20]

Both of these judges were backing into the second anchoring principle I would draw out here—another one of those foundational principles so true and so necessary that we are hardly even aware of them. The proverbial Man on the Street, again, would grasp the point at once. What do we imagine he would say if we put this question to him: From the fact that someone is tall or short, heavy or thin, that he is darker or lighter, or that he stutters, or that he is deaf—can you make any inferences as to whether you are dealing with a good or a bad man, who deserves to be welcomed or shunned, rewarded or penalized? The common sense of the matter, grasped by most people, might be explained by philosophers in this way: We are dealing here with attributes that are wholly wanting in moral significance in the sense that we cannot impute to any one of these features—height, weight, clarity of speaking or hearing—a "deterministic" force controlling or determining a person's moral character. We simply cannot draw any moral inferences from them.

To recognize this point is to recognize a truth anchored in our nature, and this reasoning threads through many of our cases without our quite realizing it. One of the most dramatic examples we can offer is that of the Baby Jane Doe case on Long Island in the 1980s.[21] The case involved an infant afflicted with "multiple birth defects." The most serious among them was spina bifida, a condition in which the spinal cord and the surrounding membranes are exposed; microcephaly, an unusually small head; and hydrocephalus, the accumulation of fluid in the cranial vault. The spina bifida produced, in turn, other deficits in sensory functions, including the control of the legs and bladder. Most of the conditions could be remedied or ameliorated through surgery, especially if the operations were performed soon. The child was transferred to a university hospital for corrective surgery, but her parents finally withheld the surgery that was necessary to keep their child alive. A third party sought to intervene as a guardian for the child, to direct the hospital to perform the surgery. But that effort was blocked in the courts in New York. The issue made its way through local courts to the federal Department of Health and Human Services. At this point the Reagan administration was engaged, and eventually it went to court. The administration did not insist that there was an obligation to operate on the child if the surgery would be futile. But the administration sought the papers in the case to find out whether the decision to withhold care had hinged on a medical judgment—or on something else. Judge Ralph Winter pointed out, in a lower court, that a decision to withhold medical treatment of a child because the child was, say, too dark or black, would not be a medical decision.[22] His ringing, instructive dissent is worth quoting at length these many years later:

> The government has never taken the position that it is entitled to override a medical judgment. Its position rather is that it is entitled under Section 504 [of the Rehabilitation Act] to inquire whether a judgment in question is a *bona fide* medical judgment. While the majority [of the Court of Appeals] professes uncertainty as to what that means, application of the analogy to race eliminates all doubt. A judgment not to perform certain surgery because a person is black is not a medical judgment. So too a decision not to correct a life-threatening digestive problem because the infant has Down's syndrome is not a *bona fide* medical judgment. The issue of parental authority is also quickly disposed of. A denial of medical treatment to an infant because the infant is black is not legitimated by parental consent. Finally, once the legislative analogy to race is acknowledged, the intrusion on state authority becomes insignificant.
>
> The logic of the government's position on these aspects of the case is thus about as flawless as a legal argument can be.[23]

If the decision in the case of Baby Jane Doe hinged on the judgment that a life afflicted with Down's syndrome and spina bifida was *a life not worth living*—that anyone bearing those conditions could be rightly consigned to death by withholding medical care—that was not a medical judgment *but a moral judgment*. It was a moral inference about a person on the basis of a characteristic—a disability—that cannot possibly establish whether we are dealing with a person who is incapable of living a life of good character and therefore deserves to die. Thus it was critical to know the grounds on which the judgment pivoted. The only way to gauge that matter was to get access to the records, and that is what the Reagan administration sought, unsuccessfully.

Now the question is whether the distinctions that Judge Winter was offering make sense to the reader: that there is a critical difference between a medical judgment and a moral judgment, that the moral judgment in this case was drawn wrongly from attributes that cannot possibly determine anything of moral significance, and that nothing in the disability of this baby can bear on the question of whether the child had a life worth living. If all of that makes sense, I submit that the decisive point here is simply grounded in the "mint" of our human nature. It is one of those inescapable facts in the way we are constituted: these attributes—height, weight, color, deafness, spina bifida—*are powerless to determine any judgment on the moral state of any person*. When Judge Winter remarked, in a statement truly rare in the courts, that the government's position in this case was "about as flawless as a legal argument can be," it is worth pointing out that the argument was indeed flawless—and compelling—because it was grounded in a *necessary truth*. It was grounded in what I would point out as nothing less than an anchoring axiom of the Natural Law. The question then naturally presents itself: If we shifted the locale—if the hospital were not in Long Island, but in Tehran or Nairobi—would the judgment be any different? Would it not be just as wrong, in any of these places, distant in space or time, to withdraw medical care on the ground that a life afflicted with spina bifida or Down's syndrome is a life *not worth living*?

If we recognize that simple point, we recognize that this judgment of ours does not reflect simply some ethic that prevails in this *tribe of Americans*. The judgment is grounded in nature, in the laws of reason themselves, in truths that can be grasped by any functional person. And there is nowhere in the world, then, where these principles would not hold true. Without any sense of astonishment—or any sense we are doing it—we would find ourselves backing again into the Natural Law. But at the same time, when we consider how these principles bear on a problem like that of withholding the medical treatment from a child with Down's syndrome, then we can see that, in striking contrast to the clichés we have often heard, there is nothing the least bit foggy about these principles of Natural Law. They bear on cases in a precise and concrete way. There is nothing inscrutable about them. And they do not suddenly become woolly or incomprehensible to any man if he is suddenly clothed with the robe of a judge. To those who say that judges should be cautious before they draw upon those axioms of reason forming the ground of *the law that will always be there*, I would say, why would you tell us that, once a man becomes a judge, he cannot understand what any functional person can understand?

There is another lesson worth noting for those of us who worry about judges flying untethered, detaching themselves not only from the text of the laws and the Constitution but from the canons of moral reasoning altogether. Judges who reason through the Natural Law as I have sketched it out here confine themselves to the narrow task of drawing out the logical implications that flow from the very idea of law, and of what it means to cast a judgment on guilt and innocence, right and wrong. They deal in axioms; they don't traffic in making predictions about what policies may prove salutary or calamitous. Judges who have absorbed this discipline are more likely to have a sharper sense of the boundaries that confine judges to judgments that are indeed more distinctly *jural*. They will not presume to tell us just how long a residence requirement is warranted before a community is obliged to pay for a publicly funded higher education. Or whether a community should fund the education of the children of illegal immigrants. Those are judgments that depend on the wealth and generosity of the community, and they should be made by politicians who have a closer connection to the conditions and sentiments of their own community. The standards for those judgments are not contained anywhere in the kit available to judges.

Conservatives have recoiled from the spectacle of liberal judges casually invoking a higher law as they blithely install as law the policies that have won the hearts of progressives. But if we have the example of judges reaching zany conclusions with affectations of moral reasoning, the apt remedy, surely, is to show where their reasoning is specious and wrong. And yet some conservatives think they have struck upon the genius of countering this vice they impute to the liberals: they would simply avoid moral reasoning altogether. And yet could it really be possible that judges, pronouncing on matters that are rightful or wrongful, can ever avoid reasoning about the standards that govern our judgments of right and wrong? To ask whether judges can actually get through their day without touching those axioms of reason, the very ground of the Natural Law, is rather like asking: Can I order the coffee without using syntax? The judges discover, with that character in Molière, that they have been speaking prose all their lives. They've been relying on the precepts of the Natural Law without the least awareness that those principles have been in play. Judges persistently have to move beyond the text of the Constitution in drawing on the principles that explain their judg-ments.[24] One way or another, they are all doing it. The only question is whether it will be done well or badly.

In the fall of 2002, I was invited to one of our leading schools of law to give a talk on my newly published book, *Natural Rights and the Right to Choose*. I had originally meant to title the book *The Genteel Treasons of the Political Class*: an account of how a hefty por-tion of our political class, especially in the courts, had been gradually talking themselves out of the moral premises of the regime in which they had risen to high levels of authority.[25] But my beloved editor at Cambridge University Press, Lewis Bateman, suggested a title far more apt by bringing together the two leading strands of argument in the book: namely, that as people came down decisively on the side of their "right to choose" abortion, they had to detach themselves quite as decisively from the moral logic that attaches to natural rights. And so even if there really were such a thing as a "right to abortion," it would be stripped of the deep moral logic we would wish to attach to anything we regard seriously as a "natural right." It would be rather more like the "right to use the squash courts," which could be revised or taken away as it suited the people who bestowed that right in the first place.

Of that logic of natural rights I will say more in the pages that follow. Here I would simply return to that night at the law school in Manhattan, where I was making the case anew for Natural Law. Following the lecture, the dean gave me a dinner, joined by members of the faculty. One professor offered this historical point: he thought it suggestive that, in the early days of the republic, almost nothing was said by the judges on natural rights or Natural Law, at least not when they were writing their opinions. On hearing my account of this conversation, my friend Daniel Robinson remarked, "Yes, and they said little about the alphabet either." Natural Law was simply woven into everything they were doing, so fundamental that it did not need to be explicitly named.

Only much later would it occur to me that what I had encountered here may have been a version of what the philosopher Gilbert Ryle named a "category mistake," a mismatching of things that misleads.[26] ("She arrived in a sedan chair—and a veil of tears.") Let's suppose that I had taken a friend visiting Amherst to see the lovely Babbott room where I taught; that I had taken him also to the library, to the earth sciences building, to the gym, to the administration building, to the fetching social center. And later, when we returned to my house and were having drinks, he said, "But I thought you were going to show me the college." I then would have said politely, to myself, "What do you think I've been doing?" In a similar way, we now find lawyers saying, *That first generation of Founders and lawyers rarely said anything about Natural Law. All you have shown us are the writings of some literate men, tracing their judgments back to the axioms of reason underlying their arguments, axioms—and rights—that would be there even if there were no Constitution. When are you going to show us how they did Natural Law?*

And we could say, now properly aloud, that we just have.

CHAPTER 4

On Aquinas and That Other First Principle of Moral Judgment

"No axiom of Euclid appears more evident than this." Those, as we have seen, were Thomas Reid's words, expressing the axiom that really stands as the first principle of all moral and legal judgment: "To call a person to account, to approve, or disapprove of his conduct, who had no power to do good or ill, is absurd."[1] Admittedly, in giving that standing to this proposition, I may have set up a rival to the axiom that Aquinas offered to us as the true "first principle of practical reason" (*primum principium in ratione practica*): "that good is to be done, evil to be avoided" (*bonum est faciendum et prosquendum, et malum vitandum*).[2] That principle captures the logic of morals: that the good is higher, more desirable than the bad; that the good should be promoted and the bad discouraged, forbidden, and at times punished. That simple point has played out in our politics and law in a dramatic way, and it continues to play out with surprising effects in our current politics.

But of course, Aquinas's principle does not tell us the substance of the "good" that we are urged to commend and support, or of the "evil" that we are enjoined to condemn and even punish. Switch the understanding of what counts as good, and we would arrive at the logic firmly in place in the Mafia: the "goods" are loyalty, obligation, and obedience, and the "evils" are any moves to undermine the criminal enterprise or save yourself by giving evidence against your brothers. The Witness Protection Program is testimony to the fact that such "evils" are punished severely as an obligatory part of the code. In that way, even members of the Mafia apply the logic of Aquinas's first principle.

In contrast, it seems to me that Reid and his most attentive American reader, James Wilson, had it right on what runs to the root in first principles. The proposition they offer gives us something substantive. It gives us the real principle that bars discrimination based on race, or the wrong of withdrawing benefits and protections for people on the basis of their infirmity, their gender, or their poverty. In putting the accent on the active powers of human beings as the predicate for the casting of moral judgments, it points to the grave wrong of making judgments about the moral deserts of human beings based on attributes that cannot possibly "determine" the moral conduct or worth of anyone. That principle also cuts more deeply because it connects with the even deeper ground of moral judgment that Kant illuminated for us: The casting of moral judgments, the praising and blaming, makes sense only in the domain of "freedom," where people have the capacity to mark off a path of conduct and cause their own acts. Casting moral judgment is out of place in the case of events that are "determined" by forces outside our control. That was the recognition summed up in Kant's "Laws of Freedom," a phrase as simple as it is baffling. The Laws of Freedom may seem odd, as laws work most often to restrict and bar freedom. But what Kant meant was that moral judgments make sense only in the domain of freedom, and what we call the Moral Laws are those laws that govern our judgments *in that domain of freedom*.[3] Kant's understanding would seem to converge then with that of Reid and Wilson, when Reid points out that "what is done from unavoidable necessity...cannot be the object either of blame or moral approbation."[4]

And yet, nothing I have said in bringing out the force of Reid's "first principle of moral and legal judgment" can possibly diminish the import of the "first principle of practical reason" captured by Aquinas. It too is one of those things so fundamental that it works on our lives without stirring much awareness. Aquinas simply followed Aristotle in his opening observation in the *Politics*: that in every act we take to seek change or oppose change, we must have at least some rough understanding of what things are good or bad, better or worse. Do we go to college or get a job? If we get a job, is it in a legitimate business or a business skirting the law? In any case, we move with an understanding of what things we find not only desirable or undesirable, but also right or wrong. Those judgments form the ground of our most practical acts. There is nothing airy about them, for they are precise enough to stir people to act. And if people are moved in their most natural acts to seek the things they find desirable, it follows that they tend to steer away or shun the things they find undesirable or wrong.[5] In other words, this first principle is something we grasp *a priori*. We can see it at once in the difference between, say, the crowd that welcomed the Red Sox back home after they had won their first World Series and a crowd gathered, in a menacing way, outside the private home of a member of the Supreme Court. Most people react to things they regard as good by applauding and celebrating, or even showing their joy in the streets. And for things they regard as egregiously wrong: throwing stones, screaming with anger, striking other people, and breaking into other acts of violence. In other words, ordinary people, people like you and me, react by celebrating and promoting what they think is powerfully good, while they condemn and show rage at things they regard as offensively wrong.

That sense of things quickly connects to the law. John Stuart Mill got to the core of the matter when he observed that "we do not call anything wrong unless we mean to imply that a person ought to be punished in some way or other for doing it." As he went on to say: "We call any conduct wrong, or employ, instead, some other term of dislike or disparagement, according as we think that the person ought, or ought not, to be punished for it; and we say it would be right to do so and so, or merely that it would be desirable or laudable, according as we would wish to see the person whom it concerns compelled, or only persuaded and exhorted, to act in that manner."[6]

And so, for example, if it is wrong to torture infants, it is the kind of thing which we are obliged to refrain from doing, the kind of thing that we may rightly be restrained from doing—or punished for doing. But *who* would be obliged to refrain from doing these wrongful things? Anyone, everyone, *as soon as we make clear that we are speaking in a moral voice.*

What is remarkable is how this elementary logic still enters our politics and confounds people at every turn, even today. And so, in the mid-1980s the Senate Judiciary Committee held hearings on the matter of fetuses' feeling pain during abortions. One witness, Dr. Richard Berkowitz, objected to the presence on the panel of Dr. Bernard Nathanson. Nathanson had been one of the early leaders in the cause of legalizing abortion, but he had later—and dramatically— shifted sides to become a pro-life activist. Dr. Berkowitz objected. He said that Nathanson was not "disinterested"—he had a settled view on the matter of abortion. Orrin Hatch, the chairman of the committee, asked Dr. Berkowitz whether he himself did not have a settled view on this matter. Berkowitz insisted that he did not; he had no moral judgment either for or against, even though he was, at the time, the director of the division of maternal-fetal health at the Mount Sinai Medical Center. But, Hatch said, Dr. Berkowitz, you *perform* abortions.[7] As far as Berkowitz could see, he was simply "pro-choice"—he would perform abortions for people who chose them, but he did not push the surgery on anyone who had an aversion to it. He was evidently far from seeing the logic that ensnarled his position. But he was joined on the panel by Professor Daniel Robinson from Georgetown, a notable figure in the neural sciences. It fell to Robinson to address these pointed remarks to Dr. Berkowitz:

> ... whether you say you favor abortion or not, if in fact you actively performed these during your professional career, this is a sufficient statement; it is a non-verbal statement. I would regard you, Dr. Berkowitz, as someone incapable of doing anything that you judge to be morally wrong, and so if you do abortion one would judge that you do not find in that act a moral wrong.
>
> I don't see what this waltz is about. If you don't regard abortion as morally wrong, why would you be diffident about reporting the number of times you have performed the service? And if on the other hand you consider that there is something tainted about the practice, why would you continue to defend it?[8]

The spurious logic followed by Dr. Berkowitz was but an echo of something far more momentous in our political life. It was a precise reflection of Stephen Douglas's position during his famous debates with Abraham Lincoln in 1858. Douglas was trying to hold together two wings of his Democratic Party: a Southern wing favoring slavery and the recent holding of the Supreme Court in the *Dred Scott* case, and a Northern and Western wing, more disposed to keep blacks and slavery out of their territory. And so he professed himself to be "neutral" on the question of slavery. He professed, that is, to have no settled moral judgment on the matter. He was simply "pro-choice," we might say, for people in the new territories of the United States: they should be free, under the banner of popular sovereignty, to vote slavery in or out of their respective territories.

But as Lincoln pointed out, Douglas was not at all neutral—he had indeed reached a moral judgment on slavery. If he thought, for example, that it was wrong for one person to own another human being as a slave, then it would be wrong for *anyone* to own a slave, and *no one* could be rightfully *free to choose* slavery:

> When Judge Douglas says he "don't care whether slavery is voted up or voted down"... he can thus argue logically if he don't see anything wrong in it; but he cannot say so logically if he admits that slavery is wrong. He cannot say that he would as soon see a wrong voted up as voted down. When Judge Douglas says that whoever, or whatever community, wants slaves, they have a right to have them, he is perfectly logical if there is nothing wrong in the institution; but if you admit that it is wrong, he cannot logically say that anybody has a right to do wrong.[9]

By Aquinas's "first principle" of practical judgment, if Douglas regarded slavery in any way as wrong, he would not be free to choose it—and neither would anyone else. But if Douglas thought that people were free to choose slavery, then slavery evidently fell, for him, into that class of things "not-wrong." And so Douglas was clearly not "neutral"—he had indeed made the moral judgment that there was nothing "wrong" in slavery.

That was the logic that Lincoln employed with even more devastating effect in the last moments of his final debate with Douglas at Alton, Illinois, when Lincoln noted that he had but ten minutes left.

In those ten minutes he brought together every strand in his argument and took the steps that led to that powerful, culminating sentence, "Why there is no greater Abolitionist in the country than Douglas after all!" In the argument leading up to that jolting last line, Lincoln not only destroyed Douglas's argument; he destroyed Douglas's party as well. He made it impossible for Douglas to receive the nomination of a united Democratic Party for president of the United States, and in dividing the Democratic Party, Lincoln made possible his own election. It all turned again on that same logic of morals—and Aquinas's first principle.

In those ten minutes, Lincoln destroyed the "straddle" that was central to Douglas's argument and his political position. Douglas's political task was to keep the main wings of the Democratic Party behind him in a run for the presidency. For his critical Southern wing, he had to offer a strong defense of the key holding in the *Dred Scott* case: that a person may not be dispossessed of his property in a slave because he enters a territory of the United States where slavery has been forbidden. On the other side, Douglas had to keep the support of the Northern and Western wings of his party, including the people who were not supportive of slavery in their states or territories. Some of them were opposed to slavery, while others were simply opposed to having blacks move in at all, in competition with the labor of whites. For those people Douglas offered the formula of "popular sovereignty": he didn't "care," as he said, whether slavery was voted up or down in the territories as long as that judgment was the sovereign decision of the people voting in those territories.

But the two policies were in evident, powerful conflict. If the Constitution meant that owners could not be deprived of their property in slaves when they entered a new territory, then the people in that territory were no longer free to vote slavery out. The holding in the *Dred Scott* case would trump, as we used to say, the whole scheme

of popular sovereignty. That new constitutional right would take pre-
cedence over any illusion of "popular sovereignty" that could keep
slavery out of the territory.

Lincoln brought out that conflict in a sharp way. And that compelled Douglas to flex his considerable genius in order to find a way
out of the contradiction. He offered the best finesse that his genius
could supply by drawing on an argument made by that notable
statesman—as he called him—Senator Jefferson Davis of Mississippi.
The argument ran this way: It was one thing to pronounce a constitutional right, as in the right not to be dispossessed of property in
slaves; but that right would remain but an "abstract right" without
local or municipal regulations to support and enforce such a right,
especially in a community in which the dominant local sentiment
was hostile to it.[10] There was the key: the local people could make
their opposition effective simply by withholding those local laws and
the willing enforcement that this new "constitutional right" would
require. In *Dred Scott* the Court had conferred a right not to be dispossessed of property in slaves. But a local community in the North
could make a virtual nullity of that right simply by withholding their
willingness to respect that right and enforce it.

Lincoln said, with genuine incredulity, that this was "a monstrous
sort of talk about the Constitution of the United States! There has
never been as outlandish or lawless a doctrine from the mouth of any
respectable man on earth."[11] As Lincoln pointed out, any officer of a
state or territory must take an oath to respect the supremacy of the
laws and Constitution of the United States. But now he would be told
that there is a new constitutional right, a right not to be dispossessed
of property in slaves. Would that officer now be free to withhold his
respect for that right—would he be free to act in such a way as to
make a nullity of that right?

Lincoln had made the decisive connection right away to the Fugitive Slave Clause of the Constitution. He himself felt obliged to respect the Fugitive Slave Clause because it was, as he said, "nominated in the bond": it was a concession that had to be accepted if we were to have this Constitution. As to the right declared in *Dred Scott*, Lincoln said that he was opposed to it and would seek to overturn it. But if he had thought that it was a constitutional right, he would have felt obliged to respect it, just as he felt obliged to respect the Fugitive Slave Clause.

And so he said, "If I believed that the right to hold a slave in a Territory was equally fixed in the Constitution with the right to reclaim fugitives, I should be bound to give it the legislation necessary to support it": "No one can show the distinction between them [in the standing imputed to them as constitutional rights]. The one is express [in the Constitution], so that we cannot deny it. The other is construed to be in the Constitution, so that he who believes the decision to be correct believes in the right. And the man who argues that by unfriendly legislation, in spite of that constitutional right, slavery may be driven from the Territories, cannot avoid furnishing an argument by which Abolitionists may deny the obligation to return fugitives, and claim the power to pass laws unfriendly to the right of the slaveholder to reclaim his fugitive."

And then, with the momentum that would carry him to his conclusion:

> I do not know how such an argument may strike a popular assembly like this, but I defy anybody to go before a body of men whose minds are educated to estimating evidence and reasoning, and show that there is an iota of difference between the constitutional right to reclaim a fugitive, and the constitutional right to hold a slave, in a Territory,

provided this *Dred Scott* decision is correct. I defy any man
to make an argument that will justify unfriendly legislation
to deprive a slaveholder of his right to hold his slave in a
Territory, that will not equally, in all its length, breadth and
thickness furnish an argument for nullifying the fugitive
slave law. Why there is not such an Abolitionist in the
nation as Douglas, after all.[12]

That devastating culminating line not only exposed the sophistry
and moral emptiness of Douglas's argument; it destroyed Douglas's
candidacy for the presidency. For what the Southerners craved the
most in the aftermath of the decision in *Dred Scott* was a slave code
for the territories that would protect the right of slaveowners to their
property in slaves even when they left their states and entered the
free territories. But that is exactly what Douglas insisted, up and
down the land, that he could not give them. That was enough to split
the Democratic Party and make Lincoln's election possible.

As we stand back to savor this conclusion to the debate, the point
should not be lost that the decisive lever in Lincoln's argument was
not to be found in either clause in the Constitution. It was not the
Fugitive Slave Clause nor the Due Process Clause that did the decisive
work here. What was decisive was simply that underlying logic of
morals and Aquinas's first principle of moral reasoning: that one
cannot say at the same time that one has a right to do X and that it
would be rightful of someone else to obstruct that right. If I have a
right, then the necessary implication of that right is that others
around me would be obliged at least to respect that right, if not to
sustain and facilitate it—certainly they would not be justified in
obstructing it. Just a year after this decisive debate, in the political
campaign in Ohio, Lincoln reduced the point to one conclusive

sentence: that according to Douglas, "a thing may be lawfully driven from a place, at which place it has a *lawful* right to remain."[13]

It may be a measure of how forgetful we are as a people that the memory of this moment has fled from the textbooks and the folklore of our people. On the other hand it may simply confirm the point that these axioms are so fundamental, so much a matter of common sense, that we can easily lose our awareness that we are using them. And yet, as we have seen, when Daniel Robinson testified before a Senate committee on the matter of fetal pain, we find that this simple principle kicks in, with surprising and notable effects, in the politics of our own day.

There is no example more striking than that of the way in which that axiom has come into play with an issue that has touched the root of the law and fostered turbulence in our politics: the controversy over same-sex marriage. And it found its clearest application in the case of the master craftsman of cakes, Jack Phillips (*Masterpiece Cakeshop v. Colorado Civil Rights Commission*, 2018). Phillips had run afoul of a statute in Colorado that barred discrimination by private businesses open to transactions with the public. Laws against discrimination on the basis of race have become quite familiar, but the Colorado Anti-Discrimination Act (CADA) had broadened the coverage of those laws to include discrimination based on "sexual orientation." Phillips readily served gays and lesbians in his establishment, but he held back when asked to make a cake to celebrate the wedding of a gay couple. The laws at that time in Colorado had not recognized same-sex marriage and when the case arose, the Supreme Court had not yet installed same-sex marriage in the laws of all the states in *Obergefell v. Hodges* in 2015. Still, the authorities saw Phillips's refusal to accept same-sex marriage as simply another instance of discriminating on the basis of "sexual orientation." But Phillips had moral reservations about same-sex marriage, anchored in religious convictions. The request for that cake, bearing that meaning, was just a step too far, for it would have signaled his acceptance of the purpose for which the cake was made. With that simple act, Phillips would become complicit in something he regarded as wrongful.

And yet his holding back marked Phillips as a serious wrongdoer under the laws of Colorado. He was faced with serious fines and with the requirement of moving, with his employees, into a regimen of compulsory counseling. The object, plainly, was to purge them of reflexes that were now stamped by the authorities as bigoted. Phillips was not compelled to speak words of acceptance and praise for same-sex marriage. But his act in making the cake could be taken as a clear enough moral endorsement. To draw on Daniel Robinson's explanation in those hearings years earlier on fetal pain, the act of making the cake would count as a "performative" act by Phillips. Dr. Berkowitz had professed to have no moral judgment for or against abortion, but that declaration of detachment was embarrassed by the fact that he actually *performed abortions*. To recall Robinson's words to Berkowitz: "Whether you say you favor abortion or not, if in fact you actively performed these during your professional career, this is a sufficient statement; it is a non-verbal statement." As Phillips's creation of a cake to celebrate a same-sex marriage would have been.

In any case, Phillips was sharply alert to the non-verbal statement that the authorities were commanding him to make in this case. And that formed the principal line of the argument in his defense in the courts. His lawyers would argue that this was a species of *coerced* speech, the kind of coercion that had been barred in the past under the protections of the First Amendment. The lawyers recalled, for example, the unsuccessful attempt to force the St. Patrick's Day Parade in Boston to accept a contingent from the Irish-American Gay, Lesbian, and Bisexual Group of Boston.[14] They distinguished what Colorado was requiring of Phillips from laws requiring the makers of packaged foods to list products' ingredients and calories or to post warnings. This was a matter of requiring the affirming of convictions that the speaker regarded as deeply objectionable. For Phillips and his supporters, this was closer to the law that required the children of Jehovah's Witnesses to speak the Pledge of Allegiance to the American flag and render a salute that was quite at odds with their religious beliefs.[15]

But that argument on speech encountered serious reservations, even among the conservatives who were on Phillips's side. The hazard lay precisely in the claim that certain "non-verbal acts" could be acts of "expression." Justice Scalia had warned that "virtually every law restricts conduct, and virtually any prohibited conduct can be performed for an expressive purpose—if only expressive of the fact that the actor disagrees with the prohibition." The act of driving through a red light could be taken as an expression of opposition to the traffic laws restraining the "liberty to travel."[16] And the right to "expression" was one of those rights that could devour itself. For if acts of "expression" have a trumping quality, a crowd of thugs that breaks up a public demonstration is itself engaged in an act of expression. On this construal, the government would not be able to protect the rights of the original demonstrators under the First Amendment! This was a right of expression so exquisite that it would extinguish itself.

In the oral argument in Phillips's case at the Supreme Court, Justice Breyer saw the connection right away to the interests at stake in the Civil Rights Acts. He mentioned Ollie's Barbecue, the restaurant in Birmingham, Alabama, that had tested the Civil Rights Act of 1964.[17] Might it not be argued, he asked, that by forcing the owners of the establishment to treat black customers in the main dining room, the law was forcing the owners to engage in performative acts of expression that ran counter to their own moral convictions? Justice

Breyer then wondered aloud whether a decision for Phillips on this ground of coerced speech would work to erode the civil rights laws. On the other hand, if the concern here was not coerced speech but religious conviction, that argument too suffered some embarrassment when put up against the case of Ollie's Barbecue. For it never occurred to anyone that the Civil Rights Act of 1964 should exempt anyone who professed a religious ground for his refusal to obey the laws that barred discrimination based on race. Or a religious ground for his own views on the rightful and wrongful treatment of black people. The legislators who framed the law in Colorado thought that law to be as deeply rightful as the laws that barred discrimination on the basis of race. And anyone who saw it in that way could not see any more ground for a religious exemption in this case than in the cases on racial discrimination. It is certainly worth reminding ourselves in that vein that even when *Loving v. Virginia* was decided in 1967—when the Court struck down the laws that barred marriage across racial lines[18]—there were earnest ministers, like the Reverend Bob Jones, who found a ground in Scripture for rejecting the mingling of the races in marriage. That reminder may bring us up with a jolt: Would anyone seriously think that the law would give a pass to bakers or florists who professed a religious ground for refusing to engage their arts in support of interracial marriage? And for the advocates of same-sex marriage, the two cases stand on the same plane. Clearly, it cannot be "religious belief" that makes the difference here. The difference between the two cases can turn—can only turn—on the fact that we have come to understand racial discrimination as deeply wrong, but many of us have not been persuaded that there is something truly wrong, in the same way, in the laws that confine marriage to the coupling of one man and one woman. We may not think it retrograde and illegitimate for anyone to harbor those moral reservations about same-sex marriage and the homosexual life. But that is exactly the understanding that pervades our laws now at every level since the Supreme Court established same-sex marriage as a constitutional right, quite apart from any provision made for same-sex marriage in the laws of any state.

As Lincoln put it in the midst of another moral split in the country, speaking of the defenders of slavery, "Their thinking it right, and our thinking it wrong, is the precise fact upon which depends the whole controversy."[19] Here is the elusive key to the puzzle of the Phillips case: Whether the argument is against coerced speech or on behalf of religious freedom, the argument in either case cannot be resolved without confronting the issue that stands at the core of the disagreement: the moral rightness of same-sex marriage.

And so in the oral argument, Chief Justice Roberts led the challenge to the law by posing this question: "Catholic Legal Services…provide pro bono legal representation to people who are too poor to [afford] it and they provide it to people of all different faiths." But if they were asked to represent the gay couple in this case, would they not be free to refuse precisely because they could not take up a cause in serious conflict with Catholic moral teaching? And if they held back, asked Roberts, would they not be in violation of this law in Colorado?

From another angle, Justice Gorsuch posed the hypothetical of a baker who offered a cake topped with a red cross. One customer buys it as a kind of celebration of the Red Cross. Another customer seeks to buy it and deck it out as a celebration of the Ku Klux Klan. Would the baker not indeed be well within his rights to refuse?[20] In a comparable hypothetical, Justice Alito offered the example of a customer who wanted to mark his wedding anniversary with a cake saying "November 9, the best day in history." But then another customer asks for precisely the same wording on a cake, but this time for the purpose of celebrating Kristallnacht, the attacks on Jews in Germany on that same day in 1938.[21] May the baker not refuse even though it is the same product, with the same inscription, but marked now for a purpose so strikingly different?

Once again, though, the matter hinges on the fact that we think that people are quite warranted in opposing the KKK or the Nazis. But we don't think that the people who would preserve marriage as we've known should be put on the same plane with the KKK and the Nazis. The people who brought forth the law in Colorado would not quite say that, and yet that doesn't shake their conviction on the depth of the wrong here. For they truly cannot see any plausible ground on which one may find fault with same-sex marriage or cast an adverse moral judgment on the homosexual life.

"If slavery is right," said Lincoln in his famous speech at the Cooper Union, "all words, acts, laws, and constitutions against it, are themselves wrong, and should be silenced, and swept away."[22] In this passage he was moving again along the same path of reasoning that Aquinas had marked off long before him. And it was nothing other than the logic of that "first principle of practical reason": If slavery were right, as Lincoln said, then he could accede to the demands of the slaveholders to censor the federal mails, to screen out the incendiary broadsides of the abolitionists. There could be no holding back; nothing less would satisfy them: "This, and this only [will appease the partisans of slavery]: cease to call slavery wrong, and join them in calling it right. And this must be done thoroughly—done in acts as well as in words. Silence will not be tolerated—we must place ourselves avowedly with them."[23]

The opponents of slavery had to be made to confess the rightness of slavery and their own wrongness in opposing it. And precisely the same thing is happening now on the issue of same-sex marriage. Some of my libertarian friends have been strongly in favor of same-sex marriage, but they recoil from what they see as unnecessary and humiliating coercion. They point out that there are many other bakers and florists to serve same-sex weddings. But the libertarians, ever quick to deride the flaring up of "moral" issues, cannot seem to get hold of the hard fact that the proponents of same-sex marriage take their position as a profoundly serious moral matter. And so we find that even some quite accomplished professors have been taken by surprise, as though they had never seen or grasped that elementary first principle set forth by Aquinas. They somehow fail to notice that the advocates of same-sex marriage are seized with deep conviction of its *moral rightness*—and therefore of the *moral wrongness* of those who oppose it. For them, it does not matter at all that there are other bakers available who would readily fashion those cakes. Jack Phillips, in making an issue of denying the rightness of same-sex marriage, was a wrongdoer. And as a wrongdoer he had to be publicly reproached and punished by the law.

We would have to run back to Aristotle and Plato, of course, to find anything as venerable in moral philosophy as Aquinas's first principle of practical reason. And what do we make of the fact that it still comes as a surprise to so many people with advanced degrees, when it suddenly breaks into our politics to reveal that one side or another is suffering from incoherence? It may be, again, something so obvious and fundamental that we no longer notice it—until one day, when someone recovers to see it, it comes crashing into our lives once again.

CHAPTER 5

Are There Natural Rights?

I t is never out of season to recall James Wilson's line that the purpose of the Constitution was not to invent new rights "by a human establishment," but to secure and enlarge the rights we already have by nature.[1] In radical contrast, the celebrated William Blackstone said in his *Commentaries on the Laws of England* that when we enter civil society, we give up the unrestricted set of rights we had in the State of Nature, including the "liberty to do mischief."[2] We exchange them for a more diminished set of rights under civil society—call them "civil rights"—but they are rendered more secure by the advent of a government that can enforce them. To which Wilson responded, "Is it part of natural liberty to do mischief to anyone?"[3] When did we ever have, as Lincoln would say, a "right to do a wrong"?[4] The laws that restrained us from raping and murdering deprived us of nothing we ever had a "right" to do. And so when the question was asked, *What rights do we give up in entering into this government?*, the answer tendered by the Federalists was, "None." As Hamilton said in *Federalist* no. 84, "Here...the people surrender nothing."[5] It was not the purpose of this project to give up our natural rights. And so what sense did it make to attach a codicil, a so-called

"Bill of Rights," reserving against the federal government those rights we had not given up? How could we do that without implying that in fact we had given up the corpus of our natural rights in coming under this Constitution?

There has been a curious forgetting, among lawyers and judges as well as ordinary citizens, that there was a serious dispute at the time of the Founding about the rationale and justification of a "Bill of Rights," and that the reservations did not come from men who had reservations about the notion of "rights." The concern, rather, was that a Bill of Rights would work to mis-instruct the American people about the ground of their rights.[6] That concern can be glimpsed—and confirmed—in that line we hear so often in our public arguments, when people earnestly insist on claiming those "rights we have through the First Amendment." Do they really think that without the First Amendment they would not have a right to speak and publish, to press their views in public, to assemble with others who share their views? That was precisely the point made by Theodore Sedgwick when the First Congress was presented with the proposal for a Bill of Rights. Was it really conceivable in a republic and a free society that people would not have these rights even if they were not set down in a constitution?[7] As John Quincy Adams would later argue, the right to "petition the government" was implicit in the very logic of a republican government. That right would be there even if no one had thought to set it down in the First Amendment. It would be there even if there were no First Amendment. *It would be there, in fact, even if there were no Constitution.*

But the challenge may quickly arise: If you are saying that those deep principles of a regime of law were there *before* the Constitution, and they would be there even if there were no Constitution, are you saying that we don't really need the Constitution? And the answer, of course, is no. The purpose of a constitution is to establish a structure of governance consistent with those deep principles that define the character of the regime. The current Constitution is our second constitution; the first one—the Articles of Confederation—had fanned centrifugal tendencies that undermined the sense of one people forming a nation with a national government.

On the night he was elected president in November 2008, Barack Obama remarked to a throng in Chicago that we had built this country "for 221 years...calloused hand by calloused hand." In striking contrast, Lincoln said at Gettysburg, "Four score and seven years ago our fathers brought forth, on this continent, a new nation." Counting back 221 years from November 2008, Obama put the beginning of the nation at the drafting of the Constitution in 1787. Counting back 87 years from Gettysburg, Lincoln found the beginning of the nation in the Declaration of Independence in 1776. It was then that we had the articulation of that "proposition," as he called it, that determined the character of this new regime arising in America: "that all men are created equal," and the only rightful governance over human beings "deriv[es] its just powers from the consent of the governed." The Declaration provided those defining principles around which the Constitution would be shaped. Lincoln explained the relationship, drawing on Proverbs 25:11, "A word fitly spoke is like apples of gold in pictures of silver": "The assertion of that *principle* ['all men are created equal'] at *that time* was *the* word, '*fitly spoken*' which has proved an 'apple of gold' to us. The *Union*, and the *Constitution*, are the *picture* of *silver*, subsequently framed around it. The picture was made, not to *conceal*, or *destroy* the apple; but to *adorn*, and *preserve* it. The *picture* was made *for* the apple—*not* the apple for the picture."[8] The Constitution was made for the Union, not the Union for the Constitution. The Union was older than the Constitution, and after all, the Constitution said in its preamble that it was brought forth "in Order to form a more perfect Union."

The Constitution was grounded in principles that were already there, but it supplied a structure, and that structure made a profound practical difference: I really do want to know—and so should everyone else—just whom the army will obey as commander in chief if the president dies. And I really want to know whether a state may make its territory available as a military or naval base for another country without the permission of the national government. The path to the enactment of Obamacare was given a serious jolt when the Constitution, for the fifty-sixth time, through peace and war, served up a midterm congressional election. That was a jolt of restraint emanating from the Constitution, but we may no longer notice the midterms as a constitutional happening because we are not litigating over this critical part of the Constitution. But the animating purpose of this whole project, as the Declaration said, was to "secure these rights," the rights flowing by nature to ordinary men and women to govern themselves.

In his famous Cooper Union speech in February of 1860, Lincoln drew attention to those black slaves who had the wit not to throw in with John Brown and his reckless, lethal escapade. As ignorant as they were, he said, and as unlearned in books, they could see that the schemes of this white man, touched with madness, were not going to conduce to their well-being.[9] That is to say, even as unschooled as they were, they were still, as human beings, "moral agents": they had a vivid sense of their well-being, of their interests, and of right and wrong. As unlettered as they were, they did not deserve to be annexed to the purposes of other men without their consent.

And so why does it not make sense to say, with Theodore Sedgwick, that in a regime of freedom—what we used to call a "liberal regime"—we begin with the premise that even ordinary men have a presumptive claim to pursue their sense of the ends rightful for them?

The burden of justification would lie then with the law when it restricts that freedom, even in the most prosaic dimensions.

When my late friend Robert Bork was a judge on the D.C. Circuit Court of Appeals, he wrote an opinion sustaining the right of a sculptor under the First Amendment to express himself in his art. But the First Amendment was really made for political speech and for arguments in a free press. It was a stretch to connect that concern to the freedom of the sculptor to express himself. But the conclusion would have made far better sense with the premises that Theodore Sedgwick sought to put in place: Yes, people could claim a presumptive freedom to pursue their interests in sculpture or writing, in cooking or plumbing, as long as they did nothing wrongful, nothing that the law could be justified in barring. No matter how prosaic the activity, people may have decent reasons for pursuing it and the law would bear the burden of establishing the *justification* for any measures that would restrict that freedom. One night in Washington I was put out of my apartment in the middle of the night because a fire had broken out in my building. I joined friends and neighbors outside as the firefighters dealt with the danger and probed its source. Clearly, my "liberty" had been impeded. But I didn't fly to the charge that my "rights"—either my natural rights or my constitutional rights—had been violated. For the regulations that restrained my freedom for a moment had the most obvious justification: the need to secure my safety and the safety of others. In another instance I encountered a young man outside the Wardman hotel on Connecticut Avenue, about to descend into the subway with a bicycle. I asked, with real curiosity, "Are you really allowed to do that—take a bicycle down there with you?" And he responded, "Yes, but not during rush hour!" He understood quite clearly that, while he was free to take his bicycle into the subway, it was eminently reasonable, or justified, to bar him from taking up extra space in a car quite packed when people are heading home from work.

I mention these simple cases to point out that these are decisions that ordinary people make every day about restrictions of freedom that we must impose on ourselves at every turn. Like the young man with the bicycle, we instantly weigh the more or less obvious justifications for the restraints—and we find nothing inscrutable about making these judgments. These judgments are not inscrutable because they engage the *common sense* that Thomas Reid pointed to, the things that ordinary people take for granted as they get on with the ordinary business of living.

But those simple cases can also yield, in a flash, some understandings of "rights" that are only dimly understood. For one thing, it is a grave mistake to speak of a natural right to concrete objects, such as cars or houses or money. The range of our rights may be as vast as the range of things that are conceivable to do with our freedom, whether spending hours trying to compose an opera or doing impersonations of Elvis Presley. But then, in every one of those dimensions, our "rights" will hinge on whether the law is *justified* or *unjustified* in restraining our freedom to pursue these passions. That youngster going into the subway knew that he had a rightful freedom to take his bicycle into the subway during the afternoon, but he had no such "right" during the rush hour. It is a critical point to bring to students at the threshold of their studies that we cannot give a moral account of any act by simply describing the overt movements that form the act. Have we said enough, for example, to describe a "theft" if we say that "Smith went to the garage of his neighbor, Jones, and took the hose hanging on the wall"? For one thing, Jones might have had permission to use the hose. But let's say that he didn't have permission, and that a fire had broken out in his house. While the fire department was being called, Smith sought to make use of the hose in an emergency, not to appropriate it as his own. The judgment of his action will hinge on the question of whether Jones was plausibly justified in borrowing for a moment a hose not his own for the sake of averting grave danger to lives and property. And when we invoke that word "justified" we draw on its moral weight to mean that we would reach the same judgment universally—at all places and times—if the situation were essentially the same.

We may replicate the same kind of analysis in virtually every instance in which our freedom is engaged. When the matter is seen through this perspective, a "lie" is not any and every act of speaking falsely. One would not be obliged to spill out the truth to one's father about the surprise party that is being planned for his birthday. Nor should one feel embarrassed about turning on lights in the house when one is not home, and in that way misleading potential burglars. To call something a "lie" is to cast a moral judgment, and it makes sense to cast that judgment when people speak falsely for the purpose of defrauding or willfully misleading for the purpose of accomplishing wrongful ends. Even Kant did not think we were obliged to tell the truth to the thief who had us by the throat: "I need not tell him the truth, because he will abuse it; and my untruth is not a lie (*mendacium*) because the thief knows full well that I will not, if I can help it, tell him the truth and that he has no right to demand it of me."[10]

Would we really stamp as "immoral" those householders in Copenhagen who did not tell the truth about the Jews they were hiding to the Gestapo at the door? Quite the opposite: for those householders to tell the truth to the Gestapo would have made them accomplices in the project of genocide, the unconditional, categorical wrong of killing the innocent. Here, as in any other instance, the judgment of a wrong will have to pivot on the question of whether the act was finally *justified or unjustified.*[11]

That recognition of a categorical moral truth, or a moral axiom, provides one of the anchoring grounds for the principles we seek to apply to particular cases. I mentioned earlier that proposition that James Wilson and Immanuel Kant both regarded as a first principle of our moral and legal judgment: that it makes no sense to cast moral judgments of praise or blame on people for acts they were powerless to effect. I pointed out earlier that the axiom does not relieve us of the need for imagination and judgment as we unravel the facts of any case: Was Jones under hypnosis, or in the intensive care unit, when the crime was committed? There may be many contingencies at work, facts that have to be read and understood, but the one thing that will never be contingent, never in doubt, is the principle itself: if Jones really was incapable of effecting a criminal act, he cannot be rightfully accused and convicted of wrongdoing.

But at the same time, the corollary kicks into place as well: if it is wrong for me to be punished for an act I was incapable of committing— and if that judgment is grounded in a necessary truth—then it can be said just as aptly that I have a *right*, in fact an *absolute right*, grounded in a necessary truth, not to be punished for something I had no power to effect. And just as the axiom itself is never in doubt, the right that flows from that axiom must bear the same qualities: it too will never be in doubt, never contingent on circumstances.

To get clear on that grounding point is to remove a vast amount of confusion from the usual discourse we hear on "rights." The "freedom of speech" under the First Amendment was never thought to cast a constitutional protection on any and all acts performed through speech. As John Marshall famously said, anyone who publishes a libel in this country can be "sued or indicted"—sued for destroying the reputation and business of a person, or indicted for the criminal libel of stirring tumults in the community, perhaps by inciting attacks on religious and political minorities.[12] Justice Scalia was making the same point when he explained that we can take seriously that right in the Second Amendment "to keep and bear arms," and yet that presumptive freedom may still be restricted in many plausible ways, with provisions on licensing and precautions for safety.[13] That "right" to bear arms is no more categorical or beyond challenge and restraint than the right to speak and publish. Absolute rights can arise only from axioms, which alone give us rights that hold true of necessity, under all conditions. Those axioms in turn give us the body of principles that come into play when we test, in a demanding way, the justifications that are offered for the law in any case when it restricts our freedom. *Detached from those axioms, or those standards for judging*, there is nothing categorically right or wrong about speaking, publishing, sculpting, playing baseball or football. By the same token there is nothing that removes any of these acts from the domain of moral judgment. When key members of the Chicago White Sox colluded with gamblers to "throw" the World Series of 1919 and become the Black Sox, the law suddenly became engaged in a new regime of moral supervision of sports. The courts would later undo some of the moral restraints that were called into question. And yet, at another point, the law would find grounds for judging the system of contracts that kept ballplayers "owned" by one team, without the standing of free agents to make contracts guided by their own interests.

But the key point that illuminates this whole dimension of freedom and moral judgment may trace back indirectly to Kant. From Kant's writing on the categorical imperative, Daniel Robinson offered this concise rendering: "In every setting in which the will is impelled by desire, there is a course of action that *ought* to be taken."[14] The corollary, of course, is that for every class of acts we can name, there is a subset of them that *ought not be done*. I found that idea a bit baffling at first, for wouldn't there be a vast domain of things in our lives that just don't generate serious moral questions? I can choose the peanut butter sandwich or the coq au vin; I may choose a suspenseful game of bingo over Beethoven's Ninth Symphony; I could fall at any moment into a preference for things coarser rather than finer, but I wouldn't be making any *immoral* choice, would I? The point may become clearer if we widen the lens and consider for a moment anything that may fall under the class of, say, cooking or cuisine. Here we might get a jolt of recognition if we recall the late Michael Flanders's song about "The Reluctant Cannibal": the youngster causing serious concern on the part of his parents because he would not even consider eating "the roast leg of insurance salesman." Our moral judgments in certain domains are so obvious that we have woven them into our practical lives without much awareness that we have indeed truncated or limited the range of our choices in this way. And we have done that in every domain of our freedom. Whether we are dealing with cuisine or baseball or performing surgeries, these acts could all be directed to wrongful and hurtful ends. We may just be unaware that, for anything we can name, we have made the choice to deny ourselves the wrongful or illegitimate uses of those things. Our choices have been narrowed for us by moral judgments so clear that they usually remain unspoken—and unnoticed. But at times the law will mark the boundary in a way we can notice.

The brute fact is that, as Kant saw, there is nothing we can name—no act, no thing—that cannot be part of a means-end change leading in a wrongful direction, a direction leading to harms inflicted without justification. The skill of driving may be used to drive an ambulance to save lives or to drive a getaway car for the Mafia. A pen could be used to write a donation to a charity or to commit a fraud.

The upshot then: Unless we have in hand a "right" that is anchored in those "first principles" of our judgment, as Alexander Hamilton called them, we are dealing with a limitless array of freedoms that may be directed to ends rightful or wrongful. Those freedoms may be plausibly restricted at many points for good reasons. The question of "rights" will always hinge then on whether those reasons for restricting freedom are *justified or unjustified*. And we gauge that matter of "justification" in the most demanding way by those measures of common sense that are anchored in the axioms of moral judgment. We know, for example, the axiom that would establish the deep wrong of harming people on the basis of race—and with that, the justification for the laws that seek to bar it. We have seen also the inescapable wrong of drawing moral inferences about people on the basis of attributes that cannot possibly have a deterministic control of anyone—attributes such as height or weight, color, wealth, deafness, Down's syndrome. But those anchoring principles would also contain a subset that could be expressed in this way: "Since we are obliged, by the logic of morals, to do what is good and refrain from what is bad, we are obliged, where we can, to do more good rather than less, and less harm rather than more."[15] When William Blackstone in his *Commentaries* sought to explain "the law of nations," he found the beginning of the law in "this principle, that different nations ought in time of peace to do one another all the good they can; and, in time of war, as little harm as possible, without prejudice to their own real interests." This was not a principle arising merely from any agreement among nations. It arose rather, as he said, from "the law of nature and reason."[16] The Marxist regime in Cuba came under rightful public censure years ago when it shot down a small plane that had wandered into Cuban airspace. The moral principle that came into play was that the Cuban authorities should have used non-lethal methods first to bring that plane down to ground or to chase it out of Cuban airspace.

That is to say, the axioms of Natural Law encompass a common-sense principle of scaling the measures of the law to the gravity of the wrong. The "justifications" for the law will then track the spectrum of what are widely recognized in common sense as "injuries." The justifications may come with different levels of gravity, but a justification there must needs be in gauging whether the law is treading on genuine rights or barring the wrongful uses of freedom.

With that sense of the ground of our rights, we can pierce the cliches that have arisen over those venerable lines in the Declaration of Independence: that "all men are created equal, that they are endowed by their Creator with certain unalienable Rights, that among these are Life, Liberty and the pursuit of Happiness. That to secure these rights, Governments are instituted among Men, deriving their just powers from the consent of the governed...." The Declaration asserts our right to life. But it was never understood to mean that the government could secure to us a right to life everlasting. Nor could it mean that the government may not oblige its people to risk their lives at times in defense of their country. Nor that the government may not take life at times, rightly, in the form of capital punishment.

Nor, for that matter, does the right to liberty mean that people have a claim to liberty unrestricted, for any law restricts the freedom of people, even the laws that put up traffic lights. And, of course, when we bar people from doing wrongful things, whether in stealing, murdering, or plagiarizing, we demonstrate that the right to freedom can never encompass "the right to do a wrong," as Lincoln had it. James Wilson put that question as a challenge to Blackstone: When did we ever have "a liberty to do mischief"? The laws that restrain us from murdering or raping or committing any other species of wrongdoing do not deprive us of anything we have ever had a natural right to do. What makes more sense is that the government seeks to protect us in our natural right *not* to have our lives or property taken, our liberties restricted in a lawless way, *without justification*. The respect for "equality" needs to be seen, I think, through the same lens. Lincoln caught it in this way:

> [The authors of the Declaration] did not mean to say all were equal in color, size, intellect, moral developments, or social capacity. They defined with tolerable distinctness in what they did consider all men created equal,—equal in certain inalienable rights, among which are life, liberty, and the pursuit of happiness. This they said, and this they meant. They did not mean to assert the obvious untruth that all were then actually enjoying that equality, or yet that they were about to confer it immediately upon them. In fact they had no power to confer such a boon. They meant simply to declare the *right*, so that the *enforcement* of it might follow as fast as circumstances should permit. They meant to set up a standard maxim for free society, which should be familiar to all, and revered by all; constantly looked to, constantly labored for, and even though never perfectly attained, constantly approximated, and thereby constantly spreading and deepening its influence, and augmenting the happiness and value of life to all people of all colors everywhere.[17]

We seem to recognize, in a commonsense way, that with all of the people who pass before our visual screen, not every one of them has a claim to exactly the same measure of respect and affection. We have reasons, after all, for finding some of those people more worthy of our respect and admiration. And when we make those judgments, we are not denying some principle deep in the character of our regime.

We see some people licensed to practice medicine and perform complicated surgery on others; we see others who fail the test of

competence and are not licensed. Some are confirmed in the practice
of their profession; some have been barred from that vocation. They
have different rewards and disappointments; they have suffered
unequal results. Have they been treated unequally, or have they been
treated according to the same standard applied equally to all, yielding
different results in different circumstances?

Seen through this moral lens, "natural rights" would mark a claim
to be treated in all instances, in all dimensions of our lives, *with justification*. That would be especially the case in those instances in
which we are faced with harms or with diminutions of our safety, our
freedom, our earnings, or our property. Our "natural right" is then,
at root, a right to be treated justly, with reasons that can establish the
ground of *justification* for the restriction of our freedom in any of its
dimensions, whether in the crafting of sculpture, the shining of shoes,
or the braiding of hair.

When James Wilson said that the Founders had not brought forth
a new government for the sake of inventing new rights, he was restating the argument in the Declaration of Independence: that the purpose of any legitimate government is the securing of those rights we
have by nature; that governments lose their claim to exist when they
show their want of interest or competence in securing those rights.
But the point that curiously needs to be made in our own day is that
this function of securing natural rights was not assigned distinctly
to the judicial branch. This dominating purpose, or *telos*, applies to
every branch of our government, to the executive and legislature no
less than the judiciary. No recent incident illustrates that point as
readily as an incident that occurred in New York City a few years ago,
when the authorities were suddenly alerted to the danger of a terrorist bringing a hidden bomb onto a subway train during the rush
hours. The police instituted a regimen for searching briefcases and
bags that passengers were bringing onto the trains. The American

Civil Liberties Union (ACLU) instantly moved into action, insisting that these searches offered potential threats to "constitutional rights." But which "constitutional rights"? The assumption, quickly engaged, was that it was that right in the Fourth Amendment not to be subjected to "unreasonable searches" of "persons...papers, and effects." And yet, what is curiously screened out here is the American Founders' understanding of natural rights. What was strikingly missed was that the government ordering the inspecting of the bags was acting to protect the right of ordinary persons not to have their lives taken in a lawless way, with no justification. And that was not a right only for citizens. The authorities evidently thought they were obliged to protect the lives of all persons entering the subways. Which is to say, they were operationally protecting the "natural rights" that flow to all human beings.

Andrew Bailey is a distinguished professor of computer science at Williams College, but when he was a youngster growing up on our street in Amherst, son of a professor of mathematics, Andy mowed lawns in the summer to make money. His plan was to buy a spiffy English racer. Toward the end of the summer he had enough money, and he bought that racer. And at the end of the summer, someone stole it. As it turned out, then, Andy Bailey had been working all summer for the thief. As John Locke would have explained it, the thief had appropriated to himself Andy's labor for the whole of the summer: Andy had been converted into a slave of the thief.[18]

The very existence of a government that could protect its people against theft was itself a force for protecting its people from involuntary servitude—long before the Thirteenth Amendment. This is what James Wilson and the Founders understood when they wrote in the Declaration of Independence that the very purpose of government, its rationale and justification, was to protect natural rights. This is what Alexander Hamilton meant when he said in *Federalist* no. 84

that "the Constitution is itself, in every rational sense, and to every useful purpose, A BILL OF RIGHTS,"—for the Constitution establishes a government with the strength and competence to protect us in these natural rights, the rights that were there even before the government was put into place.

But again, we are not identifying discrete classes of things to be protected. The question of rights will always pivot on judgments about the restrictions on freedom, the takings of property, the acts of taking of life, that are justified or unjustified. That is what the government of New York supplied when it explained the purpose for which it ordered the inspection of personal bags—and why those measures were reasonably taken for that legitimate end. And that was the purpose of a regime conceived and dedicated to the protection of ordinary people from having their lives taken in a lawless, unjustified way.

CHAPTER 6

On Civil Rights: Theories in Search of a Principle

As we have seen, there has been no more common distraction over "rights" than the tendency to fixate on rights to particular things, such as jobs or housing, while blocking from sight these underlying principles that mark the rightful and wrongful claims to these goods. And along with that distraction has come a curious want of understanding about the properties that mark a genuine "principle" of moral and legal judgment. The confusion has run, as I have pointed out, over the difference between real principles and merely "contingent propositions," or even speculations about outcomes thought to be more or less desirable. There has been no more notable example of this confusion than the issue that has recast our laws and reshaped our regime over the past fifty years: a formidable body of federal laws that would break past the barriers of privacy for the sake of banning racial discrimination in settings private as well as public.

The main confusion that has befogged this subject may be clarified by the distinction between two different kinds of propositions:

(1) If Amazon moves its offices into the community, the community will prosper.

(2) It is wrong to hold people blameworthy or responsible for acts they were powerless to effect.

Proposition number 1 may be true, but then it may not be. It is an empirical prediction, at most a statement of probability. The desirable result it predicts is contingent on many other things. In contrast, the second proposition, as we have seen, states a truth that is logically necessary. There are no circumstances or contingencies in which it will fail to be true. And yet the litigation over civil rights, going back eighty years, has been cast along the lines of that first proposition, supported by a series of speculations, often quite tenuous and problematic, about material injuries that *may* result from racial discrimination.

I have made the case over the years that the surest anchoring ground for the laws on civil rights could be found in that second kind of proposition, one that supplies a rationale that would never fail. I have argued that behind the will or passion to discriminate on the basis of race is a species of "determinism": the notion that race exerts a kind of *deterministic* control over the character and moral conduct of persons, so that if we know someone's race, we can draw some plausible inferences about him. We can gauge whether he is, on balance, a good or bad man, whether his presence in the firm or the neighborhood would improve the business or the community or if that presence would have a degrading effect. In short, we would have ground for assigning benefits and disabilities to people on the basis of their race.

But if that were true, then no one could plausibly bear responsibility for his own acts, for everyone would qualify as a member of some known race. It might be said that the willingness to discriminate on the basis of race denies the moral autonomy or freedom that gives us our standing as "moral agents." If we were not in control of our own acts, we would never deserve punishment at the hands of the law—and neither would we ever deserve praise. It is an axiom of the law, and indeed of moral judgment, that we cannot hold people responsible for acts they were powerless to effect. And so in all strictness it could be said that if discrimination on the basis of race were not wrong, then nothing literally could ever be "wrong," for there would be no plausible standards of right and wrong to which persons could be held accountable. The whole language and logic of moral and legal judgment would be stripped of its meaning. The words "right" and "wrong" might imply a vague approval or disapproval, but they could not supply the grounds for casting judgments of right and wrong on anyone, either on others or oneself.

Or so I have argued over a good number of years—that this is what is deeply wrong *in principle* with racial discrimination.[1]

I have thought that this understanding would rescue us from the bag of speculative theories and predictions that have been brought forth to explain the wrong of racial discrimination. But it has come back to me only recently that I managed to stumble into this account years ago only because Robert Jackson, that most urbane of jurists, fell into a stance that was strikingly wrong—something quite rare for him.

The moment came in *Beauharnais v. Illinois* (1952), a case dealing with the defaming of racial and ethnic groups.[2] Coming out of the war and the history of racial conflicts in Chicago, the Illinois statute made clear what it wished to forbid, and so it was charged that Beauharnais "did unlawfully...exhibit in public places lithographs, which publications portray depravity, criminality, unchastity or lack of virtue of citizens of Negro race and color and which exposes citizens of Illinois of the Negro race and color to contempt, derision, or obloquy...."

The offending publication was a leaflet cast in the form of an appeal to the mayor and city council of Chicago "to halt the further encroachment, harassment and invasion of white people, their property, neighborhoods and persons, by the Negro," adding, "If persuasion and the need to prevent the white race from becoming mongrelized by the negro will not unite us, then the aggressions...rapes, robberies, knives, guns and marijuana of the negro, surely will."

When Beauharnais was arrested, he invoked his "freedom of speech" under the First and Fourteenth Amendments. The judge drew from the script of Justice Holmes and told the jury that they would be warranted in convicting if they thought that "the article complained of was likely to produce a clear and present danger of a serious substantive evil that rises far above public inconvenience, annoyance or unrest."[3]

The jury did convict, and the Supreme Court sustained the conviction in *Beauharnais*. Civil libertarians would argue that virtually all political speech may involve attacks on some groups, whether businessmen, pharmaceutical companies, or opponents of transgenderism. But the incitement of hatred toward racial, ethnic, and religious groups came with a different edge—and a vivid history. In the aftermath of the Holocaust, the idea of banning racial incitement had a new justification, in Europe and in the journals of law. And in the temper of those times, even a liberal Court had no trouble judging that the incitement to racial hatred and violence fell outside the kind of speech that the Constitution protects.

Justice Jackson thought the judgment by and large right, and yet he was moved to dissent out of a serious concern for the details of procedure: In cases of libel or defamation, the "truth" of the speech is usually offered as a defense against the charges of libel. In this case, as Jackson said, the question of truth had not been tested or given an airing for the jury. Jackson was willing to overturn the conviction because that test of truth was not given to the jury. And yet he conceded that, in his own estimate, "This defendant [did not stand] even a remote chance of justifying what impresses me, as it did the trial court, as a reckless and vicious libel": "A publication which diffuses its attack over unnamed and impersonal multitudes is likely to be harder to justify than one which concentrates its attack on named individuals, but the burden may properly be cast on an accused and punishment follow failure to carry it."[4]

The burden was to be cast upon the accused even though, in Jackson's judgment, he had no chance of carrying it. When a smart and seasoned jurist takes to the public stage to offer solecisms with a style of gravity, that should be reason enough for the accomplished man to look more closely into why he has twisted himself into that position. Why was Jackson so unshakably convinced that Beauharnais did not have the remotest chance of proving the truth of his charge that black people carry with them into the community a culture of "aggressions...rapes, robberies, knives, guns and marijuana"?

Is it not plain? Even if there is a higher incidence of crime in certain ethnic enclaves, we know that it would be deeply wrong to discriminate against a particular family because of what is known in the aggregate of the racial or ethnic group of which they happen to be members. We know that even in an area with high levels of crime, many or most in that enclave will be completely innocent. In our central cities, violent crime emanates mainly from young males between the ages of fourteen and twenty-four. If we could put them all under detention until they reach their mature years, we would no doubt lower the level of homicides. But of course we would never do such a thing. Even if crime is rampant in certain ethnic or religious enclaves, we know that there will be men and women, and even boys and girls, who manage to hold themselves back from a dominating ethic of crime and violence.

This point, so critical and yet so long overlooked, may spring out from an elementary problem: If we place people in different "groups," where would we be warranted in drawing adverse judgments about the people who are placed accurately within these clusters? We might consider here the difference between: (1) arsonists, and (2) black people. No one falls into the class of arsonists unless he has engaged in the crime of setting fires for nefarious purposes. His fit with that label provides the sufficient ground for condemning and shunning him. But in contrast, it should be obvious that merely by knowing the color and race of any person we know nothing reliable and necessary about his moral reflexes—about any disposition to wrongdoing, as against a life of moral self-control or even saintliness.

These should be rather obvious points that one doesn't need a graduate degree to grasp. But when we speak in this way, are we not imputing to all people a certain critical *autonomy* in reaching their own understanding of right and wrong apart from the ethic that may prevail in their racial or ethnic group? Are we not saying that it would be the gravest mistake to assume that the conduct of anyone is "determined" or controlled by his race or ethnic group, by forces outside his control? I would submit to a candid world, then, that if we look at the matter in this searching way, we will discover that the wrong at the root of racial discrimination is that it denies to black people their very standing as moral agents to bear responsibility for their own acts and receive the praise or blame that is theirs alone. As we will see presently, that sense of the wrong of the matter will hold even when it is not clear that the victims have suffered any material injuries.

Now of course the ordinary man will not see a logic of "determinism" at work in the scheme of racial discrimination—any more than he is likely to mention the difference between things "contingent" or "categorical" even though the awareness of these differences is well lodged in his natural understanding. At every turn he is aware of things whose wrongness or harm will turn on matters of degree and moderation. And in contrast he has a sense of things so wrong that their wrongness will not be tempered by matters of degree or excused under different "circumstances." The decisive and telling test can be seen whenever we find people simply willing to turn away, in a sweep, from all blacks or other racial or ethnic groups. ("Whites only." "No Irish need apply.") In this broad brush of aversion, we find no interest in considering the innocence or the redeeming goodness of anyone in the group. To discriminate in that undiscriminating way is to absorb, operationally, the premise that race essentially controls or "determines" anything of moral consequence that we would need to know about any person we are judging.

The rulings of our courts, refracting the laws on civil rights, have given us a train of misadventures and distortions, all springing from the fact that the key judgments could not find that anchoring ground of principle. They have been contrived, instead, to fit an array of "contingent" theories about the wrongs done in racial discrimination. The result has been a certain confusion in our public policy, as people in and out of politics have blurred the distinction between real principles and merely contingent theories, which may or may not be true. To recall the train of notable cases is to see the problem unfolded for us with almost comic sadness.

Those confusions had already been accumulating on the way to the famous decision in *Brown v. Board of Education* in 1954. But that case launched a new era, both by rejecting racial discrimination and by stirring the courts to break through the conventions that had limited and constrained the powers of judges. In *Brown*, the Court struck down a system of racial segregation in public schools mandated by the law.[5] In the years following the case, there seemed to be certainty on all sides that the correct decision had been made. And yet from the first reactions to the case, even thoughtful liberal critics found it difficult to explain the reasoning that made that decision either defensible or comprehensible. For where had the Court found the *wrong* in racial segregation? The Court had said that the system of segregation would impart a sense of inferiority to black children, and that that sense of themselves was likely to have a demoralizing effect, impairing their capacity to learn.[6] But no empirical evidence had been gathered to show that segregation had indeed produced any measurable decline in the performance of black children in the schools of Topeka, or in any of the other cities that had been collected in the case. The only empirical studies brought forth were from schools in Springfield, Massachusetts, and Little Rock, Arkansas. The sociologist Kenneth Clark had used a combination of dolls and coloring books. In a series of questions, Clark asked the children to identify the "nice doll," or the color that little girls and boys ought to be, or the dolls that looked like themselves. The experiment elicited accounts of black children sobbing or trying to see themselves as a different color. These reactions seemed to reveal that black children had indeed absorbed a sense of themselves as part of a lower caste, ready to reject their blackness. But the embarrassment for the Court was that this tendency was more pronounced among students in Springfield, Massachusetts, at the *racially integrated school*. If there was something truly wrong causing black children to reject the color of their own skin, that wrong could not be imputed to segregated schools.[7]

And quite beyond that, the very setup of the problem invited the challenge: What if the children had been separated on the basis of race and their reading scores had gone up? Would the segregation have ceased to be wrong? Was the wrong here really contingent on the performance of the children in the schools, or was there something wrong with this segregation *in principle*, quite apart from whether the students did well or badly? And if so, what exactly was the operative principle? It would have made an evident and profound difference to explain that principle—to explain what made it wrong, of necessity, to draw moral inferences about the worth and deserts of people on the basis of attributes such as race.

That this was no trivial confusion was reflected in a seminar years later at the University of Chicago, in the mid-1960s. Philip Kurland, the revered professor of constitutional law, found himself earnestly asking how we got from *Brown v. Board* (racial segregation in schools) to the *Palmer* case, involving racial segregation in a public swimming pool.[8] Kurland remarked that the holding in *Brown* rested on the claim of impairing the performance of children in schools. Was the claim now being made that if black children were denied the freedom to swim in a pool, their academic motivation would be chilled, along with their performance?

Once again, was the "wrong" remedied in the *Brown* case simply *contingent* on the effect of segregation on the motivations and performance of the children? If there had been something wrong in principle with that segregation, then Kurland had fallen into the familiar mistake of confusing principles with the instances in which they happen to be manifested. We may recall the classic experiment of a ball rolled down an inclined plane: as the angle of inclination becomes steeper, the rate of acceleration quickens for the ball rolling down the plane. Once we are clear on that principle, it doesn't matter whether we try out the same experiment with wooden or plastic balls or red, blue, or white planes. The principle is virtually indifferent to the numberless variety of instances in which it may be manifested. And the same elementary point is engaged in that freighted matter of racial segregation: If we encountered a case of black people barred by local law from the use of public swimming pools or tennis courts, would it be necessary to articulate a new "constitutional right to swim" or a "constitutional right to play tennis"? Or does it make more elementary sense to say that we need no new rights here: we are simply dealing with the same principle, the principle that bars "racial discrimination," manifested in a variety of instances?

But the confusion noted by Philip Kurland would have its most dramatic expression in a case that would eventually facilitate some of the most radical changes in our law and culture as it bore on the subject of marriage. The problem was revealed in the very opening lines of Chief Justice Warren's opinion in 1967 when the Court faced the question of the laws in Virginia and other places that barred marriage across racial lines. "This case presents," he said, "a constitutional question never addressed by this Court: whether a statutory scheme adopted by the State of Virginia to prevent marriages between persons solely on the basis of racial classifications violates the Equal Protection and Due Process Clauses of the Fourteenth Amendment."[9] A "question never addressed by this Court"? But what was the nature of the question the Court had never yet addressed? Was it about legal discrimination based on race? Or was it about marriage? I raised the question once of what the judges might have done if the case had involved a law in Virginia forbidding partnerships in business across racial lines.[10] I imagined a case of two friends, black and white, who together purchased a delicatessen, and I called the case *Zabar's v. Virginia*. Would the judges have said that they had never seen before a case involving *delicatessens*? And when they struck down the law, would they have articulated nothing less than a new constitutional "right to own a delicatessen"? That would have made as much sense as the judgment that the justices announced in *Loving v. Virginia*, that the case brought forth a new constitutional right to marry.[11] As the justices acknowledged, that so-called right could be restricted at many points, as the law forbade incestuous couplings and the marriage of children.[12] The drift of the justices into new confusions about marriage was yet another sign of the fact that they had not been clear on the principle in the case. For if they had, they would have recognized that this case could have been resolved without saying a thing about marriage—just as the case of the partners in business would have been decided without saying anything about a right to own a delicatessen. The case could have been resolved on the grounds that we had merely another instance of racial discrimination, of something wrong in principle, wrong then *categorically, under all conditions and instances.* Instead, with this careless flinging about of labels, the Court created a right to marriage that it did not strictly mean, for the justices would take occasion over the years to keep pointing out that marriage could rightly be restricted on many plausible grounds.[13] But the "right to marry" would become woven into the precedents of the Court until it finally set the ground for that right to be claimed by couples of the same sex.[14]

[handwritten margin note: Loving v. Virginia did not come to this conclusion or principle that led to Obergefell v. Hodges]

When we are alerted to the problem in this way, it becomes even more revealing to pose anew the original question: What did the justices have to say finally about the wrong of racial discrimination? Where did the wrongness lie? In dealing with that question, central to the case, Chief Justice Warren stated as his leading point that "this Court has consistently repudiated" distinctions based on race. That is, he did not explain the ground of wrongness in these discriminations; he merely reported that he and his colleagues on the Court had rejected those discriminations in a line of cases. But clearly the Court had not "consistently repudiated" those racial distinctions. The Court had upheld those distinctions, after all, in *Plessy v. Ferguson* (1896),[15] and the justices had by and large sustained those distinctions until a slight turn beginning in the 1930s. What Warren meant was that the Court had rejected that discrimination over the preceding twenty or thirty years. In a rough estimate, Warren was talking about a cohort of about twenty-nine judges sitting on the Supreme Court when *just about all of those twenty-nine* were willing to reject racial discrimination *most of the time*. That was quite different from saying that the discrimination was categorically, in principle, wrong—and indeed Warren noted that only two judges had come close, of late, to making that claim. All that Justices Stewart and White had said was that they themselves could not "conceive of a valid legislative purpose... which makes the color of a person's skin the test of whether his conduct is a criminal offense."[16] That is to say, all we were offered here was a report on the *sensations* of Justices Stewart and Douglas—a report of what *they* could *see* or *conceive*. That was quite far from explaining how racial discrimination is wrong in principle—wrong categorically, in all instances, regardless of its effects in any case and regardless of what judges are able to "conceive" or "see." Neither Justices Stewart nor Douglas ever articulated a categorical proposition, defining something morally wrong under all conditions. And what Stewart and Douglas had left unexplained, no one else over the years has bothered to supply.

When people were moved to say something deeper about the wrong of racial segregation, the most attractive temptation was to look back to Justice Harlan's dissent in *Plessy v. Ferguson*. The laws of Louisiana had mandated the separation of the races in railway carriages. Homer Plessy, a rather light-skinned man of color, had been assigned to a car reserved for black people. Justice Harlan insisted that to take the side of Homer Plessy in this case was not to impose a scheme of social equality any more than the civic service of blacks and whites on the same jury marked a presumption of social equality. Harlan declared, in memorable, resonating lines, that the Constitution was "color blind," that "there is no caste here." He argued that "in [the] view of the Constitution, in the eye of the law, there is in this country no superior, dominant, ruling class of citizens."[17] And what else was to be inferred from this separation of races in public places but that "colored citizens are so inferior and degraded that they cannot be allowed to sit in public coaches occupied by white citizens."[18]

But again, putting the question severely, where in principle lay the wrongness in regarding a race of people as "degraded"? Was it something more than a matter of personal preference? Did it have something to do with regarding a whole class of citizens, defined by race, as degraded, without knowing anything about the character of the individual persons who made up the group? Harlan had insisted that it was wrong to stamp *citizens* as members of a superior or subordinate class based simply on their race ("there is in this country no superior, dominant, ruling class of citizens"). But then was it inadmissible, in the same way, to create superior and subordinate classes of "persons" based on race in gauging their fitness to be given the standing of "citizens" in this country? On that point, Harlan revealed the flaw that called his whole argument into question. In the sweep of his opinion, he remarked that "there is a race so different from our own that we do not permit those belonging to it to become citizens of the United States. Persons belonging to it are, with few exceptions, absolutely excluded from our country."[19] Harlan made it clear that he was referring to "the Chinese race." His rhetorical point was this: even "a Chinaman," he said, "can ride in the same passenger coach with white citizens of the United States, while citizens of the black race in Louisiana, many of whom, perhaps, risked their lives for the preservation of the Union, who are entitled, by law, to participate in the political control of the State and nation," were treated as unfitted, as a class, for the company of white people.

Harlan's sentiments on blacks and race were rightly animated, but it must be said that he never did explain the wrong in principle here. He never really explained why it was wrong to draw moral inferences about people on the basis of race, to judge them more or less fitting for acceptance or rejection, for honors or disparagement, in settings private or public. The want of that argument may explain why Harlan's dissent offered no particular help in the later arguments about affirmative action. It may also account for why it offered no guidance when the justices, in the 1940s and '50s, were searching for some way of explaining whether segregation on the basis of race was not only wrong in relation to this or that particular case, involving schools or lunch counters or swimming pools, but whether there was something *in principle* wrong with discrimination based on race, wherever that wrong was manifested. As Akhil Amar has reminded us, the Court did not overrule *Plessy* in *Brown v. Board*, because *Plessy* involved segregation in *transportation* and the cast of the Court's opinion in *Brown* confined its holding to racial segregation *in education.*[20]

The judges never quite broke out of the scheme of identifying the wrong in any case as contingent—contingent, that is, on the injuries that could be produced in, say, schools or the assignment of jobs. There would be a string of cases involving black students at universities forced to sit by themselves in classrooms, libraries, and dining halls.[21] Just to describe the segregated arrangements is to have the wrong of the situation spring out. But when it came to homing in on the legal wrong at issue, the Court fell into the speculation that the black students would lose the chance to be recognized and respected by white students and perhaps miss connections that could be highly useful for their careers.

But simply bringing students together offered no guarantee that a student would gain recognition of his merits, or indeed that he would have merits to compel admiration. And whether it is good in any case to gain acceptance depends on the character of those people whose acceptance is being sought. Instead of invoking a clear, applicable principle, this argument draws a hazy and dubious series of inferences about what might happen. The argument here resembles those against barring entry to certain private clubs on the basis of race or gender on the ground that it prevents people from meeting and making connections that may be critical to their careers. That is all, of course, speculative and problematic: to be in the club, to be in the university or the law school, is no guarantee that one will make friends and connections that lead to success in the vocation.

But when it comes to offering a chain of predictions, hardly anything compares with the chain of speculations that the Court relied on in sustaining something as momentous as the Civil Right Act of 1964. That landmark act barred discrimination based on race in "public accommodations": certain private businesses open to transactions with the public. The act ran into a constitutional tangle. The Fourteenth Amendment, which provides for the equal protection of the laws, dealt only with policies imposed by the *laws*. That was strikingly different from conventions of racial separation that were adopted by people as a matter of private right in managing their own homes or businesses or clubs. The most familiar legal justification for the federal government to regulate private businesses was found in the Commerce Clause. But the jurisprudence there had long been built on a pyramid of fictions, often implausible and at times even comic. (It used to be said that if a window washer, high in a skyscraper, could see a railroad track, and that track carried trains that crossed state lines, the federal government could regulate the wages of that window washer!) The reasoning offered by the Court was no less implausible as it unfolded its argument in the first case to test the Civil Rights Act of 1964, the case of *Katzenbach v. McClung* (1964).[22] The case involved Ollie's Barbecue in Birmingham, Alabama, a notable local establishment that refused to admit black people to its main dining room. Mr. Justice Clark, writing for the Court, sought to bring the case under the Commerce Clause in this way:

The record is replete with testimony of the burdens placed on
interstate commerce by racial discrimination in restaurants.
A comparison of per capita spending by Negroes in restaurants, theaters, and like establishments indicated less spending, after discounting income differences, in areas where
discrimination is widely practiced. This condition...was
especially aggravated in the South.... This diminutive spending springing from a refusal to serve Negroes and their total
loss as customers has, regardless of the absence of direct evidence, a close connection to interstate commerce. The fewer
customers a restaurant enjoys, the less food it sells, and consequently the less it buys. S.Rep. No. 872, 88th Cong., 2d Sess.,
at 19; Senate Commerce Committee Hearings at 207. In addi-
tion, the Attorney General testified that this type of discrimination imposed "an artificial restriction on the market," and
interfered with the flow of merchandise. [23]

In other words, the argument moved in this way: If black people
faced the prospect of discrimination in public inns and restaurants, they
might be discouraged from traveling among the states. If blacks were
discouraged from traveling, the effect would be to reduce the total vol-
ume of trade available to restaurants, inns, and other places of public
accommodation. That shortfall of trade would, in turn, reduce the orders
that these businesses would place with other businesses (for example,
for meat, linens, and silverware). The effect would be to depress even
further the level of trade and the general standard of living.

In the eyes of the law, then, the problem of discrimination in
places of public accommodation did not lie in any injustice that was
done to black people, but in the hindrance it might cause to the
interstate transport of meat. As a colleague of mine once pointed out,
the problem stated here by the Court might have been resolved quite

as well if the racists in the country had simply made up the shortfall by eating more meat!

This confusion between things wrong in principle and things merely contingently wrong was brought out in the most striking way in one of the classic cases in the 1930s, *Missouri ex rel. Gaines v. Canada* (1938).[24] In the 1930s the state of Missouri refused to admit blacks to the law school supported by the state. Instead of establishing a separate law school for blacks, the state offered to pay "reasonable" tuition fees for any of its black citizens who gained admission to law schools in adjacent states where segregation was not practiced. The Supreme Court struck down this arrangement. The fact that the state supported a legal education for blacks as well as whites was not enough. Black students would not have the chance to meet lawyers of their own age who might become important to know in practicing law in Missouri. In furnishing a law school for whites only, the state was establishing privileges or benefits for white students that it was denying to blacks solely on account of their race. The conjecture was that the policy was barring black students from the possibilities of serious material benefits in the future. But skipped over by the Court was an indelicate question: What if the law schools in neighboring states were in fact *superior* to the law school at the University of Missouri? The embarrassing point here was that black students could in fact be "forced," in this arrangement, to attend a better law school than the one they were barred from attending in Missouri. That this was indeed the actual experience in a number of cases was suggested in an interview given a while back by Cecil Partee, a prominent black politician in Cook County, Illinois. Partee recalled that he had graduated in 1938 at the top of his class at Tennessee State University. As a native of Arkansas, he applied to the law school of the University of Arkansas, but Arkansas had a policy similar to that of the state of Missouri. The state offered to pay Partee's tuition at another school.

Partee happened to be admitted to the law schools at the University of Chicago and Northwestern University, both notably superior to the law school in Arkansas. Partee ended up choosing Northwestern. He later commented, "I laughed all the way to Chicago."[25]

Cecil Partee did not suffer a material injury as a result of being excluded on the basis of race from the law school of the state, but he was nevertheless wronged. That is to say, he was treated unjustly, treated according to an unjust principle. Partee found the situation laughable. It is one of the ironies in the record of the law that the victims themselves can be quite unaware at times that they are adopting the very principle they think they are resisting. That curious want of noticing was on display, of all places, in the classic case *Plessy v. Ferguson*, in the argument made by Homer Plessy, the plaintiff in the case.

Plessy fell into the same groove of convention that had been at work in the notorious cases of racial libel. In Germany in the 1930s, good Aryans could sue for damages if they had been identified in published reports as Jews. And in the American South, white people could sue if they were identified falsely as "Negroes" or blacks. In their trials, the defense would try to show that the accuser did indeed have features that looked "negroid," and in Germany the defense would try to show that the accuser did bear features that appeared quite "Jewish." These empirical offerings were brought forth without the doctors' of the law noticing that the very premises of the law contained a vicious falsehood: namely, that if certain persons were known to be blacks or Jews, decent people would naturally draw adverse moral inferences, and of course seek to avoid their company.

And that is exactly the groove of argument that Homer Plessy fell into when he and his lawyers made their case about the wrong he had suffered. Plessy was assigned to the car reserved for colored people not because anthropologists had carefully studied his physiognomy and speech, but because one of the lead conductors for the train had to make a judgment call and thought that Plessy, even as light-skinned as he was, looked like a colored man. And indeed, Plessy and his supporters were counting on the fact that he would be seen that way, as they sought to test the law with this lawsuit. Still, in pressing that case, Plessy and his lawyers were willing to invoke anything in the arsenal of the law, and so they reached for this familiar lever: Plessy was willing to argue that by placing him in the carriage marked for black people, the management of the railroad had deprived him of his property in being a white man![26] The action deprived him, that is, of the advantages of being known as white, and opened him to all of the material disadvantages of being identified as black. All of the confusions that would arise in later years might have been foretold in the confusions of the principal figures in *Plessy v. Ferguson*. Even John Marshall Harlan in his great dissent could not quite give an account of the principle that established the deep wrongness of the racial discrimination. And the chief victim in the case invoked on his own behalf the same flawed principle that stood behind the laws he was resisting.

One of the enduring oddities of moral judgments is that people may be observed doing exactly the same things, even though their acts are motivated by notably different principles. Consider, in this vein, two restaurant owners in a liberal academic town—perhaps my own Amherst, Massachusetts.[27] Or it could be Ann Arbor, Michigan, or Berkeley, California. And let's suppose that the owners of both establishments have settled on this policy for their restaurants: they will not discriminate among their customers on the basis of race. Imagine that Restaurant Owner A operates on this maxim: it is wise to accord the rules of your establishment with the ethos, the moral outlook, that prevails in any place. In liberal Amherst (or Berkeley) it would be quite bad for business if word got around that a restaurant refused to accept black customers.

In contrast, let's suppose that Restaurant Owner B holds to this anchoring maxim: it is incoherent to draw any inferences about the goodness or badness of people as persons or customers on the basis of race, as though race controls and determines the moral character of persons. Therefore he will make no discriminations among his customers on the basis of race. The two owners are conducting themselves in the same way, but with underlying maxims that are radically different.

Now let us imagine that both owners are somehow transported to South Africa in the 1970s, when apartheid was still in effect. What happens now to the conduct of these two owners and their establishments?

Restaurant Owner A does a flip. His animating maxim is to accord the rules of his establishment with the dominant ethos wherever it is. A policy of racial exclusion would have been bad business in Amherst, but it may be the means of commanding the right clientele in Johannesburg.

Restaurant Owner B's policy remains the same. For his position has been anchored in a proposition that *will not have altered with the shift in locale.* Whether we are in Johannesburg, South Africa, or Amherst, Massachusetts, it is incoherent to claim that we can draw moral inferences about people on the basis of race, as though race essentially determines or controls the conduct of every person.

Restaurant Owner B may quickly come to see that he will have trouble surviving in business if he continues to hold to this underlying principle. But nothing in the change of locale alters in any way the validity of the principle guiding his action. Whether we are east or west, the language of moral judgment would lose its meaning and coherence if we worked on the premise that none of us was in control of his own acts, that we are not properly the subjects of blame or praise because our acts are "determined" by forces outside our control.

Restaurant Owner B was governing himself according to a maxim that springs directly from the logic of morality itself. It springs, that is, from a principle that is true of necessity—a principle that, as Alexander Hamilton said, contains its own "internal evidence, which...commands the assent of the mind." His act was grounded in the laws of reason that will be true in all places. And therefore, as Kant would say, it is *fit to be installed as a universal rule*. Its validity will not be affected even by the melancholy results of the owner's finding his business failing. The goodness or rightness of his policy is *not contingent* upon the success of his restaurant. His policy is right or good in itself—it is, we can say, *categorically* right and good.

Lincoln once remarked to a young man aspiring to be a lawyer that if he really worried that he could not be honest and be a lawyer, it was preferable that he remain honest rather than be a lawyer. This bit of advice wisely and soberly offered to lawyers would not become utopian if offered to the owners of restaurants—or to anyone else.

The force of the principle here is that we have in hand a necessary truth that furnishes one of the anchors of our moral and legal judgment. There is no case, there will be no set of circumstances, in which it could fail to be true. When producers need to cast actors to play the roles of Jackie Robinson or Martin Luther King, they of course must turn away white actors and choose only from among black men for the roles. But that is strikingly different from a case of drawing moral inferences about people—either rewarding or punishing them—solely on the basis of race, as though race could exert a force that reliably "determines" actions or character. And if it is truly wrong *categorically* to visit penalties or punishments on people solely on account of their race, then it is wrong to do that *even some of the time,* just occasionally. If it is wrong to kill people on the basis of their race, it is wrong to do it even if we do it "only at the margins"—perhaps just "taking race into account" as part of an ensemble of other attributes. Race may be only one ingredient that fuels the rage of people with a murderous bent, but if that is the criterion that the would-be murderer acts on, decisively, then the full wrongness of the act is undiminished. A wrong in principle is quite indifferent to matters of degree. And so if racial discrimination is so deeply wrong, wrong of necessity, it must surely be indefensible to say that *we are taking race into account, as one among a rich host of diverse criteria,* in deciding admissions to colleges and graduate programs. If the decision does pivot, at the margin, on race, then that is indeed the decisive point, and the deep wrong cannot be disguised by the stylish dance. At the end of the day, if applicants are given the gift of admission to Harvard or Yale on the basis of race, then it follows, as night follows day, that other candidates are being turned away, decisively, on the grounds of their race.

That was the point that made the critical difference, at least at the threshold, for the late Justice Lewis Powell in the famous case of *Bakke v. University of California, Davis* (1978).[28] Allan Bakke, a middle-aged white man, was turned away from the UC Davis medical school even though he presented with "board scores" that were outstanding by any commonsense measure. In the standard tests measuring aptitude on matters "verbal" and "quantitative," Bakke placed in the 96th and 94th percentile. In contrast, the applicants who had been set aside for special admission to a cluster of places reserved for ethnic and racial minorities showed an average score at the 46th and 24th percentiles. The "regular admittees," accepted without any racial or ethnic preferences, had average scores in the 81st and 75th percentiles.[29] In other words, Bakke's performance had placed him well above the run of students thought good enough to be accepted, even without a racial tilt to the scale. Justice Powell and his colleagues reacted to the grossness of the numbers, which bespoke a "quota." They recognized that the advantages of admission had been assigned unequivocally and decisively on the basis of race. Even if it were true that blacks and Hispanics had suffered disadvantages that had accumulated over the years, it was not clear that Allan Bakke had borne any responsibility for them. In making this strong case, at least in the first phase of his opinion for the Court, Powell came to the very threshold of explaining the deep wrong, in principle, of racial discrimination. He remarked that the Court had "never approved a classification that aids persons perceived as members of relatively victimized groups at the expense of other *innocent individuals* in the absence of judicial, legislative, or administrative findings of constitutional or statutory violations" [emphasis added]. He recognized that if a preference had to be given now to one race or ethnic group over another, there would be a need to explain just why the miseries suffered in the past by certain groups could be converted into a ground for favoring one group over others now, in a racial lottery. The Irish had fled the famine in their country and suffered humiliating discrimination in employment. So too had the Chinese and Japanese. Poles and Jews had been driven from Europe and the killing fields of the Nazis. And that is to say nothing of the "boat people" and refugees fleeing later from Vietnam and Cambodia. Powell set forth the problem aptly:

> The white "majority" itself is composed of various minority groups, most of which can lay claim to a history of prior discrimination at the hands of the State and private individuals. Not all of these groups can receive preferential

treatment and corresponding judicial tolerance of distinctions drawn in terms of race and nationality, for then the only "majority" left would be a new minority of white Anglo-Saxon Protestants. *There is no principled basis for deciding* which groups would merit "heightened judicial solicitude" and which would not. Courts would be asked to evaluate the extent of the prejudice and consequent harm suffered by various minority groups. Those whose societal injury is thought to exceed some arbitrary level of tolerability then would be entitled to preferential classifications at the expense of individuals belonging to other groups. [Emphasis added.][30]

Might the matter just be left to local majorities voting in, say, San Francisco or Los Angeles? Might they be invited to decide which racial or ethnic group should receive this largesse in the scheme of racial and ethnic favorites? That would surely set one group against another in racial conflict. On the matter of academic admissions, Gallup surveys have shown over the years that whites and Hispanics have been firmly on the side saying that "applicants should be admitted solely on the basis of merit even if that results in few minority students being admitted." In the same surveys, blacks have been emphatically tilted to the side saying that "an applicant's racial and ethnic background should be considered to help promote diversity on college campuses, even if that means admitting some minority students who otherwise would not be admitted." But by 2016, 50 percent of the black respondents came down on the side of "merit," edging out for the first time those who would give some weighting to race in admissions. But all of this depends, of course, on the vagaries of the sampling, and also on the ups and downs in our politics. In the aftermath of the killing of George Floyd in Minneapolis in

2020 and the conflagration it set off, even soothsayers will lose their
certainty in offering their readings of the data. Still, that may not
throw off an attitude settling in among black people in favor of a
policy of "neutrality," rather than letting governments decide which
will be the favored races in any city or state.[31]

In *Bakke*, Justice Powell seemed set to pronounce on the wrongness of racial preferences under all conditions, no matter who ends
up with the spoils. But then he suddenly did a turn and fell into the
familiar lingo of judges. The racial discrimination was grave enough,
he said, to trigger the test of "strict scrutiny." Strict scrutiny supposedly stands for the most demanding standard offered by the Court,
and yet by its own terms it turns away from recognizing the depth of
a wrong that is truly "categorical." For it tells us that certain acts are
so presumptively wrong that they require a demanding set of reasons
to justify them. But in all strictness, there is no way for a categorical
wrong to be justified—no coherent way of explaining why, say, it
could ever be justified to punish people for acts they are powerless
to perform. Or, in the case of "racial preferences," to punish people
for the acts done, or forborne, by persons with whom they had no
connection.

For Powell, raising the flag of "strict scrutiny" was the sign of
moving into the second phase of his opinion, where he would lose
the colleagues who had joined him in striking down racial quotas
and clearing the way for Allan Bakke's admission to medical school.
In this second part of his opinion, Powell would give new meaning
to the word "diversity." He would trigger a dynamic that would recon-
figure the administrations of our leading colleges and universities.
Race could not supply a ground, he said, for favoring one race at the
expense of the other—unless it was done at the margins. Race might
be "taken into account," but as one among a host of "diverse" criteria
that could weigh in a candidate's favor. With this decision, "diversity"

[margin annotation: as tho some is OK under strict scrutiny.]

became the mantra that gave a new veneer of justification to racial preferences. Beneath that veneer, the system of racial preferences would become ever more entrenched, enforced by a growing cadre of administrators bearing labels such as "diversity coordinator."

But just as there was no principled ground for choosing one race over another in the carnival of racial claims, there was no principled ground for choosing, among the array of "diverse" groups, the features that should make some candidates rise to the top in the crowd of applicants. Yes, the school could need a quarterback and a flute player, but how would one weigh an aspiring actor in the dramatic arts against a black child coming from a dangerous neighborhood? Faced with such a wide array of choices, could there be any quibbling with a director of admissions who finally confessed that he finds the race of the applicant far more compelling as a ground of judgment than anything else? The elaborate contrivance of "diversity" could be easily seen through as the most transparent fig leaf. But it would go on covering a scheme of racial preferences with moral pretensions ever more elevated.

And so it was understood by the eight colleagues who sat with Powell on the bench. Four of his liberal colleagues would not join with him in the first part of his opinion, as he came close to making the strong case in principle against racial preferences. But those colleagues who could not join him in rejecting racial preferences quickly moved into support for Powell in the second part of his opinion. For there he was offering the kind of fetching rationalization that would rescue racial preferences not only for this day in court, but into the next millennium. In this distracting dance of an opinion, the colleagues who were willing to join Powell in the first part of the argument now swung into opposition to the second part of his opinion. The result was one of those truly rare cases with one judge writing for the Court, along with eight justices in dissent. Powell was the only member of this accomplished Court who supported both parts of the opinion. That made him precisely the swing vote who could determine the outcome. Eight colleagues had registered their own judgment that the opinion in *Bakke* simply could not hold together as a coherent opinion.

For the judges to come up with a scheme of "taking race into account" in dispensing benefits and disabilities, either they must have failed to grasp what is deeply wrong in racial discrimination or else they had become enthralled with the kinds of theories that can be served up as the occasion requires by clever people. As Jefferson said, the ploughman is more apt than the professor to get the moral questions right because he will not be dazzled and distracted in the same way by "artificial rules" or *theories*. Theories are the products of the educated classes. The judges and lawyers have produced a legion of rationalizations while ordinary people, uninstructed in those theories, seem to have recognized all along that there is something not really right about the government's rationing out benefits to some and disabilities to others solely on the basis of their race. Lincoln remarked in another one of his simple and enduring lines, "As I would not be a *slave*, so I would not be a master."[32] Since he rejected slavery in principle, his rejection was utterly indifferent as to whether he stood on the advantaged or the disadvantaged side of that relation. If racial preferences are wrong in principle, their wrongness will be quite detached from the question of whether we happen to be the beneficiaries or the victims of the policy. And the acquiescence of the victims no more attenuates the wrong than does sheepishness on the part of the beneficiaries.

In that vein, the lingering last line must come from the dissent in the case of *Parents Involved in Community Schools* (2007) by the redoubtable Judge Carlos Bea. A community with educated and liberal families had sought to apply its collective genius in a strenuous way to arrange the assignment of children to schools by race: with all of the intricate schemes of ranking and fine-tuning, race would still be the tiebreaker, the decisive test in assigning children to schools. The liberal Ninth Circuit was content to sustain this scheme, but the Supreme Court would come down on the side of Judge Bea. Chief Justice Roberts wrote for the Court, and he offered the most telling compliment to Judge Bea by ending his opinion with an echo of the words that Bea had set down as the culminating line of his own: "The way to end racial discrimination is to stop discriminating by race."[33] That may be, after all, the last word that need be spoken on the subject.

CHAPTER 7

Speech and the Erosion of Relativism

Two vignettes may lead us back to discover anew the understanding that once governed our laws on the regulation of speech.

Vignette #1: I was in the courtroom of the Supreme Court on January 10, 2012, to hear Seth Waxman arguing, successfully, for the Fox network in *FCC v. Fox*, over the matter of bad language on television.[1] He was arguing against rules he regarded as too restrictive to be defensible. The case involved these kinds of outbursts, as recorded in the opinion for the Court: "The singer Cher exclaimed during an unscripted acceptance speech: 'I've also had my critics for the last 40 years saying that I was on my way out every year. Right. So f*** 'em.'... Second, Fox broadcast the Billboard Music Awards again in 2003. There, a person named Nicole Richie made the following unscripted remark while presenting an award: 'Have you ever tried to get cow s*** out of a Prada purse? It's not so f***ing simple.'"[2]

This is how the Supreme Court, in its official report, chose to put on the record the words that the majority were about to defend as not at all unfitting to be sounded in public, on nationwide television. Apparently those words were not thought fit to be published in the official documents of the Court. And in his argument before the Court, denying that there was any tenable ground for regarding them as unfit, Mr. Waxman omitted speaking any of these words. What inference might we draw? Perhaps that Mr. Waxman, an urbane, skilled advocate, thought these words were not fitting for a public occasion of this kind of seriousness, with a grave judgment hanging in the balance? That there was something about these words that could coarsen and cheapen the climate of discussion, quite apart from whether anyone would be hurt by them? It is worth pointing out that the omission of these words did nothing to impair or weaken the force of Waxman's argument or prevent its success. For he did win the case for the Fox network. But in a telling way, his reticence, and its success, actually confirmed the main line of the argument made by Justice Frank Murphy in the classic case on "fighting words," *Chaplinsky v. New Hampshire* (1942).[3] Waxman's argument confirms again that we will keep backing into the common sense of *Chaplinsky*, even as judges and lawyers remain under the illusion that the law has moved on from that classic case. That the main ingredients are indeed confirmed in common sense may be found in the second vignette I would recall:

Vignette #2: The scene: Amherst College, at a time of commencement in the mid-'90s: A dear former colleague was speaking to a vast audience of parents, grandparents, brothers and sisters, and aunts and uncles of the graduates gathered in the gymnasium. He chose on this occasion to sound again the cause of freedom of speech. And he focused on that signal case of *Cohen v. California* (1971), the case of a young man in the courthouse in Los Angeles wearing a jacket with the words "F— the Draft." Paul Robert Cohen had been asked to remove the jacket, and his refusal brought forth a case that made it to the Supreme Court. The Court would come down on the side of Cohen and his jacket in a decision that upended the settled doctrines on the regulation of speech in public settings.[4] My colleague sought to offer an earnest defense of the rights at stake in the case of Cohen and his jacket, and yet, tellingly, he took care *never to mention the words* on Cohen's jacket. He described them simply as an "epithet." But of course, that refined word, "epithet," did not exactly convey the tone and character of the words on the jacket. My colleague, with his own sense of propriety, had backed into the commonsense understanding that lay behind the legal ordinance that Cohen had violated. It was that very understanding that the Court had upended in *Cohen v. California*. Evidently, my colleague didn't think the words "F— the Draft" were appropriate to speak in a public setting. He may have held back out of a concern that those words could be needlessly upsetting to many people in the audience, or because—like Seth Waxman arguing before the Supreme Court—he didn't think that they were strictly necessary to the substance of the argument he wished to put before that audience.

That commonsense understanding had been articulated by Justice Frank Murphy in his opinion in *Chaplinsky v. New Hampshire* (1942). In that case Murphy wrote about the kinds of words and gestures—or we might say, "speech acts" (for example, the burning of a cross)—that could never be part of the rightful freedom of speech covered by the First Amendment: words or gestures that "are no essential part of any exposition of ideas." Those utterances, said Murphy, were "of such slight social value as a step to truth that any benefit that may be derived from them is clearly outweighed by the social interest in order and morality." They could be barred for the simple but compelling needs of civility, to keep the climate of serious discussion from a coarseness that erodes any serious exchange of reasons.

And so, a short while later (in 1972), Mr. David Rosenfeld made a scene at a meeting of a school board in New Jersey with the repeated use of the adjective "motherf—ing."[5] But asking Rosenfeld to restrain himself, to forgo the use of that vulgar expression, would not have impaired in the least his freedom to make the most searing critique of the school board. And in another case, Chief Justice Burger thought that a couple joined in a sexual embrace on the steps of city hall would not be protected by the First Amendment even though they could have been acting out a political metaphor of what the local mayor was doing to his city. The couple could be barred from this inspired and gratuitous act of shocking the sensibilities of ordinary people in a public place, and yet they would still be quite unimpaired in their freedom to offer the most penetrating critiques of the mayor and his administration.[6]

But what were those words and gestures "of such slight social value as a step to truth" that they were unnecessary to the argument? And how did my colleague and Seth Waxman have such a precise surety as to what they were? The answer is of course grounded in the understanding of "ordinary language," and that was the key to the *Chaplinsky* case as well. The line used to be that ordinary language is "system dominant"—that if we wish to be understood in the ordinary intercourse of life, we are compelled to use words in the way that they are commonly understood by the people around us. We can't just walk into a delicatessen, make up our own private language, and order a "gossamer of delight" when we mean a "corned beef sandwich." Of course, the meanings of words in common usage will alter over time, but at any given moment there must be a sense of what they mean, if they have retained any meaning at all. And that sense of things applies just as well to that class of words that formed the problem in the *Chaplinsky* case, the terms and gestures understood as "fighting words."

To recall the circumstances of the *Chaplinsky* case is to confirm again that words may lose their sting over time. If we were faced today with the circumstances of that case, it does not seem likely that they would trigger the reactions of the law. And yet the case still rings with an enduring aptness precisely because it is rooted in certain functions of language that will simply not be effaced with time. In *Chaplinsky*, a Jehovah's Witness was being especially sharp and provocative in his denunciation of other religions. He was restrained for using that assaulting language in public. And when he was taken in by Marshal Bowering in Rochester, New Hampshire, he spat out this reproach: "You are a God damned racketeer" and "a damned Fascist and the whole government of Rochester are Fascists or agents of Fascists." It is hardly likely, these days, that a man would be prosecuted because he was moved to emphatic, heated language when he thought he was being subjected to a wrongful arrest. Chaplinsky was prosecuted under a law that said, "No person shall address any offensive, derisive or annoying word to any other person who is lawfully in any street or other public place, nor call him by any offensive or derisive name, nor make any noise or exclamation in his presence and hearing with intent to deride, offend or annoy him, or to prevent him from pursuing his lawful business or occupation."[7]

The key words were: "offensive" and "derisive." As a look back at the case shows, conventions in what ordinary people take as demeaning and insulting terms may change over time. A person today may not take offense so quickly if he is called a "racketeer" or even a "Fascist" in a heated exchange, but at any time there will always be some terms of insult or denigration that carry a sting and elicit outrage from the targets. The root of the matter can be found in the understanding long accumulated in the common law: that "assaults" do not strictly require the laying on of hands and bodily touching. A person could hold an unloaded gun on another man and click the trigger. Or he could shoot and deliberately miss. One afternoon in Amherst, Massachusetts, a young woman was riding a bicycle, and a young man passing slowly in a car put his hand above her hand and moved it up and down without touching her, as though patting her in a dismissive way. That act was seen as a gratuitous act of belittling or mocking. He was charged with "assault." And in one case arising in Maryland in the early '80s, a cross was burned outside the home of a black family. The family had been away, and by the time they returned, the debris had been cleared away. The putative victims had felt no tremors of the terror that the cross-burners must have hoped to stir. And yet, people in the community had the sense nevertheless that something gravely wrong had taken place among their neighbors, even though no one had suffered a material injury.

But this understanding and the wisdom long stored up in the law were overthrown in a stroke by Justice Harlan and his colleagues that day in 1971 when they published their judgment in *Cohen v. California*. That was the moment when Justice Harlan gave us the aphorism that would live on in opinions in lower courts, and in the better class of fortune cookie. "One man's vulgarity," he said, "is another's lyric."[8] According to Harlan, the meaning of words was so subjective that no clear import could be attached to them. And that was especially the case with moral terms of faultfinding or criticism, which can be taken as insults too readily by people who may be overly sensitive. Writing of the key *F*-word at the center of the case, Harlan asked, "How is one to distinguish this [word] from any other offensive word? Surely the State has no right to cleanse public debate to the point where it is grammatically palatable to the most squeamish among us. Yet no readily ascertainable general principle exists for stopping short of that result were we to affirm the judgment [against Cohen]." And precisely because there was no "principle," no standard of judgment that could distinguish between obscene and lewd language on the one hand and quite innocent language on the other, the

Constitution, said Harlan, must "[put] the decision as to what views shall be voiced largely into the hands of each of us."[9]

With this stroke, Justice Harlan established his reputation for novelty by rediscovering the doctrines of "logical positivism" from his undergraduate years. He was trumpeting them anew about thirty years after they had been refuted and abandoned in the schools of philosophy. For his argument here was that the meaning of moral terms was essentially "emotive": When a person tells us that he condemns racial segregation or genocide, he is telling us that he has quite powerful feelings about these practices. But the report on his feelings is quite different from his judgment that the act is *wrong*. In Harlan's view, harkening back to "logical positivism," moral judgments may reflect passions but they have no *cognitive* content: they do not hinge on standards accessible to others as well as oneself, standards that can be judged finally as true or false. As G. E. Moore pointed out long ago, if moral judgments rested on mere feelings, how could one ever have a *moral argument*? How could one tell a man that he doesn't feel what he claims to feel?[10]

But that flaw touches the incoherence at the heart of Justice Harlan's opinion in *Cohen v. California*. For there is a critical discord between Harlan's premises and the grounds on which he sought to protect Cohen's jacket as a species of "political speech." What Cohen was doing with his jacket, Harlan thought, was taking a political stand. In the justice's construal, Cohen was "asserting the evident position on the inutility or immorality of the draft."[11] One is tempted to ask earnestly just which judgment Harlan thought Cohen more nearly meant by "F— the Draft"—that the draft was "immoral" or that it was "inutile"? Might it serve an analytic purpose to point out that the *F*-word strictly means neither one of these things? That was even more emphatically true if Harlan himself was right when he said that the import of these terms was irreducibly subjective and emotive, that they had no cognitive meaning. If that were true, how would Harlan have known that Cohen was making a "political" statement? For all we would know about it, "F— the Draft" could have meant "Make Love to the Wind."

But of course we know what those words meant, especially in the context of the time, with protests against the war in Vietnam roiling the country. "F— the Draft" could not be construed as praise for the draft or support for the war. "F—" was not a term of praise or encouragement. "F— the Draft" signaled a condemnation of the war in Vietnam. Harlan may have claimed that the meaning of some words was subjective, or that meanings changed from time to time, but he recognized that *the moral functions of commending or condemning* will always be at work in our language. For we are, most distinctively, moral agents, given to making judgments at every turn about things that are right or wrong, good or bad, desirable or undesirable, just or unjust. As Aristotle pointed out in the first sections of the *Politics*, animals can emit sounds to indicate pleasure or pain, but human beings can give reasons about the things that are advantageous or disadvantageous, good or bad.[12] The human species cannot get through the week without expressing judgments on matters high and low, from the service at a restaurant to abortion and assisted suicide. Our language reflects our nature as moral beings. Words may vary in meaning over time, with some words losing their moral edge: "opportunist," for example, used to be a pejorative, but announcers in football began to treat it as the descriptor for a player quick to pounce on the opportunities suddenly opened on the field. But within the class of words that convey moral reproach, there will always be a discernible cluster of words that are understood as insulting, denigrating, or assaulting. Such words will exist as long as there is, within this human tribe, the inclination to convey revulsion, disgust, or moral rejection.

And of course, it is the force and beauty of "ordinary language", that one doesn't need a degree in law to recognize these clusters of meaning. Truck drivers and construction workers may show antennae as sensitive as those of any professor of comparative literature in recognizing when they have been "dissed"—treated in a dismissive way. Indeed, the whole scheme of regulating "fighting words" and other verbal assaults may work best when the words are submitted to a jury of ordinary people. And it works nicely, in the framework of classical liberalism, to give instructions of this kind to the jury: *We work under the premise that people are presumptively free, that the burden falls to the government to show that something wrongful was done. We would ask you, then, to hold back from finding guilt in the speaker unless you judge that his words or gestures would have been seen plainly as gestures of insult or assault. If there is any doubt—if a word seems ambiguous, or if it seems to stand on the borderline between derision and severe criticism—then do not convict.* And then, to illustrate the difference, we might give the panel this list of terms:

- Nigger
- Kike bastard
- Wop
- Urologist
- Registrar
- Meter maid
- Saint

Or gestures:

- Burning crosses outside the home of a black family
- Nazis parading with swastikas in a community containing Jews who survived the Holocaust in Europe

- Welcoming the Red Sox back home after they won the World Series
- Writing a love letter

In my own city of Washington, D.C., there might be some question at the margins about "meter maid," for meter maids sometimes give tickets even before the meters run out. But we will find most people converging on the terms and the gestures that would be recognized at once by people at every level of education or refinement as terms or gestures of assault and wounding. The way we have set up the problem here reflects the sober and modest character of a liberal order. The presumption is in favor of freedom, with the burden of proof on those who would accuse speakers of wrongdoing. But there is an absorption of the deep premises of prudence as found in, say, Aquinas. The law cannot hope to extirpate all evils; at best it can hope to limit evils to a level that can be more readily borne. The law cannot convert human beings into angels, and a government that would strain to that impracticable end would require powers well beyond anything that is safe to put in the hands of those bipeds walking among us. As Aquinas put it in the *Summa Theologica,* the aim of the law is to lead people "to virtue, not suddenly, but gradually." One needs to take care, he said, not to "lay upon the multitude of imperfect men the burdens of those who are already virtuous"—namely, "that they should abstain," with stringency, from all manner of vice. "Otherwise," he wrote, "these imperfect ones, being unable to bear such precepts, would break out into yet greater evils. As it is written (Proverbs xxx. 33): *He that violently bloweth his nose, bringeth out blood;* again (Matt. ix. 17): *if new wine...is put into old bottles...the bottles break, and the wine runneth out.*"[13]

That sense of prudence has ever been present in the laws, as the best mayors and district attorneys sought to deal with intractable problems such as prostitution, gambling, or abortion. Frank O'Connor, the legendary DA of New York City, would every so often administer the sting of arrest to a doctor on Park Avenue arranging abortions. He knew he could not reach all abortionists operating in the shadows, outside the law, but he could convey, in a notable stroke, that the practice would not be countenanced in a respectable city, with a decent people. One keeps encountering conservatives who recoil from licentious, vicious speech in public places and yet would rather stay the hand of the law than confirm the power to make these decisions in the hands of the authorities. There has been a reluctance to engage the law even when the standards of judgment are so clear that they can be understood by truck drivers as well as professors. For some reason one of the oldest truisms of political life seems to evade them: that there is no power of government that may not be abused. If the very prospect of making mistakes and doing wrongful things is a decisive ground for rejecting the law, then that injunction would apply to the laws on welfare and civil rights, along with the laws that offer support to widows and orphans. For those laws, too, may be diverted to corrupt ends, along with every other part of the law. The law cannot hope to reach every assaulting act of speech or to right the wrongs done to all of the victims of burning crosses; but it may be enough for the law to concentrate on the clearest cases, the cases that will teach the clearest lessons.

In *Cohen v. California*, there was a curious passage in which Justice Harlan remarked that "no individual actually or likely to be present could reasonably have regarded the words on appellant's jacket as a direct personal insult." Harlan wanted to confine the definition of "fighting words" to words said in a face-to-face encounter. I had read him here to be thinking ahead to what he might have said if the jacket had said, "F— the Jews" or "F— the N-word." Would his judgment really hinge on a prediction about whether a Jew or a black man was likely to enter the building? Was it unthinkable that even people who are not Jews or blacks might object to that kind of language as unfitting for a public place? The same concern was raised by the speech of Seth Waxman as he argued the case on bad language before the Supreme Court and avoided the very language he was defending. And it was the same concern shown by those who pleaded for the New Jersey parent to stop wrecking the climate of discussion by weaponizing the word "motherf—ing." Again, it is clear that we are not dealing here with material injuries. What was at stake was the danger of destroying the prospect for a serious, substantive discussion by degrading the climate of civility.

Few decisions of the Court have had a more profound effect than *Cohen v. California* in coarsening the climate of public discourse in this country and degrading the way people encounter one another in public settings. Before *Cohen* those who ventured into public places could reasonably expect that people would restrain themselves out of a respect for the sensibilities of others. But *Cohen* reversed those expectations: the reigning premise now was that if people were offended by coarse, assaulting speech, they should avert their eyes and ears, develop tougher skin, or simply avoid public places altogether.

And yet the Court has enforced one notable carve-out from the near-relativist tolerance for virtually all species of political speech installed by *Cohen v. California*: those speakers and demonstrators known as "pro-life." When it comes to pro-life groups standing outside abortion clinics with signs, or simply in prayer, the people entering those clinics have not been asked to avert their eyes or forgo walking past the demonstrators. For they would find the sting of reproach in the very presence of those demonstrators, and to the courts that is a sufficient ground for silencing or muting the protestors. Pro-lifers have been pushed further from sight and earshot.

They have been banned at times from approaching women entering the clinic in the hope of engaging them in conversation. In one case they were barred from coming closer than eight feet to someone entering a clinic.[14] And in another case, the government sought to bar a priest and a bishop from praying silently in front of an abortion clinic in Dobbs Ferry, New York.[15] For, after all, people entering the clinic may decode this act of praying as a gesture of moral condemnation. Even in this age of freewheeling relativism, with claims to an expansive protection of speech, the law does seem to find a way to brand some speech acts as insulting and illegitimate.

And this has been taking place even as the Court has been ever more forcefully affirming that there are no grounds for restricting "offensive" speech. Meanwhile, there is no place now where even a muffled reference to the *N*-word does not set off an explosion of outrage and condemnation, even in Mark Twain's *Adventures of Huckleberry Finn*, where it is used for the purpose of ridiculing racists. The outrage flares even when people make references to that word for the sake of condemning it! There is no doctrine of free speech these days so sweeping in its tolerance that it will protect even the non-assaulting use of that word. All of which may merely confirm a truth that cannot be effaced: human beings, as moral agents, will always bring forth words that commend and condemn, praise and assault; and no matter how liberal the doctrines of the law may be on the freedom of speech, the people most ardent for that freedom will still identify some words and gestures as unfit for respectable company—and for the protections of the law. That state of affairs will persist, even when justices of the Supreme Court, seeking the widest protection for speech, declare it "a bedrock First Amendment principle" that "speech may not be banned on the ground that it expresses ideas that offend."[16]

We have absorbed now a grave confusion in our doctrines governing the regulation of "speech"—with some enduring, unlovely effects on the character and tone of our civic and public life. The mistakes made in the regulation of speech cannot, of course, bear all the guilt for what has befallen us. The larger dynamic at work here has been the erosion of confidence in the test of truth itself, and the emptiness of so many of the slogans that have gained currency all about us. To take just one notable and familiar example, is it not a wonder that, when the subject of abortion arises, we find so many people with college educations who profess not to know when human life begins? Can it really be that they are incapable of simply reading what the textbooks on embryology or obstetric gynecology have to say on the subject? Or have they not had an elementary course in biology, even in high school? Have we really reached the point in this country where the passions of our political life have extinguished the common sense that ordinary people typically bring to their ordinary lives, when they never doubt they can tell the difference between men and women? Or when the news of a pregnancy is greeted with the awareness of a baby soon to arrive?

But the drift away from truth cannot be detached from the relativism that has become ascendant in our jurisprudence governing speech. That relativism has been in the air, so to speak, for about a hundred years now, but especially since the end of the Second World War. It was the problem that brought forth from Leo Strauss the lectures that formed his classic book *Natural Right and History*—and that telling line about the relativism that came to America along with the "historical school" in Germany: "It would not be the first time," wrote Strauss, "that a nation, defeated on the battlefield and, as it were, annihilated as a political being, has deprived its conquerors of the most sublime fruit of victory by imposing on them the yoke of its own thought."[17]

Since Justice Murphy's opinion in the *Chaplinsky* case, there has been an erosion in the moral understanding that needs to govern the regulation of speech. The moral case for freedom of speech has faded, along with the moral sense of the rightful limits to that freedom. What has befallen us since then could be characterized as an "iatrogenic" problem—which is to say, a malady produced by the doctors themselves. We can say that the problem in the regulation of speech has been precisely engineered and sustained by the doctors of the law, bedecked with robes and, at times, a smattering of third-rate philosophy. But the progress of a malady made by the doctors themselves can be seen more readily if we turn for a moment to a colorful case that has been consigned to the folklore of our law.

Terminiello v. Chicago was a 1949 case that arose out of a public gathering headlined by the combative Father Arthur Terminiello.[18] Father Terminiello, then based in Birmingham, Alabama, had etched a sharp figure for himself in the media as an impassioned anti-Communist with an anti-Semitic edge. Terminiello was hardly a model of nuance or of moderation in utterance, and that want of modulation had led his bishop to suspend him. At the time of the case, Terminiello had flown in to address a large gathering in Chicago organized by Gerald L. K. Smith, a notorious anti-Semite. Terminiello, touted by such public figures on the right, offered a target that Communists and Socialists could not resist, and they organized their own crowd to demonstrate against the rally. The result was that, by the time Terminiello arrived at the auditorium, the surrounding streets were the playground of clashing mobs. Terminiello made his way into the hall in the face of a howling, pushing crowd. He managed to begin his speech, with taunts and yells coming from the crowd, until he exploded in outrage and invective. At that moment the police, who had shown remarkable patience, felt pressed to intervene and remove Terminiello from the podium.

Terminiello was charged and convicted on the basis of a statute in Illinois that read as follows:

> All persons who shall make, aid, countenance, or assist in making any improper noise, riot, disturbance, breach of the peace, or diversion tending to a breach of the peace, within the limits of the city...shall be deemed guilty of disorderly conduct, and upon conviction thereof, shall be severally fined not less than one dollar nor more than two hundred dollars for each offense. [Ellipsis in original.][19]

But in the prosecution of the case, the emphasis was put on the content of Terminiello's speech, with the standards that came into play with the *Chaplinsky* case in gauging offensive, derisive "fighting words." Justice William Douglas wrote for the Court in striking down Terminiello's conviction. He didn't contest the fact that over-heated and provocative language had brought the hammer of the law down on Terminiello. For Douglas the truly decisive part of the case involved an instruction that the judge had given to the jury at trial. The judge had suggested that there would be a violation, or a "breach of the peace," if the "misbehavior" of the accused "stirs the public to anger, invites dispute, brings about a condition of unrest, or creates a disturbance, or if it molests the inhabitants in the enjoyment of peace and quiet by arousing alarm." But as Douglas noted, political speech is usually heated speech, speech about the most vexing issues of right and wrong that divide people. We cannot pronounce speech to be wrongful merely because it ignites anger in some people.[20]

The case had been prosecuted with the focus provided by the *Chaplinsky* case—the focus on words that are understood, in ordinary language, by ordinary people, as insulting and provocative.

Douglas would have none of that. "The pinch of the statute," he said, "is in its application." Terminiello, said Douglas, may have been convicted on the ground that his speech invited "dispute" and brought about a "condition of unrest," but those features could not justify the punishment or restriction of speech.[21]

That construction was offered so earnestly, with a joyous blindness to the details of the case. Forty-three years later, those lines by Douglas would be invoked by several of Justice Scalia's colleagues as they derided his opinion striking down an ordinance that barred the burning of crosses outside the homes of black families. Justices White and Stevens would shower ridicule on Scalia's reasoning, even as they felt compelled to *concur in his judgment*—but to concur on no ground other than that same facile formula offered by Justice Douglas in the *Terminiello* case.[22]

Justice Robert Jackson had acted as the lead attorney for the Americans prosecuting Nazi leaders at Nuremberg. For Jackson the judgment in *Terminiello* was an example of jurisprudence soaring in the heights of lofty sentiment, quite untethered from the unlovely facts that marked this case. The scenes on the streets of Chicago reminded Jackson of the brawls between Nazis and Communists that had gripped the Weimar Republic and propelled the Nazis to power. He was moved to invoke an old proverb that says we should "take heed lest we 'walk into a well from looking at the stars.'" Douglas, said Jackson, had made barely a passing reference to the facts on the ground, writing as if Terminiello "had spoken to persons as dispassionate as empty benches, or like a modern Demosthenes practicing his Philippics on a lonely seashore." "The local court that tried Terminiello," he added, "was not indulging in theory. It was dealing with a riot and with a speech that provoked a hostile mob and incited a friendly one, and threatened violence between the two."

Jackson sought to "bring these deliberations down to earth by a long recital of facts." A bare review of the record told the story in a detail quite vivid enough. As Jackson recalled the scene,

> the crowd reached an estimated number of 1,500. Picket lines obstructed and interfered with access to the building. The crowd constituted "a surging, howling mob hurling epithets" at those who would enter and "tried to tear their clothes off." One young woman's coat was torn off and she had to be assisted into the meeting by policemen. Those inside the hall could hear the loud noises and hear those on the outside yell, "Fascists," "Hitlers" and curse words like "damn Fascists." Bricks were thrown through the windowpanes before and during the speaking. About 28 windows were broken. The street was black with people on both sides for at least a block either way; bottles, stink bombs and brickbats were thrown. Police were unable to control the mob, which kept breaking the windows at the meeting hall, drowning out the speaker's voice at times and breaking in through the back door of the auditorium. *About 17 of the group outside were arrested by the police.* [Emphasis added.][23]

The police, in other words, had sought to deal with the violence outside the hall by arresting those who had ginned it up. The sense of things inside the hall was conveyed precisely enough in Terminiello's own account at the trial:

> I saw rocks being thrown through windows and that continued throughout at least the first half of the meeting, probably longer, and again attempts were made to force

the front door, rather the front door was forced partly. The howling continued on the outside, cursing could be heard audibly in the hall at times. Police were rushing in and out of the front door protecting the front door, and there was a general commotion, all kinds of noises and violence—all from the outside.

Between the time the first speaker spoke and I spoke, stones and bricks were thrown in all the time. I started to speak about 35 or 40 minutes after the meeting started, a little later than nine o'clock.[24]

Even a Buddhist priest might have had trouble restraining himself from answering back with his own sense of outrage. As it happened, Terminiello gave what could be taken as a familiar, fiery political talk. And for a man accused of anti-Semitism, he seemed careful to make clear that his criticism of certain prominent Jewish Communists was not to be taken as a blanket condemnation of the Jewish people. (These assurances may have been discounted by the fact that he was appearing under the auspices of Gerald L. K. Smith, a man not exactly given to making those fine distinctions.) But as the crowd grew more ferocious and intransigent, and Terminiello rose to the challenge, it was foreseeable that his rhetoric would turn a corner:

I know I was told one time that my winter quarters were ready for me in Siberia. I was told that. Now, I am talking about the fifty-seven varieties that we have in America, and we have fifty-seven varieties of pinks and reds and pastel shades in this country; and all of it can be traced back to the twelve years we spent under the New Deal, because that was the build-up for what is going on in the world today....

First of all, we had Queen Eleanor [Roosevelt]. Mr. Smith said, "Queen Eleanor is now one of the world's communists. She is one who said this—imagine, coming from the spouse of the former President of the United States for twelve long years—this is what she said: 'The war is but a step in the revolution. The war is but one step in the revolution, and we know who started the war.'"...

Now, let me say, I am going to talk about—I almost said, about the Jews. Of course, I would not want to say that. However, I am going to talk about some Jews. I hope that—I am a Christian minister. We must take a Christian attitude. I don't want you to go from this hall with hatred in your heart for any person, for no person.... [This ellipsis in original.]

Now, this danger which we face—let us call them Zionist Jews if you will, let's call them atheistic, communistic Jewish or Zionist Jews, then let us not fear to condemn them. You remember the Apostles when they went into the upper room after the death of the Master, they went in there, after locking the doors; they closed the windows. (At this time there was a very loud noise as if something was being thrown into the building.)

Don't be disturbed. That happened, by the way, while Mr. Gerald Smith was saying "Our Father who art in heaven;" (just then a rock went through the window). *Do you wonder they were persecuted in other countries in the world?*... [Emphasis added, ellipsis in original.][25]

The audience was evidently primed to fill in the ellipses with a fuller sense of the villains, for these remarks, as Jackson said, moved the audience to "expressions of immediate anger, unrest, and alarm":

"One called the speaker a 'God damned liar' *and was taken out by the police.* Another said that 'Jews, niggers and Catholics would have to be gotten rid of.' One response was, 'Yes, the Jews are all killers, murderers. If we don't kill them first, they will kill us.' The anti-Jewish stories elicited exclamations of 'Oh!' and 'Isn't that terrible!' and shouts of 'Yes, send the Jews back to Russia,' 'Kill the Jews,' 'Dirty kikes,' and much more of ugly tenor" [emphasis added].

"This," said Jackson, "is the specific and concrete kind of anger, unrest and alarm, coupled with that of the mob outside, that the trial court charged the jury might find to be a breach of peace induced by Terminiello."[26] For Jackson, that mob formed a critical part of the total context in which these verbal assaults had taken place. For him, coming from Nuremberg, the action in the streets recalled Hitler's explicit teachings on the strategic use of the streets.

"We should not work in secret conventicles," Hitler had written, "but in mighty mass demonstrations, and it is not by dagger and poison or pistol that the road can be cleared for the movement but *by the conquest of the streets.* We must teach the Marxist that the future *master of the streets* is National Socialism, just as it will some day be the master of the state" [emphasis added by Justice Jackson].[27]

The action in the streets, the howling mob trying to break into the hall, the unruly people picking fights inside—all were material for an explosion waiting to be ignited. And the trigger could be found, for Jackson, in the "fighting words" of the *Chaplinsky* case. In a train of invective, Terminiello responded to the venom of his antagonists in the hall by calling them "slimy scum," "snakes," and "bedbugs."[28] At that moment, the police finally intervened to keep a battle from breaking out in the auditorium.

For Jackson the case was a moment of soul-searching that ran deep, for it brought him to wonder aloud about the wisdom of the Court, in 1925, in the *Gitlow* case, when it had taken the step of applying the First Amendment to the states through the Due Process Clause of the Fourteenth Amendment.[29] That was the notable first step in the gradual "incorporation" of the Bill of Rights to apply to the States. Jackson looked back to the precedents running up to the *Gitlow* case, and his reaching back brought him to Justice Holmes's opinion in the memorable case of *Schenck v. United States* (1919).[30] And what Jackson offered now, as the doctrine that should govern the *Terminiello* case, was Holmes's famous "clear and present danger" test from *Schenck*. "The question in every case," Holmes had said, "is whether the words *used are used in such circumstances* and are of *such a nature* as to create a *clear and present danger* that they will bring about the substantive evils that Congress [or the State or City] has a right to prevent" [emphasis added by Justice Jackson]. For Holmes— as for Jackson—the most incontestable "substantive evil" that speech could bring about was a riot, an outbreak of violence.[31] And for Holmes that concern preempted the moral question of whether the speech itself was provocative or thoroughly innocent. Nor would it matter whether the reaction of the crowd might have been warranted by a provocation or an unjustified verbal assault.

For Holmes, ever seeking to purge moral judgments from the law, those distinctions just did not matter. The brute fact was the riot, and it needed to be put down for the public peace and safety. But that Holmesian detachment from the moral character of the speech is the key to the failure of Jackson's otherwise rich and insightful commentary in *Terminiello*. For if the silencing of Terminiello hinged on the prospect of his bringing about the "substantive evil" of rioting, then Terminiello could have been barred from speaking *before he had even reached the podium*. For as the record showed, the riot was in full force by the time Terminiello had arrived. And when the opening of doors offered the occasion for ice picks to whirl through, there could be no question that a riot was already in progress.

If Jackson was prepared to use the "clear and present danger" test as the most apt or serviceable test for the Constitution, then he would have done even more than bar the speaker from the chance to speak. He would have put in place a doctrine that yields deeply illiberal effects, "the heckler's veto": the success of adversaries in bringing out a mob in the street—or on a campus—and serving up a hostile protest can be enough to bar any speaker from speaking. The heckler's veto has recently shown its primitive force once again in the thoroughgoing barring of conservative speakers from many of the colleges and universities in this country.

Jackson had no need to go back as far as *Schenck* for a constitutional test so dubious. He already had in hand the much better rule of *Chaplinsky*, with an opinion he had joined, and that case offered a guidance that could be readily understood by ordinary people. When the matter is seen through the lens of *Chaplinsky*, it was the police on the scene in Chicago who turned out to be the best jurists in the *Terminiello* case. They worked with a careful and deft hand precisely because they were guided by the commonsense understanding in *Chaplinsky*. They knew that they could recognize at once the kinds of words and gestures that were meant to insult and denigrate and taunt an audience to the edge of a violent outburst. What they saw, from the first moments, was a crowd itching for trouble long before any speaker reached the podium to speak. And so their first reflex was to restrain the violent. They would not use the violence of some people in the crowd as a predicate for dispersing the audience or silencing the speaker. As Terminiello recalled, when he arrived at the building, the protestors were there "body to body and covered the sidewalk completely, some on the steps so that we had to form a flying wedge to get through."[32] It took the police to escort Terminiello and his hosts to the building. As Jackson noted, seventeen people outside the hall were arrested. Once inside, the police sought to deal with the people who were shouting and trying to prevent the speaker from speaking. One man in the audience sprung up and called the speaker a "God damned liar"; he was removed by the police. The operating mode of the police, we might say, was to protect the freedom of the speaker while dealing with the violent opposition that could disrupt the speech and produce a minor riot. In this way the police sought to preserve a certain public order—until Terminiello began responding to his assailants with the kind of language ("slimy scums," "bedbugs") that threatened to drive things over the edge. That was the moment when the police finally intervened to take Terminiello off the stage. It was his use of those words, in that context, further inflaming the crowd, that was taken as the ground of his responsibility here—and the justification for the $100 fine that he was assessed.

But as judges and scholars look back at the *Terminiello* case, the judicious performance of the police, guided by the standards in *Chaplinsky*, goes wholly unnoticed. Only fragments of Jackson's fine opinion are recalled, detached from the dissenting judgment that they helped to explain. The one thing that remains, echoing afresh, with the power to keep our jurisprudence on speech in permanent disarray, are those lines from Justice Douglas on the instruction given to the jury: whatever the circumstances of the case, judges must not sustain any restriction of speech on the ground that the speech "stirs the public to anger, invites dispute, brings about a condition of unrest." Twenty-two years later the Court would turn another critical corner with *Cohen v. California*, and twenty years after that it would confront the case of burning crosses outside the homes of black families. With these turns, those simple lines from Justice Douglas in *Terminiello* would have a deep, crippling effect on our law. The pieces finally came together in the most revealing way in that case on the burning of crosses, *R.A.V. v. St. Paul* in 1992.

Justice Scalia set forth the plain facts of the case: "In the predawn hours of June 21, 1990, petitioner and several other teenagers allegedly assembled a crudely made cross by taping together broken chair legs. They then allegedly burned the cross inside the fenced yard of a black family that lived across the street from the house where petitioner was staying."[33]

As Scalia noted, this conduct could have been prosecuted under other ordinances, as, for example, the laws barring trespassing. But that was not exactly the wrong that the authorities were seeking to condemn in this measure for the burning of crosses. Their sense of the problem was reflected in the language of the ordinance: "Whoever places on public or private property a symbol, object, appellation, characterization or graffiti, including, but not limited to, a burning cross or Nazi swastika, which one knows or has reasonable grounds to know arouses anger, alarm or resentment in others on the basis of race, color, creed, religion or gender commits disorderly conduct and shall be guilty of a misdemeanor."[34]

Anyone who had absorbed the common sense of *Chaplinsky*, with its dependence on the understanding of ordinary language, would have had no trouble decoding what was taking place here. Anyone who had lived in this country, and known something of our experience as a country, could instantly tell the difference between, say, a burning shoe box and a burning cross. Materially speaking, there may be little difference. But people who know the meaning of ordinary words and expressive gestures—the raised middle finger, the well-placed jeer or sneer—understand the difference at once. They have no trouble telling the difference between a crowd welcoming the Red Sox home after winning the World Series and a crowd outside the home of a black family burning a cross. And that is why the Supreme Court of Minnesota, in construing the statute, could put aside many of the words about arousing "anger, alarm or resentment" and find the core of the statute in those "fighting words"—those words or gestures of assault and denigration.

But that is where Justice Scalia offered a refinement that would imperil the ordinance—and stir disagreement with his colleagues. Scalia was quite prepared to sustain restrictions on the forms of speech that were arguably obscene or lewd or denigrating. For their content, he wrote, "embodies a particularly intolerable (and socially unnecessary) *mode* of expressing *whatever* idea the speaker wishes to convey" [emphasis in the original].[35] Scalia did not think that bans on that kind of offensive speech could be averted by attaching a political message to it. A "shockingly hardcore pornographic movie" could not be saved from proscription if the filmmakers simply included a model "sporting a political tattoo."[36] In that vein, we may recall Chief Justice Burger's hypothetical couple locked "in sexual embrace" on the steps of city hall. The couple could have been acting out a metaphor of sorts, characterizing what the administration of the day had done to the city. But the message could be conveyed in other ways without engaging in this gratuitous bit of theater to assault the sensibilities of ordinary people in the middle of the day. Scalia's concern drew on *Cohen v. California* in its opposition to restrictions based on the "content" of the speech. For Scalia, the decisive point was discrimination based on "viewpoint." The law could bar all speech threatening the president, but not the speech threatening only presidents of one political party or only presidents holding to liberal or conservative policies. The law may bar libel, but not solely libels directed at officials in the government. Scalia did not deny for a moment that "burning a cross in someone's front yard is reprehensible."[37] But the flaw he found here was that the law restricted speech based on certain "disfavored subjects." It was directed at those groups that the people in political office cared about beyond others. As Scalia argued, the ordinance in St. Paul "applies only to 'fighting words' that insult, or provoke violence, 'on the basis of race, color, creed, religion or gender.'" But since he agreed that these gestures of assault on black people were reprehensible, who was being left out? Who was not being shown a comparable concern? Not covered, said Scalia in a telling passage, were those attacked on the basis of "political affiliation, union membership, or homosexuality."[38]

On the campuses in the country—and in our public discourse—we hear people labeled as "homophobes." They are characterized as bearers of a disease, rather than as people who may have reasons, and at times religious convictions, that lead them to serious reservations about the homosexual life. People who have done no more than defend marriage as a union between one man and one woman have been treated as lepers. They may be even barred from employment in leading corporations, as in the notable case of Brendan Eich. Eich was forced out of Mozilla, the company he had shaped, because he had contributed to the referendum in California that sought to preserve marriage as the union of one man and one woman. People with Eich's beliefs don't seem to command much sympathy or concern from those who pass these statutes on racial discrimination and the burning of crosses. But might these people not be protected, as well, from denigrating attacks that affect even their prospects for making a living?

Still, there are ample grounds on which to find the act of hostility aimed at black people in the cross-burning to be a serious assault. The fact that legislators are not moved to cover other victims attacked in similar ways is not an argument for failing to vindicate the wrongs that the law does reach.

For Justices White and Stevens, the Court seemed to be losing its moral and jural bearings as it showed a willingness to pass over this odious assault on black people. As Stevens remarked, all of the cases dealing with classes of speech based on the content of speech had involved "precisely the sort of regulation the Court invalidates today."[39] And Justice White was even more severe: "The decision," he wrote, "is mischievous at best and will surely confuse the lower courts. I join the judgment, *but not the folly of the opinion*" [emphasis added].[40] There was the censure—and, at the same time, the evasion. Both judges were being snippy and gratuitous in their commentary on Scalia's opinion—and yet both of them were *concurring* in the judgment. Justice Stevens wrote that he would certainly have voted to sustain this law had it not been "overbroad." And Justice White noted, as the decisive ground of his complaint, that the Supreme Court of Minnesota had been willing to uphold an ordinance barring expression that "by its very utterance" causes "anger, alarm or resentment."[41]

Virtually every member of the Court expressed a willingness to sustain a law involving this classic assault on black people, and most of them refused to share Scalia's aversion to casting judgments on the "content" of the speech. What held them back from following their convictions in this particular case? It was nothing other than those lines lingering from Justice Douglas's opinion in the *Terminiello* case: that we may not restrict speech simply on the grounds that it stirs "anger," incites "unrest," or arouses "alarm"—for do we not know that all political speech can do that?

The court in Minnesota had read the statute through the lens of the *Chaplinsky* case: there was an expressive act, understood readily in our language and experience as an act of assault. And an assault directed solely on the basis of racial hostility was clearly unjustified. Why did the language from the *Terminiello* case come into play here at all? The answer may be supplied by reminding ourselves of the surgery that had been done on the *Chaplinsky* case with Justice Harlan's quick scalpel in *Cohen v. California*.

Justice Murphy's opinion in *Chaplinsky* had summarized the nature of an offense that the law may rightly forbid: "the insulting or 'fighting' words—those which by their very utterance inflict injury or tend to incite an immediate breach of the peace." There were two categories of "fighting words" there: words "which by their very utterance inflict injury," as distinguished from words that "tend to incite an immediate breach of the peace."[42] The first test reminded us that assaults do not strictly require the laying on of hands or bodily touching. They can be found in a threatening or lewd phone call in the middle of the night, or in a public insult. People can be hurt, with lasting effects, even if they don't have the means of striking back at their assailants. After all, the black family in the house may not have the opportunity to assault the crowd burning a cross outside.

The surgery done by Justice Harlan in the *Cohen* case removed that first category established in *Chaplinsky*. According to Harlan, the meaning of words was too elusive, and perhaps too emotive, to have any fixed meaning. The restraint on speech could be cabined, then, by confining "fighting words" to those words spoken or spit out in a face-to-face encounter that was more likely to produce actual "fighting." Gone was the recognition of those words "which by their very utterance, inflict injury."

And now, in the post-*Cohen* world, the city council in St. Paul was no longer free to bar the burning of crosses as an act that "by its very [execution] inflict[s] injury." That commonsense understanding was no longer available to legislatures in the country after the *Cohen* case. All that was left was the possibility of barring words that "tend to incite an immediate breach of the peace"—words or gestures that provoke people to violence. And how might a legislature explain a bit more precisely what those words might be? Well, the legislature might try to explain that it is forbidding the kind of language that "stirs the public, invites dispute, brings about a condition of unrest."

But those are the key words from *Terminiello*. And they will produce now, each time, the same result. No matter how firmly grounded the law may be in identifying words and gestures truly assaulting, the statute will be readily overturned whenever a legislature seeks to explain that it has in mind the gestures and words that...truly *make people angry, outraged, and ready to strike back.*

It is a surefire formula for striking down virtually any law seeking to apply even the most minimal restraints that a civilized community would seek to establish in its public life. The whole thing resembles the old Monty Python bit of a training officer inviting his men to attack him with a banana. One man makes a try...and he is shot. The men keep trying, in a series of sallies, this time a man wielding a pomegranate, followed in succession by others with other pieces of fruit. One after another, the mock assailants are shot, confirming anew the same lesson.

The justices have brought about a situation in which laws regulating speech cannot recognize those acts of speech that "by [their] very utterance inflict injury." To pass constitutional muster, a law would have to be defended by showing what in the speech it bars is likely to inflame and incite fighting. But at the same time, *the very description of those qualities—provoking people to anger and unrest—becomes enough, under the formula of* Terminiello, *to strike down the law.* We might as well try next time with bananas.

As we have seen, what we have here is the jural equivalent of an iatrogenic disease. The current disarray and incoherence in our laws governing speech is a disarray brought about and sustained by judges. The marvel is that the incoherence has not been obvious enough, to minds tempered in the law, to alert the judges that somewhere along the way something has gone notably wrong. The only saving grace is that the *Chaplinsky* case is still there to be read, a model of common sense to be discovered anew and to offer a kind of lighthouse for jural minds still adrift.

With the advent of John Roberts as chief justice in 2005, Justice Scalia's position became even more entrenched, and the Court began to strike down restrictions on speech that would have been accepted in the past even by the most ardent defenders of free speech. And so the Court would come to the rescue of the Reverend Fred Phelps and his Westboro Baptist Church as they harassed the funeral of a dead marine with signs saying "Semper Fi Fags" and "Thank God for Dead Soldiers."[43] In this new willingness to protect all speech, no matter how scurrilous and vicious, only Justice Alito seemed attentive to that light that still lingered, growing ever fainter, from the ruling in *Chaplinsky*.

But something suddenly changed again sometime in the middle of 2017. Perhaps it had something to do with the rising intolerance of the left on the campuses, with the widely spreading "cancel culture." Limiting speech was no longer a matter of fastening on that tight class of insults and epithets instantly and widely understood. The move now was to ban from the campuses genuine substantive arguments on the most contested moral questions of the day. It might have occasioned no surprise that even conservative judges, faced with a wave of illiberalism, would have sought some line of defense for speech that did not depend on reasoning overly refined. But what came suddenly was a lurch to the side of what might be called, sympathetically, a "soft and strategic relativism," or a relativism decorously covered over in the hope of shoring up more protections of speech. This sudden move seemed to be born of desperation. The conservative justices seemed to be seeking some tenable line that would slow the wave of repression running through the campuses and flowing over into our political life out of doors. But with that move, it might be said that the bottom fell out of their First

Amendment jurisprudence. For on the basis of moral relativism, it becomes ever harder to explain why an affable willingness to tolerate and protect even the assaulting and the vicious counts in any way as a "good" to be savored and preserved and woven into our laws. What began as move of desperation soon revealed itself as the mark of a jurisprudence on a downward spiral.

CHAPTER 8

The Conservatives and the Lure of Defensive Relativism: Spiraling Down

O ver forty years ago, a dear friend and seasoned lawyer in New York told me that corporations were not permitted under the law to have obscenities in their names. Were that not the case, we could expect to see the telephone directories at the time filled with such listings as "The Amherst F—ing Fuel Co." And yet recently, in two rulings within the space of three years, this rather prosaic issue, which had stirred hardly a tremor in the world of law, caused two justices of the Supreme Court to do a flip that promises to unsettle the laws on "speech" even further.

Matal v. Tam (2017) involved a musical band composed of young people with Asian backgrounds who styled themselves "The Slants."[1] The federal Patent and Trademark Office, taking that name as a term of derision, denied the band a trademark, invoking a provision in federal law that barred the registration of any trademark that may "disparage...or bring...into contemp[t] or disrepute" any "persons, living or dead." But the Supreme Court struck down this use of the power of the law to restrict the freedom of businesses to name themselves. The name "The Slants" was evidently an effort to make light of a snide epithet for Asians. Justice Alito caught the sense of the matter, in his opinion for the Court, when he remarked on the belief held by members of the band "that by taking that slur as the name of their group, they will help to 'reclaim' the term and drain its denigrating force."[2]

There was nothing novel in the understanding behind the statute. As we have seen, the law had long recognized that certain terms or expressions are widely understood as terms of derision and insult. "Slants" seemed to be part of that same family of expressions and could be barred from respectable discourse for that reason. Whether the Trademark Office got that call right or wrong can be readily answered using the formula of the *Chaplinsky* case. The question of whether this, or any other particular term, was in fact a term of derision could be established by consulting surveys that might have been taken on the matter, as in the case of the surveys that sought to gauge the question whether the name "Washington Redskins" was a term of insult or denigration. But wanting a survey, the matter could have been addressed by any panel of ordinary folk who might be called on as a jury. And if the evidence suggested that the term "Slants" did not carry anything close to the opprobrium of the infamous *N*-word, the Trademark Office could have waived its objections. Or it could waive them even after the decision against the trademark if there had been a public protest or a query raised in Congress. That might have been enough to nudge the office to take a second look at what it had done.

In other words, the whole matter could have been resolved without the Supreme Court's treating this as a question of high moment. The Court could have shied away from creating nothing less than a constitutional right to give names to businesses without the restraints of that civility that may still be applied to the ordinary speech of daily life. And yet this case moved even Justice Alito to break from the position he had held, often in lonely dissent, as his conservative colleagues had thrown over almost every lingering justification for judging and restraining speech that denigrates and assaults. Alito had been the sole dissenter in *Snyder v. Phelps* (2011), when, as we have seen, the Reverend Fred Phelps and his crew harassed the funeral of a young Marine with signs saying "Semper Fi Fags."[3] It was clear to Justice Alito that what had occurred in that case was a "vicious verbal assault." As Alito understood, restraining Phelps from such an unwarranted, unjustified assault interfered in no way with his religious or civic freedom. Almost alone among judges over the previous forty years, Alito seemed to have hold of that key point in Justice Murphy's opinion in the *Chaplinsky* case: that gross words of assault or denigration "are no essential part of any exposition of ideas, and are of such slight social value as a step to truth that any benefit that may be derived from them is clearly outweighed by the social interest in order and morality."

For many years already, the Court had been drifting to a kind of decorous relativism, given a cover of innocence because it came with lofty language emitted by men and woman in robes enthroned in a kind of temple. This shift had gone on gradually for a long while, with the current becoming more confirmed with each case, and plainly it was running beyond the powers of Alito to arrest its progress. Something evidently tipped for him in, of all things, the case of *Matal v. Tam* on "The Slants." Somehow the question of denigrating terms in the names of businesses finally moved Alito to abandon his earlier position and step into the current that had been carrying his colleagues. Seeing the matter anew, Alito was moved to take the doctrines governing speech onto an entirely new plane: "We now hold that this provision [on derogatory names of companies] violates the Free Speech Clause of the First Amendment. It offends a bedrock First Amendment principle: Speech may not be banned on the ground that it expresses ideas that offend."[4]

The shift was simple, but unsettling. For the implication here was that "offense" is entirely subjective—that different words or modes of expression may offend people for reasons that may be wholly personal or idiosyncratic. What is ruled out here is that something may indeed be done in an act of speech, or other expressive acts, that is offensive in principle—that may inflict harm without justification. The assumption now was that nothing ever done through the instrument of speech may ever be, in principle, offensive and wrongful.

Alito's lines brought back to me the scene from forty years earlier, when I was brought into a meeting with the American Civil Liberties Union (ACLU) to state "the other side" in a case dealing with a band of Nazis in Skokie, Illinois. The self-styled Nazis were seeking to parade, with swastikas and armbands, in a community containing many Jews who had survived the Holocaust. David Hamlin of the ACLU declared at the time that the First Amendment "protects all ideas—popular or despised, good or bad...so that each of us can make a free and intelligent choice." In Hamlin's translation, it was a matter of being "popular" or "despised"—to be despised was merely to be "unpopular."[5] It was no part of his understanding that certain things may be, in themselves and in principle, *truly* despicable. And now it may be the height—or the depth—of irony that this position of the ACLU seems to be settling as the position even of conservatives on the Court.

But during the debate over the Nazis in Skokie I had pointed out that the real threat did not come from that ragtag bunch calling itself the American "Nazis." The more serious danger was a political class talking itself into the notion, as David Hamlin had it, that *we must be free to hear the Nazis because we must be free to choose the Nazis* and their policies in a free election. The assumption, in other words, is that democracy is all process and no substance: that people are free to choose anything—to choose slavery or genocide—as long as it is done in a democratic way with the vote of a majority. In this under-standing it would be legitimate for the American people to choose the Nazis or the white supremacists because their ends are no less legitimate than any other set of ends on offer in our politics.

But the very freedom to choose a candidate or a party in a free election sprang, of course, from the "proposition," as Abraham Lincoln called it, that "all men are created equal," that the only right-ful government over human beings depends on "the consent of the governed." The Nazis, on their racial principle, rejected that found-ing premise and, with it, the regime of free elections. To say that it was legitimate to choose the Nazis in an election was to say that it was legitimate to choose the party that would end free elections. And as it acted out its character, it would sweep away also that regime of absolute freedom of speech that the ACLU affects to trea-sure. But if that regime of freedom was good in principle, we could not be warranted in choosing to sweep it away. If that regime is not rightful in point of principle, then the principle of "all men are cre-ated equal" could not itself be true. It could not be, as Lincoln thought it was, a "self-evident" or necessary "truth, applicable to all men and all times."[6] It could be, at best, only something true now and then. If it is not an enduring truth, it must only be an opinion, no more or less true than any other set of opinions on offer in the political landscape.

Again, the real danger posed by that case in Skokie was not that of the gaggle of a dozen would-be Nazis on the street. The deeper danger was that lawyers from the best schools, heading the ACLU, would talk themselves out of the very principles that marked this regime and the ground of their own freedom. But the even sadder move is that a corps of gifted conservative judges, bracing for a wave of intolerance, seem willing now to adopt as their own the jural doc-trines on speech established by the ACLU.

Only a year after *Matal v. Tam*, this slide into a tactical relativism would be taken a step further in the famous case of Jack Phillips, the Masterpiece Cakeshop baker who had refused to design a cake to celebrate a same-sex wedding. The case did not exactly have a resounding resolution. For Justice Kennedy, the swing vote, the case turned on the fact that the Colorado Civil Rights Commission had gone out of its way to show a gratuitous contempt for Phillips and for the Christian convictions that reinforced his moral judgment. Justice Alito rightly sensed the need to say something more emphatic in defense of religious freedom. He drew to his side his new colleague, Justice Gorsuch, and together they risked taking this emerging, half-hearted relativism just a bridge too far. For now the two justices were moved to say that "just as it is the 'proudest boast of our free speech jurisprudence' that we protect speech that we hate, it must be the proudest boast of our free exercise jurisprudence that we protect religious beliefs that we find offensive."[7]

Is the assumption now that nothing going under the name of religion may ever embrace anything that is in principle wrong or despicable—that offensiveness is simply in the eye of the beholder? But what of Satanism? How can the affirmation of radical evil be consistent with anything that we could consider "religion" rightly understood? And yet, as bizarre as it sounds, that is precisely the argument that some conservatives have fallen back upon: that in order to secure religious freedom from the prejudices of the irreligious or the people hostile to religion, it is necessary that we stop presuming to cast judgments on any religious teachings as legitimate or illegitimate, defensible or indefensible. But this affirming of relativism, this radical denial of the grounds of moral judgment, has the perverse effect of undercutting the very ground on which we would offer a moral defense of religion. Or an account, in other words, of just why religion is worth protecting.

This emerging relativism would be given a further test two years later in a case in which the obscenity in the name of a business was quite plain and unmistakable. And for the first time in a long while some of the justices showed a deep uneasiness over pulling away any remaining restraints of the law. The recognition seemed to be finally breaking through to them of just what might be done to the sensibilities of the public when the vulgarity and coarseness they were licensing could be proclaimed now openly and loudly, from the language on television to the advertising signs blazing throughout the country.

The case was *Iancu v. Brunetti* (2019).[8] Erik Brunetti had sought a trademark for a brand of streetwear he would call "FUCT"— "Friends U Can't Trust." The name was close enough to the *F*-word that the federal Patent and Trademark Office refused to register the trademark. During the oral argument on the case, Chief Justice Roberts voiced a concern that advertisements for this brand of clothing would be posted in malls where children could see them—a concern that would spring up at once for ordinary folk. But even apart from the effect on children, the case made Roberts question whether the government should be "facilitating this kind of vulgarity."

Roberts did not back away from his concerns even as he concurred with the main opinion written by Justice Kagan, an opinion that struck deeply at any law that would impose moral restraints on the names of corporations. Remarkably, Roberts's concern about opening the floodgates on vulgarity was expressed in terms even more vibrant and fearful in the liberal wing of the Court by Justices Sotomayor and Breyer. And yet in registering those deep qualms, these three judges were described only as "dissenting in part." And there we find the true puzzle of this case: Virtually all of the justices writing separate opinions revealed their keen awareness of the corrosive damage in the culture that this decision was highly likely to license. Since the day that the decision was handed down in *Matal v. Tam*, the Patent and Trademark Office had been flooded with appli- cations for trademarks using the word "nigga" for everything from tablecloths and headgear (hair bands, hair holders) to athletic apparel (shirts, pants, jackets). Now, as the Court took a step further into explicitness, Justice Sotomayor seemed to experience a moment of sharp wariness, a kind of presentiment of something like the N-word's being brandished about, making the appalling now routine. Every justice speaking on the question voiced the wish that Congress replace the current law with a measure more narrowly focused to deal with vulgarity, obscenity, and lewdness. And yet, each one of them fell in line to strike down the law as it was, finding its prohibi- tion of "immoral" trademarks too broadly phrased. So convinced were they that the law was too vague to be sustained that they some- how failed to notice that the administrators applying the law were applying it precisely as these justices would have wished.

What the justices failed to see was that there was in fact no prac- ticable way for the law to be rewritten. It could not have been made more precise. Just why that was so had been explained many years ago by the redoubtable Thomas Reid, the Scot philosopher of the eighteenth century who was studied so closely by that fellow Scot, James Wilson, and read with deep respect by both John Adams and Thomas Jefferson. Passages from his works were threaded through James Wilson's lectures on law, and Wilson invoked Reid in one of the first cases in the Supreme Court, *Chisholm v. Georgia*, in 1793.[9]

The lesson from Thomas Reid came in the early pages of his classic book *Essays on the Active Powers of the Human Mind*. His targets were the moral skeptics led by David Hume, and among the things that Hume professed not to know was the very meaning of such things as "active powers" possessed by human beings. But here, as in other cases, wrote Reid, "the philosophers have found great difficulties about a thing which, to the rest of mankind, seems perfectly clear." The ordinary man understands, without the need for reflection, the "active power" he exerts to perform his own acts, from the prosaic to the grand, whether choosing to open a bottle or to join the army. Reid was referring to things so elementary that the ordinary person grasps them as a matter of course, and virtually has to take them for granted. "It is well known," he said, "that there are many things perfectly understood and of which we have clear and distinct conceptions, which cannot be logically defined": "No man ever attempted to define magnitude; yet there is no word whose meaning is more distinctly or more generally understood. We cannot give a logical definition of thought, of duration, of number or of motion.... When men attempt to define such things, they give no light. They may give a synonymous word or phrase, but it will probably be a worse for a better."[10]

Take, for example, the notion of "number." A dictionary would tell us that by "number" we mean "a member of the set of positive integers; one of a series of unique meaning in a fixed order which may be derived by counting." Something "unique"?—meaning "one" of its kind? "A member"? That is, "one" part? There is a "fixed order" or "series," derived by "counting"—but what is it that is counted, and what are the units that make up the series? As Reid suggested, every attempt to provide a definition will end up offering synonyms or saying the same thing in another way.

We might imagine what Congress could do if it were asked to make more precise a statute that depended on terms such as "up" and "down." I would suggest that this was essentially the problem that the justices were asking the Congress to solve in the *Iancu* case, to deliver them from their moral perplexity.

Justice Sotomayor was even more certain than the chief justice that the decision she was joining would "beget unfortunate results." With this decision, she said, "the Government will have no statutory

basis to refuse ... registering marks containing the most vulgar, profane or obscene words and images imaginable." Sotomayor thought
that the majority had been too facile in collapsing the difference
between "scandalous" and "immoral." Justice Alito thought that both
words were too imprecise, that they could "easily be exploited for
illegitimate ends." But Sotomayor thought that "scandalous" could
be more readily cabined to "the small group of lewd words or 'swear'
words that cause a visceral reaction, that are not commonly used
around children, and that are prohibited in comparable settings." She
concluded that the situation could be saved if the Court simply
adopted "a narrow construction for the word 'scandalous'—interpret-
ing it to regulate only obscenity, vulgarity and profanity."[11] And that
move would save the policy of regulating trademarks from
unconstitutionality.

Which is to say: Back to *Chaplinsky*! Back to the commonsense
understanding. But how does that differ from the standard of judgment that the Trademark Office had actually applied in this case? The
statute governing the Patent and Trademark Office authorized the
withholding of trademarks that consisted of "immoral or scandalous
matter." Justice Kagan was good enough to recall that as the office
sought to apply that statute, it asked whether the public would view
a trademark as "shocking to the sense of truth, decency, or propriety";
"calling out for condemnation"; "offensive"; or "disreputable."[12] The
office had simply sought to explain in different ways how ordinary
people would understand what it means to say that something was
"immoral" or "scandalous." *And it offered precisely the same translation that Justice Sotomayor offered for "scandalous."* As Thomas Reid
could have explained, people were simply offering different words
for the same thing as they sought to explain what they could mean
by "insulting," "derogatory," "obscene," "offensive," and "stirring anger
and conflict."

In his own rambling way, Justice Breyer thought these were "attention-grabbing words" that risked making public spaces "repellant, perhaps on occasion creating the risk of verbal altercations or even physical confrontations."[13] In his usual manner, tripping into an insight rare and novel, Justice Breyer rediscovered the meaning of "fighting words" seventy-seven years after Justice Murphy had set down that standard in the *Chaplinsky* case. But the fact that everyone writing was saying the same thing seemed not to shake Justice Kagan in her belief that no one could exactly define something rather basic, which everyone essentially grasped. She did not see how the meaning of "immoral" and "scandalous" could be narrowed, as the government rightly argued, to words that were "lewd, sexually explicit, or profane." She and her clerks consulted a dictionary and found that "immoral" might mean "inconsistent with rectitude, purity or good morals," "wicked," or "vicious." And "scandalous" would typically mean "giv[es] offense to the conscience or moral feelings," "excite[s] reprobation" or "call[s] out condemnation."[14] Exactly as Reid foretold to us: everyone seeking out different ways to explain the same rudimentary thing.

We might as well ask the Congress to give us more precise definitions of "higher" and "lower." "Elevated" and "sunken"? But the problem with Kagan's argument ran even deeper, for if we take her seriously, this accomplished jurist must have suffered a moment of forgetting Aquinas's first rule of practical reasoning, whose logic is grasped instantly by ordinary folk: that we commend and applaud what is rightful and good while we condemn, discourage, and even punish the things we regard as wrongful and wicked. And so Kagan found something arbitrary in the fact that the Trademark Office "allows registration of marks when their messages accord with, but not when their messages defy, society's sense of decency or propriety." The statute, she observed with laser-like clarity, would favor phrases such as "Love rules" rather than "Always be cruel."[15] That is to say, the office would be guided by the commonsense understanding, widely diffused, of the kind of things that should be commended and encouraged and the things that should be condemned and discouraged. There was nothing novel about that "logic of morals," which in this case led to nothing more astounding than the sense that love is better than cruelty.

And yet even in the face of writing of this kind on the part of his colleagues, Justice Alito sought to assure his friends following the work of the Court that "our decision is not based on moral relativism."[16] But then that understanding of the case was instantly and indecorously undercut by Justice Kagan in her opinion for the Court: She noted that the Trademark Office had "rejected marks reflecting support for al-Qaeda (BABY AL QAEDA and AL-QAEDA on t-shirts) 'because the bombing of civilians and other terrorist acts are shocking to the sense of decency and call out for condemnation.' ... Yet it approved registration of a mark with the words WAR ON TERROR MEMORIAL."[17]

For Justice Kagan, "viewpoint neutrality" evidently means that we must be willing to treat on the same moral plane the killing of the innocent in terrorism and the opposition to the killing of the innocent. If that is not "moral relativism," words have lost their meaning.

Justice Alito touched on the concern that a law too broad, with ill-defined limits, "can easily be exploited for illegitimate ends." Conservatives are haunted by the specter of "speech codes" and of the outright repression of conservative speakers and professors on college campuses. Nothing accounts more for their willingness to swing over to the side of a sweeping relativism on the matter of speech. By drawing a clear, unequivocal line—by their willingness to protect even "immoral" and "scandalous" trademarks—they hope to shore up the protections for speech on the campuses and in the public arena. That concern seemed to have been at work when Justice Scalia took the dramatic step of striking down laws barring the burning of crosses in 1992. But the climate of intolerance and repression on campuses has only become ever more aggressive, without a trace of apology. And why should the conservatives affect to be surprised? Once we sign on to the premises of even a mild moral relativism, we can no longer explain or defend the rightness or goodness of the regime we are seeking to preserve. We have cut the moral ground out from under our defense of free speech—or of anything else.

Now of course these seasoned jurists would not see themselves as "relativists," and would quickly scorn the title. But we may have here a flashback to John Finnis's line about the man who is singing "I'm not singing."[18] It is one of those "performative" contradictions. If judges really hold that nothing in speech is so offensive that it cannot be regarded as legitimate, then they are regrettably putting in place the premises that do the work of relativism even if they are not flying with the brand name. With the best intentions, and disclaiming all the way, conservatives have backed themselves into a spiral of relativism. That is not a path that conservative jurists should have helped prepare for us, and they should not be riding this spiral all the way down.

CHAPTER 9

Recasting Religious Freedom

Belated entries for two diaries, nearly fifty years apart.

June 7, 1965

My wife Judy and I, both twenty-four years old, arrive in Washington, D.C., for the first time, to look for an apartment. I had won a doctoral fellowship at the Brookings Institution, and Judy had given up a scholarship at my own place, the University of Chicago, in order to be with me in Washington. A special committee called together at George Washington University will give Judy the same scholarship she had given up in Chicago, to do a master's degree in teaching.

But on that day we arrive in 1965, the Supreme Court leads the news, handing down the momentous decision in *Griswold v. Connecticut*. What was heralded that day in the press was a new "constitutional right to contraception." More precisely, the holding was that people would be freer to purchase contraceptives without the restrictions of the law, especially if they were married and invoking their marital "privacy." The right to "privacy" that contained a right of access to contraception will be extended fairly soon to unmarried couples and ensembles.[1] And in time that "privacy" will be converted into an understanding of "autonomy" for people to practice their own understanding of "sex." That autonomy will become, in turn, the ground for recognizing—and protecting—the homosexual life. The circuit will be completed in quick steps: same-sex couples will be brought under the laws on marriage—and insulated from any adverse judgment cast in the law. Or rather the reverse: the adverse judgment will be rendered, with the threat of serious penalties, on people who *pronounce an adverse judgment* on the homosexual life, especially if they decline, as bakers or florists, to lend their endorsements to same-sex weddings. But long before that, the right to privacy, springing from *Griswold*, would be expanded in *Roe v. Wade* into a "constitutional right to abortion."

March 25, 2014

I am on my way to the Supreme Court to hear the oral argument in *Burwell v. Hobby Lobby Stores*, a case that brings together all of the "rights" that radiated from the *Griswold* case and *Roe v. Wade*. But those rights would be taken to a radical new level now in challenging the religious freedom to withhold support and approval for these new rights to contraception and abortion. With the sweeping force of Obamacare and a new right to medical care, the federal government has mandated private employers to cover contraception and abortion in their medical plans. The Green family, who own the Hobby Lobby craft stores, offered generous medical coverage to their employees. But they had religious and moral objections to abortion and contraception. So they refused to offer as a "benefit" things they regarded as morally objectionable and harmful.[2]

As I approach the Supreme Court on the day of the argument, I encounter a scene that captures at once the dramatic changes that the Court has sparked in the culture in the intervening years since *Griswold* in 1965. I find the landscape overflowing with the colors and shouts of people on both sides. Especially noticeable is the presence of young women not shrinking in reticence but carrying signs proclaiming such slogans as, "My employer has no business touching my contraception." (I can't help thinking that Mr. Green, of Hobby Lobby, would surely agree with that line. He had no inclination to have the laws bar young people from making their own decisions and purchasing their own contraception.) But in a glance, the vast cultural shift since 1965 could be taken in at once: By 2014, the teaching of the laws has produced a generation of young people who not only believe that they have a "right" to acquire and use contraception without the restraint of the law or the reproach of people around them. That right to contraception and abortion has become, for them, one of those deep, fundamental rights of the Constitution—it has become a deeper anchor of personal freedom under the Constitution than the freedom of speech and "the free exercise of religion." Contraception and abortion are now bound up with their standing as "persons." So critical are these medicines, devices, and surgeries that, regardless of whether it makes more rational sense for these young people to pay for these things themselves, they deserve to have those services paid by someone else, whether their employers or the taxpayers next door.

But what has been added to the mix most recently is a liberal administration sprung from a political party far more detached from religion than any party in our history had ever been. That party was now showing a barely guarded contempt for the religious. The party of the left had become fixed on abortion and contraception not merely as legitimate private choices but as intrinsic goods, which deserve to be encouraged and promoted with *public* funds—and now, public obligations. Once the provision of medical care was given the standing of a constitutional right, once anyone had freed himself from moral or religious hesitations about abortion and contraception, the authorities could shed any lingering reservations of their own. They could regard the directives on abortion and contraception as quite as binding now on the religious as the laws that bar discrimination based on race.

That scene caught precisely enough the changes that have now made our politics far darker and more threatening to the religious. What made the problem even thornier was that the same moral logic posing the challenge here to religious freedom in *Hobby Lobby* would remain quite the same even if the people so persuaded of the rightness of abortion and contraception were utterly free of any hostility to religion. Meanwhile, on the other side, the defenders of religious freedom managed to encumber their own cause by confounding moral judgment with religious "belief," or detaching their religious convictions from the grounds of a distinctly moral judgment.

But in that respect, it turns out then that there is nothing novel here: The confusions revealed in our own day can be traced back to the most moving and earnest statement for religious freedom that sprang from America's leading figure at the very beginning of our national life under the Constitution. Surely there could be nothing more eloquent on the matter of religious freedom than George Washington's notable letter to the Hebrew congregation in Newport, Rhode Island, in 1790. Washington expressed the character of this new American regime, or what it wished to think of itself in its best light. And as he knew, that ideal of religious freedom did not accord, at least not yet, with the state of living practice at the time. In that notable letter, so characteristically terse, and yet with it all magnificent, Washington remarked to the Hebrew congregation in Newport that "it is now no more that toleration is spoken of, as if it was by the indulgence of one class of people, that another enjoyed the exercise of their inherent natural rights":

The Citizens of the United States of America have a right
to applaud themselves for having given to mankind examples of an enlarged and liberal policy: a policy worthy of
imitation. All possess alike liberty of conscience and
immunities of citizenship. It is now no more that toleration
is spoken of, as if it was by the indulgence of one class of
people, that another enjoyed the exercise of their inherent
natural rights. For happily the Government of the United
States, which gives to bigotry no sanction, to persecution
no assistance requires only that they who live under its
protection should demean themselves as good citizens, in
giving it on all occasions their effectual support.

Ordinary folks may invoke their rights under the First Amendment
without quite realizing that they are appealing merely to the "positive
law" contained in the first nine amendments in the Constitution. But
clearly their understanding runs deeper—to something closer to the
sense of things conveyed by George Washington. In their natural
understanding they do seem to think that they are appealing to something in principle right, something closer then to a natural right,
which would be there even without the Constitution. Several years
before George Washington's letter, James Madison had invoked a comparable notion of the freedom of religion as nothing less than a natural
right. In his "Memorial and Remonstrance against Religious
Assessments" (1785), Madison insisted that "this right [of religious
freedom] is in its nature an unalienable right."

Of course, that "natural right" to be left undisturbed in the religious life did not necessarily entail the fuller set of "civil" rights that
attached to citizens. The novelty in Washington's letter, so easily overlooked, is that the regime in America was one of the rarest since
biblical times in which Jews might eventually claim the standing of

citizens, on the same plane as Christians. But it was a possibility as of yet unfulfilled. For we remind ourselves that "natural rights" could mark simply the right to live with the protections of the law, the securing of life, property, and some elementary liberties. "Natural rights" did not necessarily entail "political rights," and Jews could not yet vote or hold public office in Rhode Island when Washington wrote his letter to the congregation in Newport. We may recall that the Thirteenth Amendment delivered black people from slavery and recognized their standing as persons with a "natural right" to freedom. But citizenship was not conferred on the former slaves until three years later, in 1868, with the Fourteenth Amendment. And "political rights" were not conferred for two more years, when the Fifteenth Amendment provided that the right to vote "shall not be denied or abridged...on account of race, color, or previous condition of servitude."

The natural right to practice one's religion would not necessarily entail a right to citizenship or voting, and it was certainly never thought to confer a right to be exempted from the laws that governed everyone else. For those laws were understood to spring from the same ground of moral reasoning and Natural Law that entailed and protected the freedom of religion. The laws that barred homicide would bar the burning of wives on the funeral pyres of husbands even if the act were done in accord with a religious code.

And yet, if we take seriously the claims to freedom of religion as a "natural right," we discover, with a sobering jolt, that the conventional and familiar arguments for religious freedom in the courts suffer a critical embarrassment. For those arguments are not offered in the currency of "natural rights," with reasons that are accessible even to people who do not share the convictions of the religious. The defenders of religious freedom offer foremost an avowal of their earnest *beliefs*, sincerely held. But on that basis, a religion may claim respect only from people who share those earnest beliefs. The case for religious freedom as a natural right must mean a more demanding test, and Washington's letter should not be misunderstood on this cardinal point: To say that Jews had a natural right to be left undisturbed in the practice of their religion was to say that Jews possessed a right that had a claim to be respected even by people who did not take seriously for a moment the revelation recorded in the Hebrew Bible. Somehow, those who were not Jewish had to be able to grasp *through reason alone* why they were obliged to respect the freedom of Jews to practice their religion even if those Gentiles understood and respected nothing in the religion that they were enjoined now to respect.

In this vein, it becomes critical to remind ourselves that the Catholic position on abortion does not appeal to faith or revelation. Rather, it draws upon the facts of embryology woven with reasoning from moral principles. Catholics argue that there are no principled reasons for removing the child in the womb from the circle of human beings that would not apply equally to many people walking around outside the womb. It is the moral reasoning of the Natural Law.

And so it was telling when Bishop William Lori spoke for the U.S. Conference of Catholic Bishops in resisting the controversial mandates under Obamacare on contraception and abortion. Bishop Lori made it clear that Catholics were not seeking an *exemption* from the mandate on contraception and abortion based on beliefs of their own that may not be shared by others. They were pronouncing the mandates to constitute an "unjust law, no law at all," and therefore *rightly binding on no one*. This was not, he said, "a Catholic issue. This is not a Jewish issue. This is not an Orthodox, Mormon or Muslim issue. It is an American issue."[3]

Bishop Lori framed the argument for religious freedom around the claims of "conscience," but he made it clear that he was not using "conscience" as it has been used—and virtually unraveled—over the years in the claims of "conscientious objection." In that cluster of cases, "conscience" has been taken to mean any conviction that a person holds with earnest passion. The bishop was appealing, rather, to "conscience" in the sense once explained with exquisite care by John Paul II in *Veritatis Splendor*: as an understanding ordered to a body of objective moral truths. John Paul II remarked on the facile tendency to accord to the "individual conscience the status of a supreme tribunal of moral judgment which hands down categorical and infallible decisions about good and evil": "But in this way the inescapable claims of truth disappear, yielding their place to a criterion of sincerity, authenticity and 'being at peace with oneself,' so much so that some have come to adopt a radically subjectivistic conception of moral judgment."[4]

What is lost, then, is the recognition that conscience is not directed inward to the self and one's own feelings, but outward to the Natural Law and moral truths: With the corrupted or relativized version of "conscience" and religion, religious moral teaching can be reduced simply to "beliefs," in the modern, vulgar sense. Step by step, even the religious began to fall in with what John Courtney Murray called a libel or abasing of religion—the tendency to reduce religion simply to claims of "belief," or "simply a matter of personal experience, and religious faith to be simply a matter of subjective impulse, not related to any objective order of truth," and not valid then for anyone who does not share those beliefs.[5] Hence the line grown familiar among Catholic political figures from Edward Kennedy and Mario Cuomo to John Kerry and Joseph Biden: that they are personally opposed to abortion but would not impose their Catholic beliefs through the law. (In fact, of course, as the joke runs, they would not even impose those beliefs on themselves.)

But when it became clear that the argument for religious freedom is cast now as an argument in Natural Law, moving beyond "beliefs," the problem of Obamacare and the mandates was transformed. The landscape for lawyers and judges was suddenly altered, leaving them less certain on the terms that would guide them. For consider this problem of two owners of businesses: Both of them object on moral grounds to the mandates of Obamacare on abortion and contraception. One is a Catholic, whose understanding has been informed by the Catholic reasoning on these matters. The other man claims no religious attachment; he has formed a moral objection to abortion, say, solely on the grounds of that principled reasoning that the Church itself offers as a teaching in Natural Law. Would we really say that the Catholic businessman had a stronger claim to challenge the law on grounds of religious freedom? For his reasoning was in no way different from that of the non-Catholic businessman, who reached his moral conclusion by drawing on the same empirical evidence of embryology, amplified by principled reasoning. Are the claims distinguishable on any grounds that matter? Does one position have a certain dignity as a claim of "religious conviction" or religious freedom that is not available to the man standing against the law *with the same moral reasoning used by the Church*? We might ask, then, with the labels stripped away, Is one man being deprived of his religious freedom, and the other deprived of nothing of comparable moral or constitutional standing?

This confusion over beliefs and reasoning came into sharp display when the Obama administration decided to move ahead to impose the mandates of the Affordable Care Act (or Obamacare) even on the religious owners of private businesses. The defenders of religious freedom chalked up a victory of sorts in the courts in Colorado and finally made it to the Supreme Court in *Burwell v. Hobby Lobby* (2014). The courts came to the aid of the Green family, the owners of the Hobby Lobby craft stores and Mardel, a chain of Christian bookstores. The Greens offered a program of health insurance to their employees, and under Obamacare they would have been obliged to cover, in their plans, contraceptives and abortifacients. The Greens asserted that they could not do that without violating their religious convictions. The Greens would win at the Supreme Court, but true to form, the Court was content to treat it as a telling and decisive point that the Greens offered as the grounds of their moral convictions their "sincere beliefs"—notably the "belief that human life begins when sperm fertilizes an egg." Their "belief"? That would surely have come as news to the authors of all of the texts in embryology, who report that point as one of their anchoring truths.[6] The Greens also professed to "believe" that they would be "facilitating harms toward human beings" if they helped to provide drugs that prevent implantation on the uterine wall. Since the blocking of implantation does kill the nascent life, we may ask: What belongs here to "belief" rather than truth?

My friends litigating religious freedom feel pressed to argue within the grooves of "sincere beliefs," because that is the term that the courts have confirmed and the judges recognize. But in this way they have fallen in with a trend of cases that has seen "conscience" reduced, or relativized, to virtually anything that a person sincerely believes. At the same time, with the same line of reasoning, religion itself has been relativized until it is detached from any notion of God and the laws springing from that God. Well into the nineteenth century judges could invoke Madison's understanding of religion as "the duty which we owe to our Creator and the manner of discharging it."[7] But as the judges dealt with claims of conscientious objection, the "conscience" they were protecting did not require the commands of a Lawgiver.

As the years and the cases rolled on, then, "religion" was gradually purged of its defining substance. First it was divorced from any claims of truth. And in a further, exquisite move, the definition of religion was detached even from theism, let alone the Creator who endowed us with natural rights. The Congress had sought to preserve at least some plausible connection to "religion" in the statutes on conscientious objection. In 1948 Congress stipulated that "religious training and belief" referred to an "individual's belief in a relation to a Supreme Being involving duties superior to those arising from any human relation, but [not including] essentially political, sociological or philosophic views or a merely personal moral code."[8] But that statute was tested and overridden in a series of cases of young men who explicitly denied that their religious views were connected to a Supreme Being. After this run of cases, the Congress removed the ingredient of belief in a Supreme Being. But then, with the *Welsh* case in 1970, Justice Black was willing to honor any convictions springing from "deeply held moral or ethical beliefs"—as though any views held passionately would take the place of religion. Justice Harlan remarked that Justice Black had "performed a lobotomy" on the statute. But he thought that the changes were plausible because he thought that it was wrong, finally, to give the preference to those people who claimed that their convictions sprang from *religious belief.*[9]

And so what were we left with? An understanding that reduced religion to a set of beliefs without knowable truths. The Court was willing to treat on the same plane as "religion" anything that a litigant professed to regard as a serious doctrine governing his life, even it were composed of clichés drawn from a superficial reading of philosophy, sentiments read on the back of a cereal box, or any species of nonsense. Working, then, within the broad reach of this reasoning, we have come to see "ministers" of the Church of the Flying Spaghetti Monster, with colanders on their heads, offering invocations before the meetings of local legislative assemblies. They have done it with a sense of parody, being honest with themselves—and after all, is there any moral doctrine that requires that all religions be "sincere"?

Imposing a test of sincerity is just another way of smuggling in a moral test for religions. And in one of the most remarkable tricks of the eye we have administered to ourselves, we seem no longer to recall one of the most momentous cases in which the law did indeed invoke moral reasoning in making a judgment on what would stand as a legitimate religion in this country. Once the Church of the Latter Day Saints was purged of polygamy, it would stand on the plane of legitimacy in our laws and claim the right of "free exercise."[10]

The truth that dare not speak its name is that even many friends of religious freedom have been content to argue for that freedom on terms that accept the reduction of religion to "beliefs" untested by reason, for they don't wish to put themselves in the position of speaking the uncomfortable truth: that not everything claiming the name of "religion" in this country may be regarded as a legitimate religion.

But there is another hard fact that should come as a consolation: the canons of reason will ever be woven into the laws on religion. It is the enduring problem of reason and revelation.

It has been common, of course, to set reason apart from revelation, as two radically different ways of knowing. Protestants, especially, have seen a radical tension between reasoning from Natural Law and the word of God to be found in the Scriptures. A sense of that radical difference was sharpened by Karl Barth in the twentieth century, but more recently there has been a strong surge of scholarship showing how Natural Law was readily absorbed as part of Christian teaching by figures such as Richard Hooker and John Calvin.[11]

But it was Saint John Paul II who cut through the problem with his striking encyclical *Fides et Ratio* (*Faith and Reason*).[12] John Paul II recalled that when Saint Paul undertook his mission to Athens, he entered into discussions with "certain Epicurean and Stoic philosophers." As he reached outside the circle of Jews, he could not appeal to Moses and the prophets. He had to appeal to an understanding more widely accessible; as John Paul II wrote, he had to appeal to "the natural knowledge of God and to the voice of conscience in every human being."[13]

Here, as he said, the fathers of the Church would build on the achievements of the Greek philosophers. For Greek religion had been polytheistic, with a persisting inclination, as John Paul II noted, to "divinizing natural things and phenomena." But it was the considerable service of the "fathers of philosophy to bring to light the link between reason and religion":

> As they broadened their view to include universal principles, they no longer rested content with the ancient myths, but wanted to provide a rational foundation for their belief in the divinity. This opened a path which took its rise from ancient traditions but allowed a development satisfying the demands of universal reason. This development sought to acquire a critical awareness of what they believed in, and the concept of divinity was the prime beneficiary of this. Superstitions were recognized for what they were and religion was, at least in part, purified by rational analysis. It was on this basis that the Fathers of the Church entered into fruitful dialogue with ancient philosophy, which offered new ways of proclaiming and understanding the God of Jesus Christ.[14]

Greek philosophy was a powerful lever in fending off sophistry, and so it could become, as John Paul II recalled, "the hedge and protective wall around the vineyard" of the Church.[15] As he put it in *Fides et Ratio*, a faith deprived of reason runs the risk of falling into feeling and sentiment, and "so run[s] the risk of no longer being a universal proposition."[16] He recalled the First Vatican Ecumenical Council, arguing against a divorce between reason and revelation: even if faith were superior to reason, the council declared, "there can never be a true divergence between faith and reason, since the same God who reveals the mysteries and bestows the gift of faith has also placed in the human spirit the light of reason. This God could not deny himself, nor could the truth ever contradict the truth."[17]

But what is it then that revelation can reveal? John Paul II said that revelation "clearly proposes certain truths which might never have been discovered by reason unaided, although they are not of themselves inaccessible to reason":

> Among these truths is the notion of a free and personal God who is the Creator of the world, a truth which has been so crucial for the development of philosophical thinking, especially the philosophy of being. There is also the reality of sin, as it appears in the light of faith, which helps to shape an adequate philosophical formulation of the problem of evil. The notion of the person as a spiritual being is another of faith's specific contributions: the Christian proclamation of human dignity, equality and freedom has undoubtedly influenced modern philosophical thought.[18]

As he wrote in the opening lines of the encyclical, faith and reason "are like two wings on which the human spirit rises to the contemplation of truth; and God has placed in the human heart a desire to know the truth—in a word, to know himself—so that, by knowing and loving God, men and women may also come to the fullness of truth about themselves." Michael Novak would draw upon that understanding in his luminous book *On Two Wings*—on

"Humble Faith and Common Sense at the American Founding."
And there he would indeed show that the precepts of common
sense and the Natural Law were readily absorbed, without any sense
of strain, by the most deeply religious at the time of the Revolution
and the Founding.[19] If there was one document that revealed it all,
it was the sermon delivered by the Reverend Samuel Cooper to
mark the inauguration of the new Constitution of Massachusetts
in October 1780:

> We want not, indeed, a special revelation from heaven to
> teach us that men are born equal and free; that no man has
> a natural claim of dominion over his neighbours, not one
> nation any such claim upon another; and that as govern-
> ment is only the administration of the affairs of a number
> of men combined for their own security and happiness,
> such a society have a right freely to determine by whom
> and in what manner their own affairs shall be adminis-
> tered. These are the plain dictates of that reason and com-
> mon sense with which the common parent of men has
> informed the human bosom.[20]

It was vital to know, then, that there was no disconnection between
revelation and reason. As John Paul II had it, "the truth conferred by
Revelation is a truth to be understood in the light of reason. It is this
duality alone which allows us to specify correctly the relationship
between revealed truth and philosophical learning."[21] Our late,
beloved Father James Schall remarked that "if what is said to be
revealed is irrational or contradictory, it cannot be believed, even
according to revelation."[22] If Moses had come down from Sinai and
said, "The Lord, our God, said not to worry overly much about taking
what is not yours, or lying with other men's wives"—if that were the

report, we would have expected to find many Hebrews scratching their heads and asking, "Are you sure you got that one right?"

On the other hand, there has long been a curious lapse of memory when it comes to the most notable instance of man challenging God's moral judgment and having the temerity to ask God for *reasons*. That, of course, was the notable case in which God had told Abraham that he planned to go on to Sodom and Gomorrah and destroy those hotbeds of a morality that was just too far in advance of cable television. But would God unleash his punishment in a sweeping, undiscriminating way, making no distinctions between the innocent and the guilty? "Far be it from You," said Abraham, "to do such a thing, to put to death the innocent and the guilty.... Will not the judge of all the earth do Justice?"[23] If moral truth came solely from "revelation," was Abraham suggesting to God that He had forgotten for a moment His own revelation? Or does the encounter make sense only if it presupposes some standards of moral judgment, accessible to our reason, that God himself could have been expected to acknowledge?

And yet, some of our soberest conservative judges seemed have reached the melancholy conclusion that in order to secure religious freedom from the people hostile to religion, it is probably best that we hold back from a reasoning overly strenuous as we judge various religious teachings as legitimate or illegitimate, defensible or indefensible. That seems the most plausible explanation for the willingness of Justices Alito and Gorsuch to take that intrepid step in the case of the Masterpiece Cakeshop: "Just as it is the 'proudest boast of our free speech jurisprudence' that we protect speech that we hate, it must be the proudest boast of our free exercise jurisprudence that we protect religious beliefs that we find offensive."[24]

Were the justices really ready to hold that the First Amendment protects anything and everything offered under the name of religion—

including anything that is in principle wrong or despicable—that "offensiveness" is simply in the eye of the beholder? Once again there was that needling, persistent challenge of Satanism. How could the affirmation of radical evil be consistent with anything that we could consider "religion," rightly understood?

Putting aside for just a moment this strain of coherence, this detachment of religious freedom from the grounds of a *reasoned* defense, it is apt to ask, How is all of this consistent with originalism and the American Founding? As Lincoln reminded us, the Union, the American regime, is older than the Constitution.[25] The Union began, as Lincoln held, with the Declaration of Independence, with God the Creator who endowed us with unalienable rights. To recall again Madison's understanding, religion is "the Duty we owe to the Creator and the manner of discharging it."[26] That God is the Author of the Laws of Nature, including the moral laws. There is no understanding about God and religion more bound up with the American laws from the beginning. The notion of "religion" utterly bereft of grounds of moral judgment could hardly be reconciled with the God of the Declaration of Independence; it could not be part of any original understanding.

The redoubtable, late Harry Jaffa once offered this commentary on the scene of Moses coming down from the mountain with the Ten Commandments: "Imagine Moses," he wrote, "descending Sinai and finding the cult of the golden calf, and being told by Aaron that the people had just discovered their natural right to religious freedom!"[27] But what Jaffa offered as laughable is now taken entirely seriously—accepted even by some Catholic defenders of religious freedom. One scholar of the law who has worked thoughtfully in this vineyard has remarked that "the fundamental human right to religious freedom is grounded in the truth about the human person; it is enjoyed and should be protected whether or not one's religious beliefs are true."[28]

It does not require any special genius to grasp that we can have
a deep respect for people as human persons without being obliged
to credit as true and plausible everything they happen to believe or
consider true. And yet this argument for a sympathetic relativism
has gained credit even among the professoriate when it comes to the
matter of religious freedom. But, as Harry Jaffa observed, "there is
certainly a rational component of any religion comprehended by the
protections of the First Amendment. The free exercise of religion
does not include the right to human sacrifice, to suttee, to temple
prostitution, to the use of hallucinatory drugs, or to any other of the
thousand and one barbarous and savage religious practices that have
been features of barbarous and savage religions."[29]

My friends litigating cases would accept that understanding,
though they would be averse to speaking of "barbarous and savage
religions." But even so, the same friends have been willing to leave
unchallenged the acceptance of Satanism as a sect claiming religious
standing. In *Town of Greece v. Galloway* (2014) the Supreme Court
refused to find an establishment of religion when a town council
invited ministers of local churches to offer invocations. The Court did
not object when some of the prayers were quite emphatically Christian
in character.[30] But as this practice has spread in the land, the reigning
assumption has been that the invitations to speak should be available
to all sects claiming to be "religions," with no discrimination. There
is no requirement that a religion encompass the *G*-word (God), the
Creator who endowed us with the standing of rights-bearing creatures. Under this dispensation the Satanists in the country have found
a new growth industry, offering invocations before the meetings of
local legislative councils. The affirmation of radical evil no longer
counts as a point of disqualification.

It seems to go serenely unnoticed that the willingness to acquiesce in this style of ecumenism is not in fact a position of large-natured tolerance and "neutrality" toward religion. As Gunnar Gundersen has argued, it is rather a slide back into paganism. Imagine that we have a scheme that offers public celebration of a different religion every day. There will be days for Catholics, Presbyterians, Baptists, Muslims, Satanists, and the burning of incense for new sects on the scene. Implicit in the scheme is that none of these religions rests on a teaching that is arguably truer than the others. Instead of "respecting" these religions, the scheme begins by refusing to respect the truth of these religions, or *to respect the adherents of these religions as they understand themselves.*

But quite apart from any other point of embarrassment, the notion of religion purged of any standard of moral judgment contains an incoherence that destroys it from within. Gundersen made the decisive point: If we detach the understanding of religion from any moral test of what is offered in the name of religious teaching, then we have removed as well the moral ground for treating religion itself as a "good."[31] If there are no truths underlying our judgments of good and bad, then what is the ground on which we claim religion itself to be a "good" that should be respected in our public life? Why do we cast protections around religion with the Religious Freedom Restoration Act? Why do we insist that the government tailor the means to its ends more narrowly when it penalizes people for holding to their religious views? Why should religion evoke that kind of concern when we cannot impute anything true to its teaching?

And indeed we now hear that argument from the adversaries of religion. They have asked why religious beliefs should be accorded any higher degree of deference than the other things that people feel passionate about, whether it is a passion for unions and

the minimum wage or a passion to save the environment. That
challenge has been made, and it cannot be answered by a response
that seeks to protect religion by denying that it has any moral teaching. Or by denying that the religious may be rightly governed, along
with everyone else, by laws that truly command what is rightful and
forbid what is wrongful. Almost no religious group in this country
would claim to be exempted from the laws that bar discrimination
on the basis of race.

And so, in a kind of jujitsu, the new teaching offered by Justices
Alito and Gorsuch in the case of the Masterpiece Cakeshop can be
tested in a "hypothetical" of this kind, which cannot be far removed
from a case ready to happen: Suppose that, instead of Jack Phillips,
we had a baker who had been an earnest evangelical of the fundamen-
talist, Bob Jones persuasion. He sincerely believed that there is a
ground in Scripture mandating the separation of the races. And so he
refused to make a cake, not for a same-sex couple, but for a couple
who were celebrating an *interracial* marriage. He would put himself
at odds with the requirements of the law running back to the Civil
Rights Act of 1964. Does anyone seriously believe that the Court
including Justices Gorsuch and Alito would protect this baker under
the same ruling they used to protect the Masterpiece Cakeshop baker?

But why have these accomplished judges settled in with a proposition of this kind so inconveniently at odds with the understanding
of religion and God that was bound up with the Founding? The best
answer that occurs to me is that the justices have come to recognize,
often with regret, that they are actors with an inescapable role to play
in statecraft. They may have to make some of the same prudential
moves that people in the political branches are routinely pressed to
make.[32] My own hunch is that the justices have come to see the landscape of the law as growing ever more menacing for the religious. It
may be that, in their reckoning, the wave of political intolerance has

now risen so high that they think there is a better chance of securing freedom by drawing a wider line to protect all manner of political speech and all manner of religious conviction, no matter how zany. They may be willing now to protect some aggressive racists and even Satanists, if that is the cost of protecting legitimate religion and religious institutions.

But as the late Stan Evans used to say, "the problem with pragmatism is that it doesn't work."[33] The Satanists and the self-styled Nazis and racists have been a fringe minority not because most people have studied the doctrines of these groups, but because there has been a hovering sense of something deeply unrespectable and wrong about them. If the law now begins to teach that the doctrines of the Satanists and the Nazis are no less legitimate than any other principles or slogans, should we really be surprised if this sweeping away of moral judgment removes the inhibitions that may still be holding some people back from being drawn to these groups?

And then the further turn of the screw: If we declare now, in a grand casting away of moral judgment, that there are no grounds for discriminating between legitimate and illegitimate religions based on what they teach, and no grounds on which to show that religion counts as a "good," but as something no better or worse than anything else—what would hold back the large and growing party in our society that has become hostile to religion? What would prevent that party from imposing its secular religion, its new orthodoxy of abortion, same-sex couplings, and transgenderism? It is already inclined to impose this new orthodoxy, without apology, on Christian hospitals and charities and schools, and to treat the complaints as mere noise. And if religion bears no distinct truth, why would the complaints of Christians now be different in any way from the complaints of other people who find their interests overridden, their freedom diminished, because they are on the losing side when the votes come in?

But critics may rightly ask, What alternative are you offering? I would suggest that we brace ourselves for a move out of the groove grown familiar—that we detach ourselves from the impulse to defend religion by reducing it to a matter of "belief" with little claim to "truth." The issue may be joined rather by contesting the very substance and justification for the laws that have been used as battering rams against the religious. No instrument in that arsenal has been more powerful than the statutes and regulations at all levels of government that bar discrimination based on "sexual orientation." That has been the device for putting Catholic Charities out of business when it would not place children for adoption with a same-sex couple. It is also the device that has been used with such crushing effect on people who will not make cakes or arrange flowers for same-sex weddings. It was used against Jack Phillips in Colorado even before Colorado installed same-sex marriage in its laws. Almost no religious group would challenge the validity of the laws that bar racial discrimination, for we have come to see why it would be deeply incoherent to draw adverse moral inferences about the goodness and worth of people on the basis of race, as though race exerted a deterministic control on the conduct of any person. But no compelling principle of that kind can possibly explain why it would be "wrong" for people to have an aversion to such "sexual orientations" as, for example, pedophilia or bestiality. For after all, even the gay activists make discriminations and cast judgments here. There has been a serious debate among them over the years as to whether to treat as legitimate the North American Man/Boy Love Association or the pedophiles. And that says nothing about the zoophiles, the people inclined to bestiality, or sex with animals. But if even the gay activists think they can regard certain "sexual orientations" as illegitimate, how could the law be justified in barring, in a sweeping way, *all* discrimination based on sexual orientation?

To insist that these rights apply only to "consenting adults" is once again to smuggle in a moral judgment on the orientations that are legitimate or illegitimate. As the members of the Man/Boy Love Association could argue, there is no danger of pregnancy in relations between an older man and a teenage boy, and no danger of the necessity of taking life in an abortion. The youngster can be alerted to the physical or medical dangers in a sexual relationship as he may be instructed in the dangers of tractors and dangerous equipment when he works on a family farm. And since there is no prospect of begetting children—if it is simply a matter of mutual pleasure—the teenager can surely claim to be the sovereign judge of what gives him pleasure. The members of the Man/Boy Love Association would pose a challenge in asking, *Why should the "sexual orientation" of pedophilia be any less legitimate than the orientation toward any other variety of same-sex relations?*

But apart from these questions at the very core of the matter, there has been some rather striking evidence that some sexual "orientations" may be seriously unstable. Paul McHugh noted that "a 10-year study of 79 non-heterosexual women...in 2008, reported that 67 percent changed their identity at least once, and 36 percent changed their identity more than once."[34] In other words, we do not even have a clear definition of the "protected class" here, the people licensed to launch lawsuits and stir prosecutions.

In contrast, then, to avowals of feeling and "beliefs," *substantive* arguments could come into play on the question of these laws on "sexual orientation." Such arguments would make no reference to religion or "beliefs." To challenge the very premises and substance of these laws is to challenge the justification for the laws and for the punishments they mete out.

In the classic understanding, we do a portentous thing when we impose laws on other people, and that move will always call for a *justification*, an explanation of what makes it *just* or rightful for others as well as ourselves. With that sense of things we may return to the Green family, the owners of the Hobby Lobby stores, and their litigation over Obamacare: Before the law could impose the mandates of Obamacare on the owners of the Hobby Lobby stores, those proposing the law should bear the burden of showing that there is something deeply unreasonable about the understanding held by the Greens. The Greens are not contesting that, under the laws, people have a right to choose contraception or abortion for themselves. But that right has never challenged the freedom of others to turn away from those things for themselves in moral disapproval. Nor should it bar them from refusing to endorse or support abortions for those who come under their private support.

In the case of the Green family, the moral argument here may be deepened by pointing out the claims that the Greens have forgone: They did not make the kinds of arguments we have seen in the past on the part of people who object "conscientiously" to the fact that the money they are compelled to pay in taxes is being used for policies they find deeply repugnant. They were not complaining, as people complained in years past, that their money was being used to support the United Nations, provide welfare to unmarried mothers, or even to fund abortions. The Greens understood that they were already committed, through the nexus of the tax system, to the support of those abortions funded by the government. The question in the *Hobby Lobby* case was why the Greens should be compelled to support abortion directly and personally through the medical services they fund for their employees. In an earlier day, the very notion of the public authority compelling a private person A to make payments, or transfer his property, to private person B, would have been marked as the plainest example of "class legislation" and a form of legalized theft.[35] If undertaken by the federal government, it would have come clearly under the Fifth Amendment as a taking of property without due process of law. Chief Justice Chase caught the sense of this matter in the famous legal tender cases, when he remarked that the constitutional provision on the taking of property "does not, in terms, prohibit legislation which appropriates the private property of one class of citizens to the use of another class; but if such property cannot be taken for the benefit of all, without compensation, it is difficult to understand how it can be so taken for the benefit of a part without violating the spirit of the prohibition."[36]

To put it another way, if a service is mandated by the federal government, the federal government should be required to fund that service, not transfer a *public service to private persons to bear at private expense*. That convenient device simply avoids the discipline of constitutionalism. For in freeing the government from the need to raise the money to cover its own commitments, it frees the government from the need to justify to the voters the taxes it is laying upon them to raise that money. In the case of abortion, the surgery is readily affordable by most people who desire to have it. If an additional child is really an economic burden, then it would make as much sense to borrow money for the abortion as to borrow money to pay for a car or a smart phone.

The readiest general rationale for the public funding of abortions is that the measure is necessary for the public safety or health. But abortion is not a procedure that relieves any illness or cures any disease, for pregnancy is not an illness. And if the offspring in the womb cannot be anything other than human, then abortion could hardly enhance the "public safety" by withdrawing the protections of the law from a whole class of human beings.

What I have been sketching here is a mode of defending the embattled religious by appealing to the constitutional rights that are drawn from the same moral root but do not hinge on matters of ineffable "belief" or "sincerity." Just at the time that I was making this argument in public settings, two accomplished federal judges, in two different federal circuits, were offering some examples of how these arguments could be cast: in early November 2013, Judge Janice Rogers Brown writing for a panel in the D.C. Circuit in the case of *Gilardi v. U.S. Department of Health and Human Services* (HHS), and about two weeks later Judge Diane Sykes, in the Seventh Circuit, writing for the appellate panel in the companion cases of *Korte v. HHS* and *Grote v. Sebelius*. It was telling, I think, what both judges made clear was *not* at issue in these cases. As Judge Brown wrote, the D.C. Circuit case was not about "the sincerity of the Gilardis' religious beliefs, nor does it concern the theology behind Catholic precepts on contraception."[37] And Judge Sykes was willing to leave uncontested the sincerity of the plaintiffs. The judges engaged these cases at a different level. A "right to contraception" was not at issue because the owners of these businesses had not barred the access of anyone to contraceptives. Judge Brown noted that "the government has failed to demonstrate how such a right...can extend to the compelled subsidization of a woman's procreative practices."[38] The employer may not bar his employees from using contraception, but how can that create an obligation on his part to fund it?

Judge Sykes observed that the government cited two "public interests" here: first, that the "public health" would be enhanced by the wider availability of contraceptives; and second, that "gender equality" would be advanced if women could be as liberated from the prospects of pregnancy as men were. But even if it were the case that a vast public good would be served by diffusing contraceptives more widely in the land, why would any of this justify a policy of forcing an unwilling person to bear a direct personal responsibility in funding these services for any other particular person? As Judge

Sykes pointed out, contraceptives could be distributed to the population at large in many other ways: The government could provide
"contraception insurance"; it could "give tax incentives to contraception suppliers to provide these medications and services at no cost
to consumers; it can give tax incentives to consumers of contraception and sterilization services."[39] The government could also just buy
the contraceptives and give them away—but with funds it would have
to raise by taxing the public.

In other words, these ends of public policy could be accomplished
quite readily without compelling any particular person to buy contraceptives for anyone else—and to violate his religious principles.[40]

Judges Brown and Sykes both insisted that religious beliefs really
had nothing to do with this case. In their reasoning, the matter was
treated most aptly by testing in a demanding way the justifications
that should be required in any case of imposing laws, restricting
personal freedom, and commandeering personal property. It was a
style of judging that was more familiar before the New Deal and the
advent of the administrative state. But that mode of judging was
available to Judges Brown and Sykes now because, while the judgment did not hinge on religion, the cases were being argued under
the Religious Freedom Restoration Act (or RFRA). That act put upon
the government the burden of showing whether its ends could be
attained with measures that did not restrict the freedom of people to
be governed by their religious convictions. In other words, under the
banner of religious freedom, *the Congress had authorized judges to
do what judges had done in the past and ought to do under the premises
of a constitutional order*: to test in a demanding way the laws that
would restrict personal freedom in any domain, including the freedom to run a business. The Congress had carved out a domain in
which judges were free to do what they should be able to do across
the board, *in all other cases.*

What I'm arguing is that there is *nothing morally diminished* when we defend the rights of the religious by invoking the same principles of law that come into play in other instances: when we defend the rights of human persons not to be enslaved, not to have their lives taken, their earnings confiscated, their liberties restricted *without justification*. For these principles are all drawn from the same moral core, and they begin with that recognition of the human person as a bearer of rights. What people may no longer notice is just how deeply those principles of constitutionalism are woven in with our religious tradition. Or to put it another way, the whole notion of natural and constitutional "rights" is amplified when the human person is *seen through the lens of our religious understanding*. Pope Leo XIII caught this point in the opening sentence of his 1888 encyclical *On The Nature of Human Liberty*. He observed there that "Liberty, the highest of natural endowments, being the portion only of intellectual or rational creatures, confers on man this dignity," that he is the bearer of rights.[41] We don't impute "liberty" to cows and horses, creatures without reason. They cannot direct themselves to ends rightful or wrongful; they cannot impart a moral purpose to inanimate matter. Chesterton said that animals have no religious sense: When was the last time, he asked, that you heard of a cow giving up grass on Friday?[42] He might as aptly have asked, When was the last time you heard of a cow or any other animal making a promise and keeping a commitment even when it no longer accorded with its interests or inclinations? Our language of law speaks of persons, of their rights and wrongs and their "injuries," the unjustified harms they suffer. These terms are part of the logic of law, and they were woven in the laws before the advent of Christianity. But these terms are given a deeper resonance by our religious tradition. For with Christianity something else comes into play to tell us what is so deeply portentous about the taking of a human life, or why it is not trivial to restrict the freedom or take the property of those beings we call "moral agents." As the late Gertrude Himmelfarb once observed, we can be remarkably unaware of how much we are living on our religious capital—and how our ordinary language has been given its deeper meaning by a religious teaching long absorbed.[43] Our religious teaching has formed the deep moral reservoir on which the law has drawn.[44] What other teaching could have shaped Lincoln's understanding when he remarked that "nothing stamped with the Divine image and likeness was sent into the world to be trodden on, and degraded, and imbruted by its fellows"?[45] The law has lived, and continues to live, on the moral capital of our religious teaching, even while the awareness of that connection has fled the memory of most lawyers, or been happily put out of mind by them.

In my book *Natural Rights and the Right to Choose*, I recalled an incident from years before, when I had been commissioned to write a piece on the newly opened Holocaust Museum in Washington. As I moved through the halls with a friend, I suddenly came upon a sight that has been encountered by many visitors to the museum: a vast vat filled with shoes. They were the shoes of the victims, collected by the Nazis as they sought to extract anything they could use again or sell. And what came flashing back instantly, at that moment, were those searing lines of Justice McLean, in his dissenting opinion in the *Dred Scott* case: You may think that the black man is merely chattel, but "he bears the impress of his Maker, and [he] is amenable to the laws of God and man; and he is destined to an endless existence."[46] He has, in other words, a soul, which is imperishable; it will not decompose when his material existence comes to an end. The sufficient measure of things here is that the Nazis looked at their victims and thought that the shoes were the real *durables*.[47]

Some of my colleagues back in the academy had taken as their signature tune that line from Nietzsche, amplified by Dostoevsky, that God is dead and that everything is permitted, presumably because without God some lose their surety that there are real grounds for moral judgments. My colleagues have been people of large natures, and they are prepared to engage their sympathies for all species of hurts suffered by the mass of mankind. But even they would have to concede that they cannot give the account of the wrong of slavery or the wrong of genocide that Justice McLean was able to give. They cannot give the same account that serious Christians and Jews can give. And that is how our religious tradition bears every day on our law.

It is only because of how we are seen through the lens of religious teaching as moral agents that we are seen as rights-bearing persons. *And it is then that the full range of our rights comes into sight.* Those rights and freedoms may involve rather prosaic things: the right of a woman to braid hair for a living or the right of a man to shine shoes. Those rights may not take a large role on the public stage, but there is nothing trivial in the right of ordinary people to make a living—because there is nothing trivial about the human persons who bear that right. And so, when we protect the right of Mr. Green of Hobby Lobby not to be compelled to supply his employees with abortifacients or contraceptives, we are defending him in rights that are bound up in the same moral package with his rights of religious freedom. There is nothing diminished in that manner of defending Mr. Green. The Natural Law comes into play when we test the "justifications" that are offered for restricting the freedoms of people, whether freedoms grand or small. And as we defend the religious by engaging these same principles of Natural Law, we are not merely pleading for tolerance of their "deeply held beliefs." The defense of religious people like Mr. Green, in his right not to have his property confiscated, will be grounded now in principles that can stand as objectively true and rightful *even for people who do not share his religious beliefs*. And if a further dividend is to be welcomed, the law is also placed on a ground that can be understood by ordinary people, even those not burdened with a degree in law.

But to put it in another and stronger way: Mr. Green of Hobby Lobby and Jack Phillips, the Masterpiece Cakeshop baker, will find the most apt ground for their defense in the same principles that would defend the freedom of businessmen and other people who share their moral concerns on matters like abortion, contraception, and same-sex marriage even as they profess no religious ground for their convictions. To see things in that light is to bring out a more buoying truth: that our religious tradition does not come into our law and our lives as a set of eccentric "beliefs," merely begging for indulgence and *exemptions to the laws laid down for others*.

With all of the threats to religious liberty in our day, and the litigation over matters of "belief," we seem not to have noticed that the Court, in recent years, has stumbled on to one of its most powerful levers for protecting the religious—and perhaps without quite appreciating what it was putting in place.

That curious want of noticing may be due to the fact that this lever for the religious is nowhere found in the text of the Constitution. Nonetheless, even more curiously, it was Justice Scalia, that stickler for the text, who first caught the matter, in a moment of unfeigned outrage. The case was *Locke v. Davey* (2004).[48] Joshua Davey was a student at Northwest College, a Christian college in Washington State, who had been awarded a scholarship that the state had made available to students in the top 15 percent of their high school classes. But when Davey pursued a degree in pastoral ministries, he lost the scholarship. The law in Washington explicitly refused support for studies "devotional in nature or designed to induce religious faith."

With that law, the state was taking a strong, perhaps overly strong, position on separating Church and State. But that was, the Court held, compatible with the original meaning of the First Amendment, which begins with the words, "Congress shall make no law respecting an establishment of religion, or prohibiting the free exercise thereof." Strictly speaking, nothing in this policy interfered with Davey's freedom to practice his religion. Nor was Davey being barred from public office because of his religion—a "religious test" for office forbidden under Article VI. No right mentioned in the Constitution was violated. Justice Scalia, in contrast, thought there might be a denial of "the free exercise of religion" here because Davey was being punished or penalized for his religion. But there was no "right" to a publicly funded education, and if the State had not provided the scholarship, Davey would not have been considered "punished" because he didn't have one. As Scalia pursued the matter in his dissent, he summed up the wrong at issue: Washington offered a wide benefit on scholarships, but it "carved out a solitary course of study for exclusion: theology.... Davey is not asking for a special benefit to which others are not entitled.... He seeks only *equal* treatment—the right to direct his scholarship to his chosen course of study, a right every other Promise Scholar enjoys."[49] What was coming into play was the principle of equality, but joined now with a right not to suffer a disability on the basis of religion.

And then, a few years later, *mirabile dictu!*, everything came together in *Trinity Lutheran Church v. Comer* (2017).[50] The state of Missouri was trying to reduce its accumulation of used tires by bringing them into a "Scrap Tire Program," where they could be used in creating rubber surfaces for playgrounds. In the sacred cause of "recycling," the state would offer grants to schools that wished to replace their gravel yards with the safer surface. Trinity Lutheran Church had a small learning center with a playground. But when the school applied for the grant, it ran into a provision of the constitution of Missouri: "That no money shall ever be taken from the public treasury, directly or indirectly, in aid of any church, sect or denomination of religion, or in aid of any priest, preacher, minister or teacher thereof, as such...."

This time the Court came down heavily against the exclusion of the religious. Chief Justice Roberts made a game and half-hearted effort to distinguish the new case from *Locke v. Davey*, but he quickly settled into the rule that would now take hold: "Trinity Lutheran is not claiming any entitlement to a subsidy. It instead asserts a right to participate in a government benefit program without having to disavow its religious character." As Roberts recognized, the constitution of Missouri did not deprive Trinity of its rights to hold services, and it barred no one from political office. But the critical point distilled now—at long last—was that the Court would not countenance "the exclusion of Trinity Lutheran from a public benefit for which it is otherwise qualified" simply because it was a religious institution.[51]

There it is, reduced to its simplest, clearest expression. That principle had the advantage also of drawing the adherence of two of the liberal justices, Breyer and Kagan. The Court seemed almost absentmindedly to trip into this simple rule, which should have been evident long ago. But now it has been settled, with the liberal wing of the Court signing on—or at least some of the time.[52] And this rule, so long in the fashioning, promises to be one of the most powerful tools that can be used now in defense of the religious.

There are many grounds of hope, then, as well as dangers to be averted, if people can forbear taking the "low door under the wall": the lure of seeking an exemption from the law solely on the basis of a religious "belief," which disclaims any test for its truth. That move has always had a beckoning appeal. And it is all the more appealing now, in the desperation arising from the sense of having lost in the "culture

war" and with the courts seeming to have turned now decisively hostile. It is powerfully tempting to seek a safe harbor by carving out protections for "religious belief." But that is an illusion that will eventually
be dissolved, for such a move already concedes the main issue in principle: it concedes the rightfulness of compelling other people to fund
abortions as long as one can get a religious exemption for oneself. Once
that point is conceded, it is simply a matter of whether the political
class in charge is pleased to move at a decorous pace or whether it is
disposed to tighten the controls at once, even at the cost of humiliating
the religious. And so a Catholic college newly opened in Massachusetts
may be required to cover same-sex couples and abortion in its medical
insurance. Or to have an outreach program for its gay, lesbian, and
transgender students. Or it may be given a leave from those requirements so long as it admits no one but Catholics or has a governing
board composed entirely of priests. The authorities in Boston proved
willing to see Catholic Charities in Massachusetts close down entirely
if the organization would not renounce Catholic teaching and place
children with same-sex couples.[53]

The willingness to settle for "exceptions" is simply a breathing
stop on the way to surrender or dhimmitude. That outcome is made
all the more likely because the seeking of exemptions is a move to
remove oneself from the political battle and the possibility of finding
allies. The lure of religious exemptions works to deflect the religious
from the true heart of the matter: the need to engage the very substance of the issue, whether it is the undeniable human standing of
the child in the womb or the moral incoherence of the "right" to
declare one's own sex. Nothing less will settle or resolve these issues,
or give us the framework for living civilly together even as we continue to be morally divided.

We may give the last word here to the matchless Father Ronald
Knox, that notable priest, theologian, essayist, and writer of detective

stories. The full sweep of the relativist vision, in politics and religion, was encompassed by Knox in a satire in 1928, not to be surpassed. It was titled "Reunion All Around" and written in the style of a monograph of the seventeenth or eighteenth century. It offered an argument for the union of all "Mahometans, Jews, Buddhists, Papists, and even Atheists," in the Church of England, as the Church shows its willingness to water down virtually any doctrine that might get in the way of bringing in everyone. For all of its archaic typography and style, it has the chilling ring of modernity; it could have been written even more aptly last week.

In this scheme, the papists prove more difficult than the others—the author allowed that their children might have to be put to the sword. Or they might have to be barred from marriage and the privilege of having issue. But as the scheme is extended, the author finally reaches the matter of the atheists. The sticking point in their case is "only one single Quarrel to patch up, namely as to whether any God exists or not." If the consciences of the Atheists can just be eased on that point, they may be able to accept the forms of worship in the Church, especially as they are emptied of any divisive substance.

So the author encourages the theologians to take the line, in proper humility, to allow that though "God is Immanent and yet Transcendent, [still] we cannot see the whole Truth...until we have reconcil'd ourselves to the last final Antimony, that God is both Existent and Non-existent." Those of us on different sides of this question are evidently looking at just half of the truth, and that awareness gives rise to a soaring possibility of sweeping inclusion: "that when we have study'd each other's points of view, and come to understand them a little better, by common Discussion and common Worship, we shall all of us recognize the Divine Governor of the Universe as One who exists, yet does not exist, causes Sin, yet hates it, hates it, yet does not punish it, and promises us in Heaven a Happiness, which we shall not have any Consciousness to enjoy."[54]

With this happy resolution, we shall transcend altogether those vexing divisions in matters moral and religious, and so, as the pamphleteer says, "in these days of Enlightenment and Establishment, everyone has a right to his own Opinions, and chiefly to the Opinion, That nobody else has a right to their's."[55]

CHAPTER 10

The Moral Turn in Jurisprudence

The story used to be recognized at once by several students in my class, as soon as the first ingredients were set in place. But over the years I found that my students were less and less familiar with this venerable account from the Bible in Second Samuel: the story of David and Bathsheba and Nathan. David was quite drawn to Bathsheba, and so, for the worst motive, he put her husband, Uriah, at the front of a battle so that he would be killed. With that stroke, David could possess her himself and cover up the fact that she was pregnant with his child. As the story unfolds, the Lord sends the prophet Nathan unto David, and the prophet tells him this story: "There were two men in one city: the one rich, and the other poor. The rich man had exceeding many flocks and herds; but the poor man had nothing, save one little ewe lamb, which he had bought and reared; and it grew up together with him, and with his children; it did eat of his own meat, and drank of his own cup, and lay in his bosom, and was unto him as a daughter. And there came a traveller unto the rich man, and he spared to take of his own flock and of his own herd, to dress for the wayfaring man that was come unto him but took the poor man's lamb, and dressed it for the man that was come to him."

On hearing this story, "David's anger was greatly kindled, and he said to Nathan: 'As the Lord liveth, the man that hath done this deserveth to die; and he shall restore the lamb fourfold, because he did this thing, and because he had no pity.'

"And Nathan said to David: 'Thou art the man.'"[1]

Just why did Nathan do it that way? He used a rather rough analogy, to put it mildly. But the description was *impersonal*, and with that move he removed the *personal* details of David's situation and brought to his side the logic of a moral judgment: When we say it is wrong for some men to hold others as slaves, for whom would it be wrong to do such a thing? For anyone, for everyone. And for whom would it be wrong to be held in that slavery? For anyone, for everyone. We are dealing here again with the "logic of morals," and we begin to speak about the things that are more generally or universally good or bad, right or wrong—which is to say, good or bad, right or wrong for others as well as ourselves.

Nathan drew David in to acknowledge that he would call that act wrong regardless of who had done it. Then it merely remained for Nathan to point out: *that someone is you.* I used to raise this matter with my students just to point out that moral logic was there, recognized long before analytic philosophers had the wit to start pointing out that "logic of morals." (And it had another utility for me, in dealing with people like that one student of mine who suggested that the logic of morals was something I invented myself in the '60s for the sake of ruining his weekends in the '70s.)

As we have seen, that moral logic is filled out when it is combined with Aquinas's first law of practical reasoning: that the good is that which we are obliged to do, and the bad and wrong are the things we are obliged *to refrain* from doing. And so if it is wrong to torture infants, then it is the kind of thing that we are obliged to refrain from doing, the kind of thing that we may rightly be restrained from doing—or punished for doing. That was the classic connection between the logic of morals and the logic of law. When we come to the recognition that it is wrong for anyone, for everyone, to torture a child, we lay the groundwork for forbidding that wrong to anyone, to everyone. We may forbid it, that is, with the force of the law. That does not mean, of course, that we are obliged to bar with the law everything that may count as a "wrong." Prudence must always be at work. But it makes a critical difference that we get clear in the first place about the ground for banning anything: that it is a wrong serious enough to forbid.

That logic was evidently caught in the Bible, in the confrontation between David and Nathan, well before Aristotle connected the dots for us. It was contained in that ingenious casting of the problem by Nathan in *impersonal* terms. That framing of the law is a feature that pervades virtually all of our laws. And lawyers have been serenely working within that framework for generations without the least awareness of this feature as a critical *moral* strand running through their work. These inescapable ingredients are woven so closely in our common understanding of law that they are hardly recognized for their distinct moral logic. But the framing of the law in *impersonal* terms marks the necessary *universal* cast of a moral judgment. The discipline of that impersonal casting of the law is a discipline of getting clear on the ingredients that mark the nature of the wrong that the law would forbid.

The most explicit and important application of this principle has come to us in our understanding of "bills of attainder." In forbidding bills of attainder, the Constitution requires that we specify in impersonal terms the nature of the wrong the law would punish, and not merely list names of people who are to be condemned or punished.

Legislators need to get clear on the ingredients that define the wrong they would forbid; they cannot get around that troubling point by simply naming names. That was the problem that arose when Richard Nixon alone was deprived of control of his presidential papers. Justice Brennan remarked at the time that Mr. Nixon was a "class of one." [2] But there was a need for the Congress and the executive to explain more precisely what that "class" was. "Resigning the presidency" could not supply the ground of a punitive action on the part of Congress when the very purpose of the resignation and the pardon from President Ford was to preclude a punishment. This constitutional discipline of defining the law in impersonal terms brings out a *moral* dimension of the separation of powers that has rarely been noticed. John Locke caught the sense of this in his *Second Treatise*:

> [I]n well-ordered commonwealths, where the good of the whole is so considered as it ought, the legislative power is put into the hands of divers persons who . . . have by themselves, or jointly with others, a power to make laws, which when they have done, being separated again, they are themselves subject to the law they have made; which is a new and near tie upon them to take care that they make them for the public good. [3]

In other words, legislators are cautioned not to legislate for others what they would not be willing to see applied, with full force, against themselves. Which is to say: the separation of powers is a method of *making operational the logic of the categorical imperative.* [4]

The strands then are drawn across the epoch—from the Bible, from Aristotle in the *Politics*, from Lincoln on the issues that roiled the United States in his own day, and from the politics of abortion in our own time; and those strands, drawn from different times, reflect that connection between the "logic of morals" and the "logic of law." And yet the remarkable story of our own age is the trick of the eye that has screened, or even blinded, the vision of people trained in the law. What has been thoroughly screened from view is the moral logic that has ever governed and pervaded the very idea of "law."

Take as a quick, telling example, this problem: We enact a law that bars discrimination on the basis of race in private restaurants and hotels open to business with the public. These businesses, which we used to call "public accommodations," virtually beckon members of the public to enter the premises as potential customers. Now what do we understand that we have enacted? One might, implausibly, suggest that enacting this amounts to telling the public: *This rule to bar discrimination on the basis of race helps to mark off the character of a "just" society; we are encouraging everyone who shares this judgment to bring his conduct in line with the principles we proclaim here.* We haven't heard that construction offered to us because that is emphatically not what we understand a "law" to be. A real "law" is *binding*—it displaces, or closes down, private choice or personal freedom—in this case, private choice and personal freedom to engage in racial discrimination in "public accommodations." There is an *obligation* to *obey* the law. And to say that the law is binding in that way is to say that it may be rightfully enforced. Enforced on whom? On anyone who comes within its terms. In the case of this particular law, it would be the owners and managers of businesses open to these transactions with the public. A law dealing with income tax or social security will be binding for a wider circle. But the point, so instantly grasped, is that the law applies *universally* to everyone coming within its terms. If the law pronounces that it is wrong to turn away potential customers solely on the basis of their race, the law carries the logic of a moral judgment: that the wrong would apply *universally*, to any and every instance of turning away customers on the basis of race.

The law will be binding even on people who may have the deepest moral objection to what the law commands them to do or forbear from doing.

And that draws us to the point that stands at the very threshold of law for all of the great writers in political philosophy: that this state of affairs calls out for "justification." Why is it that some men have the power to have their edicts treated with the force of law, obliging everyone else to obey?

This is precisely the moment when we come up against a hard binary choice that cannot be evaded. On the one hand, we may say that the exercise of power amply supplies its own justification. On this construal of law, those who succeed in gaining and holding power have, through those very exertions, established their fitness to rule. In other words, it is a prettified version of Might Makes Right, the Right of the Strongest to Rule, as Rousseau so aptly put it. It may be decorously covered over, to be sure, with Latin phrases of wisdom drawn from venerable sages, but they are simply formulas to cover the rule of the powerful. There is no lack of urbane people who have accommodated themselves to this maxim at different times under various local circumstances. Some might even, with Montesquieu, thank God "that I was born a subject of that government under which I live; and that it is His pleasure I should obey those whom He has made me love."[5] Or they might take the brash line of Justice Holmes, seeking a law serenely purged of moral judgment and settling comfortably, as he did, with the law as the Rule of the Strong. The obligation to obey the law would not spring from any underlying moral principle of the rightful government over human beings—those beings we call "moral agents," who are so much given to arguments over matters of right and wrong. The justification for "the rule of the majority" would spring, instead, from the unvarnished reckoning that the majority can overpower the minority.

If we hold back from taking that path, the only coherent alternative is to insist that this exercise of power over other men must take on the discipline of justifying itself. To justify: to show why something is rightful or just. When we override the freedom of moral agents, people who can deliberate about the things that are good or bad for themselves, can we actually show, as the ground of our policy, a principle that would be valid and rightful for anyone who came under the commands of this law? Which is to say, we are asking whether there is a moral ground of justification for that law. And if we take that path, we open ourselves to the obligation to treat the matter of "justification" in the most serious manner: we must insist on evidence and reasons, tested in the most demanding and principled way.

But beyond the distraction of labels, we need to be clear that with that simple choice, we have chosen here the moral reasoning of the Natural Law. And we can remind ourselves that this choice of the moral path—the path of justifying the law we would impose on others—is indeed the most *natural* path. It is the path that ordinary people are most naturally disposed to follow when they find themselves engaged in arguments about the most serious things. Once again, in the style of C. S. Lewis, we could repair to the conversation and reflexes of children. In that vein, I raised the question earlier (in chapter 2 above) about a young boy set upon by schoolmates who rough him up and steal his lunch money: It was quite implausible to think that the child would feel that his assailants were right to attack him, that their very success in overpowering him meant that right was on their side. The child understands, as part of his natural reactions, this cardinal point in political teaching: that power itself cannot be the source of its own justification, that the success of some people in overpowering others cannot itself establish the rightness of the act. In his own way, the child understands what Rousseau put forth with sharp, eloquent force: "To yield to the strong is an act of necessity, not of will. At most it is the result of a dictate of prudence. How, then, can it become a duty?" As Rousseau said, "To admit that Might makes Right is to reverse the process of effect and cause": "The mighty man who defeats his rival becomes heir to his Right. So soon as we can disobey with impunity, disobedience becomes legitimate. And since the Mightiest is always right, it merely remains for us to become possessed of Might. But what validity can there be in a right which ceases to exist when Might changes hands?"[6]

I would make my bet that a jury of seven-year-olds would grasp that essential point, even without Rousseau's winged prose. The average seven-year-old will understood what evaded the well-read Justice Holmes.

How is it then that, for years, lawyers and judges have talked themselves into a state of *not seeing* the pervasive moral logic of the law, the logic that has underlain and pervaded what they do every day? How can we account for the fact that most lawyers we encounter will consider "morality" or "moral concerns" as something extrinsic to the law, something tangential and rarely to be addressed—*and not the matter that stands at the very core of law?* Have they lost that simple insight from Aristotle: that the law is grounded in the enduring nature of one kind of creature, the only creature that can honor a contract or obligation—or respect a law—even when it runs counter to his own interests and appetites? Dr. Johnson famously said that one could know a man for years without knowing how good he is at hydrostatics, but one can't be with him for minutes without forming some estimate of his character. As Johnson said, "We are perpetually moralists, but we are geometricians only by chance."[7] So we earnestly wonder: What is there in the training of lawyers that screens out from their sight the plainest things in those divided human creatures they have all about them as clients, adversaries, or in-laws? The readiest answer, I suppose, is that when it comes to the education of lawyers, Justice Holmes has won. We recall again his hope that "every word of moral significance could be banished from the law altogether."

In all strictness, there is not exactly a choice between two moral paths, for the willingness to opt for the Rule of the Strong marks a decisive turning away from any trace of moral concern that the exercise of powers over others must call out for a *justification*. My own sense of things is that the most natural reflex of human beings, as we have come to know them, is that they are drawn to the second path as a matter of course, whether on politics or on any other matter in which they have serious interests at stake. To insist that those men and women who govern me need to establish the justification for the policies they are making binding on me is, I would contend, the most natural response to this exercise of power. And in the same way, the men and women who take seriously the obligation to explain that justification—to assemble evidence and reasons that are compelling—are doing the most natural thing. Without sounding the trumpets or unfurling the banners, they are doing a jurisprudence of Natural Law.

And was this not the choice disclosed to us at the very beginning of the American republic? Was this not what James Wilson had crystallized in the first case that elicited a string of opinions set down by the Supreme Court of the United States, the case of *Chisholm v. Georgia* (1793)? As Wilson said, the law in America would be placed on a different foundation from that of the law in England. William Blackstone himself had said that the law in England issued from the command of the sovereign: "The principle is, that all human law must be prescribed by a Superior." But in America, Wilson wrote, "Laws derived from the pure source of equality and justice," he wrote, "must be founded on the CONSENT of those, whose obedience they require. The Sovereign, when traced to his source, must be found in the man"[8]—that is to say, a creature of reason who can judge the justification for the government and the laws under which he is living. There it was in its starkest form: the difference between (1) a legal positivism, unadorned, with the law claiming its sanction on the strength of power alone, as opposed to (2) a law that needs a moral justification for the acts it forbids and the good ends that it enjoins. With that move it should have been clear: the choice of the Founding was the path of Natural Law.

That is the critical "turn" we take that marks our engagement in the work of Natural Law: that central, pervading discipline that offers and tests the justifications for our law. And we may make that turn even when we are wholly unaware of "theories" contending over the ages, with plausible and implausible versions of the Natural Law. The turn I have in mind is what we see every day as serious legislators and lawyers do the work of framing the justifications for the law. Perhaps the most dramatic example in our own time may be found in the performance of the lawyers for the state of Texas in a case called *Roe v. Wade* (1973). The brief they composed managed to draw upon the most up-to-date evidence on embryology, woven with principled reasoning. The lawyers would probably have been surprised if anyone had remarked at the time that they were offering, in their work, a notable example of the moral reasoning of the Natural Law. But the brief they composed stands in the most striking contrast to the dissenting opinions that were struck off by two seasoned jurists, Byron White and William Rehnquist. In this instance, the Natural Law was not set off against any claim for the Rule of the Strong. It was set off rather against a kind of mechanistic jurisprudence, which took as a matter of high conviction—and pride—that the judges would steer around those questions of moral substance that stood at the heart of the case. The positions that White and Rehnquist took in that case would establish the approach and character that would define "conservative jurisprudence" for the next forty years and more.

In our James Wilson Institute in Washington we hold a senior seminar, meeting twice a year, bringing together some rather gifted professors of philosophy and law along with some notable figures on the federal bench who have been interested in seeing the case made anew for Natural Law. For one session we decided that we would look back with fresh eyes at the briefs and arguments that were presented in *Roe v. Wade*, a case that has become iconic now in our law and politics. It is the case that has transformed and poisoned hearings over the confirmation of judges appointed to the Supreme Court, and indeed for people appointed to federal judgeships at all levels. For liberals, every appointment of a conservative administration threatens to install a judge who will be willing to overrule *Roe v. Wade* one day. That, more than anything else, has made these hearings an occasion for scorched-earth warfare whenever a supposedly conservative administration brings forth a nominee. But as we returned to that now classic case, which we thought we knew well, the reading of the briefs dealt us some genuine surprises.

I had not begun to think seriously about abortion until the late 1960s, and the book that made a difference in shaping my own understanding was a book of essays edited by John Noonan for Harvard Press in 1970, *The Morality of Abortion*. And within that book the essay that made such a decisive difference for me was the one written by the theologian Paul Ramsey. The essay was titled "Reference Points in Deciding about Abortion." Ramsey traced the development of the fetus and embryo back stage by stage, pointing out, for example, these interesting markers. In his words:

- Between the 18th and 20th week it is possible to hear the fetal heartbeat with a simple stethoscope....

- After 12 weeks brain structure is complete, although the fetus is only 3½ inches long... [and] a fetal heartbeat can be monitored by modern electrocardiographic techniques via the mother.
- By the end of the ninth or tenth week the child has local reflexes such as swallowing, squinting, and movement of the tongue. By the tenth week he is capable of spontaneous movement, without any outside stimulation.
- At eight weeks, there is readable electrical activity coming from the fetal brain. Fingers and toes are now recognizable.[9]

As Ramsey traced the development back, he finally reached the point that proved, for me, telling and decisive: there is nothing we have now, genetically, that we did not have when we were that zygote, no larger than "the period at the end of a sentence."[10] It was all there—the genes that would determine our coloring, our height, our allergies, our disposition to certain maladies and diseases. And we ought to know by now that if any one of us had been destroyed at that stage, we would not have been the child delivered at the end of the *next* pregnancy. That zygote alone was you or I.

But as the seminar with the professors and judges returned to the original briefs in *Roe v. Wade*, we looked at them again through the lens of our concern about conservative jurisprudence. And something now sprung out: the lawyers for the state of Texas had set forth, in their brief, an even richer form of the essay produced earlier by Paul Ramsey. It was richer in that it drew more deeply and precisely on the evidence of embryology. It was richer also in the way it wove that evidence with principled reasoning. In that way, it managed to bring forth a compelling moral case for the law that cast protections around offspring developing in the womb.

But as the brief took that form, it defied the clichés that had been cast on this issue from the conservative as well as the liberal side. From the liberal side we would hear that only a "religious" perspective on abortion could induce people to see a real human being in that offspring in the womb. And from the conservative side one would hear that a moral judgment on abortion was a "value judgment" that should be left to the legislatures of the states. The brief for Texas sought to show that this was not a matter either of religious belief or the arbitrary enactment of a mere opinion (a "value judgment"). The brief drew deeply on the findings of embryology to show that the offspring of human beings is human at every stage of its development; that the offspring undergoes no change of species; that it is a separate organism, with a genetic definition of its own, and not part of the body of the mother. And of course the laws on homicide will not be affected by any alterations that this small human begins to manifest as it becomes larger, with a beating heart and features more articulated. The killing of an older, heavier man is not a more serious murder than the killing of a small child.

In the first place, the brief stated the key points that stand at the very root of the matter: "It most certainly seems logical that from the stage of differentiation, after which neither twinning nor recombination will occur, the fetus implanted in the uterine wall deserves respect as a human life. If we take the definition of life as being said to be present when an organism shows evidence of individual animate existence, then from the blastocyst stage the fetus qualifies for respect. It is alive because it has the ability to reproduce dying cells. It is human because it can be distinguished from other non-human species, and once implanted in the uterine wall it requires only nutrition and time to develop into one of us."[11]

We have here, as Professor Robert George has said, a creature with the power to drive its own growth and to integrate the features

of its own development.[12] The offspring is evidently "alive" and growing. And it cannot be anything other than a human being. If it were
not human, an abortion would be no more "indicated" or relevant
than a tonsillectomy.

As the lawyers for Texas went on to unroll their case, they
offered an even richer, more fetching account than Paul Ramsey
had set down:

- At the end of the first month the child is about 1/4 of an
  inch in length. At 30 days the primary brain is present
  and the eyes, ears, and nasal organs have started to form.
  *Although the heart is still incomplete, it is beating regu-
  larly and pumping blood cells through a closed vascular
  system.* The child and mother do not exchange blood,
  the child having from a very early point in its development its own and complete vascular system. Earliest
  reflexes begin as early as the 42nd day. The male penis
  begins to form. The child is almost 1/2 inch long and
  cartilage has begun to develop. [Emphasis added.]
- Even at 5 1/2 weeks the fetal heartbeat is essentially similar to that of an adult in general configuration. The
  energy output is about 20% that of the adult, but the
  fetal heart is functionally complete and normal by 7
  weeks....
- By the end of the seventh week we see a well-proportioned
  small scale baby. In its seventh week, it bears the familiar
  external features and all the internal organs of the adult,
  *even though it is less than an inch long and weighs only
  1/30th of an ounce.* The body has become nicely rounded,
  padded with muscles and covered by a thin skin. The arms
  are only as long as printed exclamation marks, and have

hands with fingers and thumbs. The slower growing legs have recognizable knees, ankles and toes.... [Emphasis added.]

- The new body not only exists, it also functions. The brain in configuration is already like the adult brain and *sends out impulses that coordinate the function of the other organs.* The brain waves have been noted at 43 days.... The heart beats sturdily. The stomach produces digestive juice. The liver manufactures blood cells and the kidney begins to function by extracting uric acid from the child's blood. The muscles of the arms and body can already be set in motion. [Emphasis added.]

- After the eighth week no further primordia will form; *everything* is already present that will be found in the full term baby. As one author describes this period: "A human face with eyelids half closed as they are in someone who is about to fall asleep. Hands that soon will begin to grip, feet, trying their first gentle kicks." [Emphasis added.][13]

In light of all this, I continue to find it remarkable to hear that public opinion may change on abortion because we know so much more about the baby in the womb than we did in 1973, when *Roe* was decided. For that is so patently false. The brief for Texas showed how precise and deep already was our knowledge of the child in the womb. And perhaps the most jolting refutation on that point comes in the decision that the lawyers cited from a case in New York in 1953, *Kelly v. Gregory—twenty years before Roe.* The court dealt there with the challenge emerging already to the laws on abortion: that the offspring was merely a part of the body of the mother and that a woman should have the sovereign control of her own body. But even in 1953 the study of embryology was not exactly in an antediluvian state. The court in New York explained matters in this way:

> We ought to be safe in this respect in saying that legal separability should begin where there is biological separability. We know something more of the actual process of conception and fetal development now than when some of the common law cases were decided; and what we know makes it possible to demonstrate clearly that separability begins at conception.
>
> The mother's biological contribution from conception on is nourishment and protection; but the fetus has become a separate organism and remains so throughout its life. That it may not live if its protection and nourishment are cut off earlier than the viable stage of its development is not to destroy its separability; it is rather to describe the conditions under which life will not continue.[14]

With this kind of statement, amplified by the brief for Texas, the materials were in hand to deal as precisely and comprehensively with the substantive question as we might ever deal with it, even today. In the light of that fact, it becomes even more illuminating to look at the dissents written in *Roe* and in the companion case of *Doe v. Bolton* by William Rehnquist and Byron White. Only Rehnquist wrote in dissent in *Roe*, and White wrote the main dissent in *Doe*. Both of these opinions sought to steer around the substance of the case, or step around it gingerly. That could be taken, in the minds of the justices, as one of the cardinal virtues of their manner of writing. With this oblique style of writing, they were addressing the case without truly addressing the wrong, or the injury, that the law was seeking to reach. Their slender achievement, if we can call it that, is that they managed to preserve this critical distance from the substance of the legislation only by displaying a thorough obliviousness to the most telling points of evidence and reasoning that were assembled in the brief for Texas. And yet they couldn't quite prevent themselves from letting certain muffled judgments leak out about the law they were trying to address.

With any serious attention to the argument in the brief from Texas, White and Rehnquist should have understood at once that the brief offered ample reasons to refute the very premises that White and Rehnquist were setting down to judge laws on abortion. Justice Rehnquist thought that some, but by no means all, restrictions on abortion were constitutional. He took it as given that a state could not outlaw abortions "where the mother's life is in jeopardy." But as he noted, even the majority on the Court was willing to concede that restrictions might be justified late in the pregnancy,[15] presumably because the offspring simply comes to resemble more and more the being that would soon be recognized as a child. But if Rehnquist had paid attention to the depth of the arguments and the supporting facts in the brief, it should have been clear to him that the gradation of trimesters was utterly irrelevant to the status of that small human being, which had never been anything other than a human being through the entire length of the pregnancy. The height and weight of a human being is quite irrelevant to the question of a homicide. The question is just why a difference in age bore at all on that question, once it was clear that we were dealing with nothing other than a human being.

That curious screening or blindness was all the more striking in Justice White's dissent in *Doe v. Bolton*. For White was even more emphatic than Rehnquist about the grounds on which abortions could be regarded, in his judgment, as not only unjustified, but debased:

At the heart of the controversy in these cases are those recurring pregnancies that pose no danger whatsoever to the life or health of the mother but are, nevertheless, unwanted for any one or more of a variety of reasons— *convenience, family planning, economics, dislike of children, the embarrassment of illegitimacy,* etc. The common claim before us is that for any one of such reasons, or for no reason at all, and without asserting or claiming any threat to life or health, *any woman is entitled to an abortion at her request if she is able to find a medical advisor willing to undertake the procedure....*

It is my view, therefore, that the Texas statute is not constitutionally infirm because it denies abortions to those who seek to serve only their convenience rather than to protect their life or health. [Emphasis added.][16]

The point was as sharply expressed there as it may ever be. And yet why did it not yield to a judgment even sharper and clearer: that convenience, or the avoidance of embarrassment, could not possibly be taken in any instance as a justification for killing any other human being? But that was not the judgment that White offered. Instead, he transmuted the issue into a question of the right of the people and legislatures to balance competing "values":

The Court apparently values the convenience of the pregnant mother more than the continued existence and development of the life or *potential life* that she carries. *Whether or not I might agree with that marshaling of values,* I can in no event join the Court's judgment because I find no constitutional warrant for imposing such an order of priorities on the people and legislatures of the States. [Emphasis added.][17]

It was telling that, for White, the matter was now transformed from the hard truth about destroying a human life to the task of balancing utilities and *values*. In the course of that move, the fetus was reduced to merely a "potential" life. White ignored the commanding central proof in the brief for Texas: the offspring in the womb, powering or integrating its own growth, was never merely a *potential* life; it was nothing less than a living human being from its first moments. In White's hands, that inescapable truth—which should have stood as the predicate for any serious discussion of abortion—was treated as a matter hardly even worthy of notice. But even worse, the nature of the harm and the victim were now dramatically transmuted. For what, in White's judgment, had the Court now done?

> [T]he people and the legislatures of the 50 States are con-
> stitutionally disentitled to weigh the relative importance
> of the continued existence and development of the fetus,
> on the one hand, against a spectrum of possible impacts
> on the mother, on the other hand.[18]

The killing of the child—the grave concern that had brought forth the law—was now displaced as the main question of harm and justice in the case. The harm done to the fetus was replaced now with the harm visited on the people and legislatures in the separate states, as they were barred from balancing the question of how much they value the life of a child when set against the interests and convenience of a pregnant woman. This line of reasoning becomes intelligible only if one has removed from the question before the Court the very object of the law in barring the killing of small human beings.

Both White and Rehnquist fell back into the familiar groove of claiming, as White had, that there was nothing in the "language or history of the Constitution to support the Court's judgment."[19] To reach its result, said Rehnquist in his dissent to *Roe*, the Court had to "find within the scope of the Fourteenth Amendment a right that was apparently completely unknown to the drafters of the Amendment." A majority of the states, he noted, have had restrictions on abortion going back a hundred years, all of which suggested that the Fourteenth Amendment was never understood to entail a right to abortion. And then he invoked a talismanic phrase, saying that the right to an abortion could not be claimed to be "so rooted in the traditions and conscience of our people as to be ranked as fundamental."[20]

This was, again, the familiar response of conservative jurisprudence: appeal to "tradition" as a way of evading the vexing question of whether the practice in question is, in any serious reckoning, morally defensible or indefensible. Justice Scalia was ever emphatic on this point, contending that we would find a ground of discussion far less contentious, far less open to political quarreling, if we appealed to the historical record rather than invite an argument over moral truths. But as we have come to see, arguments over the Second Amendment, or anything else of consequence, can be counted on to elicit rival, contentious readings of the historical record. And yet that has not shaken the confidence of conservative judges that the appeal to tradition has a beckoning value precisely because it is a ground of judgment safely distant from the need to weigh the moral justifications for acts of legislation.

It may be worth stepping back for a moment and reminding ourselves that, for all of their differences, the dissenting justices and the lawyers for Texas in *Roe* were coming down on the same side. With all of the gyrations and indirections, the dissenting judges were finally saying that they would have sustained that law on abortion in Texas. And yet the differences between the brief and the dissenting opinions ran deep. The dissenters could come to the threshold but not speak those simple, magic words: that the law in Texas was "justified." They did not wish to speak those words, for they wished to avoid casting judgments on the substance of the law. The judges, we might say, were governed by a "theory"—a theory that told them what was decorous or indecorous for judges to do in judging acts of legislation.

In sharp contrast, we might aptly say that the lawyers for Texas acted "naturally": They sought to show in a strenuous way just why the law in Texas was "justified"—why it was indeed "just" and rightful as it imposed a binding, uniform rule and removed the freedom to order the killing of a small human in the womb. As I have suggested, we have trouble seeing what was *natural* in what the lawyers were doing because they were acting on precepts of the Natural Law so woven in common sense that we are hardly even aware of them.

But what is more remarkable is that this "natural" reflex of the lawyers in Texas had managed to sustain itself despite several genera-tions of teaching in the law schools determined to root it out. As we have seen, Justice Holmes marked the critical turn in legal teaching when he proclaimed the hope of producing a science of "law" cleansed of "every word of moral significance." For Holmes, the majority claimed its authority to rule precisely because it had secured the strength to enact a law and impose its will. Its edicts should not be challenged by judges invoking those airy standards of judgment known mainly to philosophers. Hence Holmes's famous observation that the role of the judge was to stand back and "let the dominant power have its way."[21] But in a civilized manner, of course. Or as he said on another occasion, "If my fellow citizens want to go to Hell I will help them. It's my job."[22]

Lawyers tutored in this curriculum might have thought that they had said quite enough if they noted that the laws on abortion in Texas had been debated and enacted by reasonable men and passed in accordance with legal procedures quite settled and known. Which is to say, the legislators simply had the power to enact the law, with the trappings of legality. But the lawyers for Texas did not take that path of the Rule of the Strong. They engaged rather an older reflex, which had survived the legal revolution wrought by Holmes and his epigones because it was bound up with something more deeply planted in human nature and the rule of law. The lawyers for Texas understood that the law worked by closing down personal choice and replacing private freedom with a uniform public rule. What kicked in for the lawyers for Texas was the irreducible moral sense: if we seek to close down the freedom of people on any point, or close down their private choice, we are obliged to show that we have, as the ground of our policy, a principle of justice that would hold its validity for everyone who comes under the law. Those lawyers had taken the *moral turn*, perhaps without any lingering awareness that they had taken it.

The simplest thing to be said here is that the lawyers for Texas did the most "natural" thing, even though it ran counter to the precepts that had been taught so persistently in the schools of law for over a hundred years. The law in Texas barred the freedom of people to kill offspring in the womb for matters of convenience or advantage or for anything less than the peril posed in childbirth to the pregnant woman. With that sense of the gravity of the law, the lawyers for Texas set about assembling the empirical evidence and the moral reasoning that would justify the law in casting its protections on that nascent being in the womb. And as the lawyers for Texas summoned the discipline to face that task in a demanding way, they did more than enough to show that they were engaged in a jurisprudence of Natural Law.

But let us suppose for a moment that the dissenters in *Roe* and *Doe* had been willing to do the work—that they had been willing to put on the record the robust moral defense of those laws in Texas that the lawyers had so diligently and artfully composed for them. Still, we might ask, what difference would all of this have made for *Roe v. Wade*? The answer, I think, reveals itself readily, for it takes little imagination to see that a move of that kind would have put a heavier burden on Justice Blackmun to sustain his opinion for the Court and draw allies to his side. The dissenting opinions would have exposed Blackmun's opinion, in the plainest way, as a caricature composed of half-truths and untruths.[23] Even Blackmun could have seen that his argument would not have stood up against the array of empirical evidence that formed that brief for the state of Texas.

A telling clue in this respect was provided in an incident that offers a denouement to this story. It is a story I tell with some mild apology, for it has been withheld for years out of a decorous concern for things too seriously revealing said in a private context. But it is now a long while ago, and the story bears a lesson too important to remain unheard. Without revealing more than strictly needs to be said, the incident involved a dinner party in Washington not long after the decision in *Roe v. Wade* was announced.[24] Senator James Buckley was still sufficiently steamed by the decision that he was willing to engage at table with a friend from his days at Yale, Justice Potter Stewart. Stewart had helped form the majority in *Roe*. Buckley had the gravest moral objections to abortion, and he expressed his deep incredulity over the decision: it seemed to betray, he thought, a flippant disregard for the facts known well to embryology about the development of the child in the womb. He then rolled off, in a series of steps, the emerging features of the embryo turning into a fetus, resembling more and more the *child* we would come to know after birth. From the accounts I have heard, Senator Buckley's account ran along the same lines that I had found so riveting as they were unfolded by the lawyers for Texas in the case. As Buckley unfolded the sequence of the development of the embryo, with its implications quite unmistakable, Stewart was apparently jarred. As the story goes, Stewart recoiled; he responded with heated disbelief that this account could be true. But the details cited by Buckley happened to be quite undeniably true: they were confirmed in the textbooks on embryology and obstetric gynecology—and as Buckley pointed out, they had been set forth quite amply in the brief. Had Stewart not read the brief?

Whether he had read the brief or not, or read it with any care, his surprise virtually makes my case: For can we not readily imagine the effect on Stewart if the dissenting opinions had simply brought forth the mass of evidence so carefully arranged in the brief for Texas? It was merely the short rehearsal of that evidence that had produced a jarring effect on Stewart when it was sprung upon him by James Buckley. At the very least, we suppose that Stewart would have been given pause. And any doubts of his own could have encouraged the doubts of others, or at least undermined the glib certainty of his other colleagues. The result might have been a more closely divided Court, too divided perhaps to offer to the public such a momentous decision. The judicial politicians on the Court, doing their calculations, might have decided to hold back. Or a majority might even have been assembled to sustain the laws on abortion, as a majority on the Court had come together just two years earlier, in *United States v. Vuitch*, to sustain a law on abortion in the District of Columbia.[25]

But whether or not the dissent cast in those terms would have caused Stewart or any other justices to peel away from the majority, whether it would have made any difference to the outcome of that case, it would have made the most profound difference for the coherence of conservative jurisprudence. For it would have kept before us the clearest sense of what the case, in its deepest import, was truly about. And we could say at least this much: A style of judging that insists on focusing, in a demanding way, on whether the law, in its defining substance, is justified, is a style of judging that fits more aptly the true character of law, whether the judges get the answer in the case right or wrong. And when the judges focused their genius on that irreducible moral question, the judges would be doing all they need do, in their honest labor, to do a jurisprudence of Natural Law.

CHAPTER 11

After the Overruling of Roe: The Natural Law Moment

I t was one of those inversions of the constitutional order not widely noticed. With a mounting sense of something grave at stake, presidential elections became charged with the question of whether the Republican candidate was likely to choose the kind of judges who would cut back or overthrow *Roe v. Wade* and the "right to an abortion." And, in sharp contrast, whether the Democrats would choose the judges sure to keep that decision secure. Professor David Forte caught the unsettling truth: the president had now been converted into the Chief Elector. It would fall to him to choose the judges who would really govern us from the top of the state—on abortion and sexuality, and all things in between.

And now the moment had come when this question, contested so bitterly for forty-nine years, seemed to have been brought to a point of resolution—at least for now. Six conservative justices on the Supreme Court came together in support of a decision to overrule *Roe v. Wade* in the case of *Dobbs v. Jackson Women's Health Organization*.[1]

The fact that the decision was the upshot of so many years of constant combat by both sides, in legislatures and courts, was itself a telling sign. Ten years after *Brown v. Board of Education*, public sentiment in opposition to racial segregation had jelled to the point that Congress could enact the landmark Civil Rights Act of 1964. Forty-nine years after *Roe v. Wade*, public resistance had still not been quelled. No slogans, however loudly and persistently sounded, could counter the findings of embryology, or dislodge the conviction that abortion involved the killing of a small, innocent human being. Public opinion remained divided, with only slight shifts over the years. About 20 percent of the population would outlaw abortions in all circumstances, while about 22–27 percent would accept abortion without limits. According to the Gallup surveys, most of the country falls in the middle, saying that abortion should be "legal only under certain circumstances."[2] But that vague rubric covers many divergences. People who call themselves pro-choice have opposed abortion in the case of a woman who wants to finish school and get on with her career. About 55–60 percent of people surveyed would bar abortions when the beating heart of the child can be heard. (Among Republicans, the figure comes in at over 70 percent.)[3] But many people in these surveys probably don't know that the heartbeat can be heard with a Doppler device at five to six weeks into the pregnancy, around the time a woman may be learning that she is pregnant. What may be concealed by the reporting on the polls is the broad agreement to be found in the country: most people, both pro-choice and pro-life, readily accept abortion when a pregnant woman's life is in danger (a situation exceedingly rare these days). The remarkable thing is that the public held on so long, reluctant to sign on to a right to abortion under any and all circumstances, even while, for forty years, the federal courts had been quashing efforts in the states to enact even mild restrictions on abortion.

In the aftermath of *Dobbs*, we might bring back the words that Lincoln spoke about a country deeply and violently divided on the searing question of his day. "Neither party expected," said Lincoln, that the conflict would have "the magnitude or the duration which it has already attained." Both sides in the *Dobbs* case were bracing for a decision quite resounding and fundamental. But for the opponents of abortion the decision in *Dobbs* was far less fundamental and decisive than they hoped it would be; and for the defenders of abortion, it would not be as devastating as they feared it would be.

The decision of the Court held closely to the line that had been long settled among conservative lawyers: the declaration of a constitutional right to abortion in *Roe* was the exercise of "raw judicial power,"[4] because nothing in the text of the Constitution had even hinted at a right to kill infants in wombs. Therefore, there was no right to abortion springing from the Constitution, no right that a federal court had any authority to proclaim. The issue would simply be returned to the political arena in the separate states. In the blue states, the most populous states, access to abortion would not be in the least disturbed.

On the substantive rights or wrongs of abortion, conservative jurisprudence had nothing to say. And in the opinion for the Court in *Dobbs*, the conservative majority held to that line with tight control, even when the momentum of the argument worked strongly to pull them in another direction. That the conservative justices would hold to that line was a sober fact long accommodated by the pro-lifers who had worked so strenuously to seek the overruling of *Roe*. People had traveled from all parts of the country every January to form a massive pro-life march in the worst weather that Washington serves up, and they had never carried signs decrying a grievous mistake of jurisdiction. No rage was shown over judges crossing into the wrong legal lane. For the people assembled from all parts of the country for this annual march, the deep wrong was the dismembering or poisoning of babies in wombs. And yet now that *Roe* was overturned, they would see the massive killing in abortion going on, with no serious limits or restraints, in New York, Chicago, Los Angeles, and other cities in the blue states. On the other side, the pro-choicers would find that this right they had come to prize would still be available where most of them lived. Other people were likely to be no farther than a day's drive from a state that offered abortions with virtually no restraints. To make that trip even more encouraging, proposals were springing up to offer payments for travel and hotel expenses for women willing to make the drive.

These women had been given the confidence to think that they had a deep, constitutional right engaged here. They had a point, then, in asking why such a deep right would be lost to them if they suddenly moved to another state. That was a proper question, and something more needed to be said. What was needed were the words spoken by the lawyers for Texas in *Roe v. Wade* as they sought to address the question that any legislator should be obliged to take seriously: What made it "justified" for a community to extend the protections of the law to those living beings in the wombs, even when it meant—as in the case of every law—that the law would be binding even on people who stood in grave disagreement with it? That is the question that should be asked at the threshold of any act of legislation giving the law to people and overriding their personal choices. On that cardinal point, however, the majority in *Dobbs* took it as part of their discipline to say no more on this matter than they needed to say. The case was settled for them, as a legal matter, once they decided that the Constitution did not guarantee a right to abortion, and *Roe v. Wade* was no longer "the law of the land." But just how the majority in *Dobbs* left matters in that state is the question that draws us into the art and statecraft of Justice Alito's opinion.

In the *Dobbs* case, the law in Mississippi barred abortion after fifteen weeks in the pregnancy. The state offered the kind of "factual findings" that the lawyers in *Roe* had supplied years earlier, though its statement of the facts was rather less refined than that earlier version: according to the brief from Mississippi in *Dobbs*,

> The legislature...found that at 5 or 6 weeks' gestational age an "unborn human being's heart begins beating"; at 8 weeks the "unborn human being begins to move in the womb," at 9 weeks "all basic physiological functions are present"; at 10 weeks "vital organs begin to function," and "[h]air, fingernails, and toenails...begin to form"; at 11 weeks "an unborn human being's diaphragm is developing, and he or she may "move about freely in the womb"; and at 12 weeks the "unborn human being" has "taken on human form in all relevant respects." [Brackets and ellipsis in original.][5]

Well, to be a bit more finicky: the beating of the heart is *measured or heard* at five or six weeks, but the hearing of the heartbeat simply marks another phase in the development of a small being already living and powering its own growth. "All basic physiological functions are present" even when the unborn being is no larger than a zygotal dot.[6] The evident purpose of this account, drawn from findings in embryology far more precise, was to show that the unborn child is a recognizably human entity from its earliest moments, long before the shifting state of "viability" has been reached somewhere around the twenty-fourth week. With that move the legislature sought to break through the line that the Court had settled on thirty years earlier to mark the stage when the laws may not cast restraints on abortion. The district court first hearing the case enjoined the enforcement of the law on that very ground, holding that "viability marks the earliest point at which the State's interest in fetal life is constitutionally adequate to justify a legislative ban on nontherapeutic abortions."[7]

Justice Alito would have to deal decisively with that matter of viability, along with the curious theory that the "stages" in pregnancy have any bearing on the human standing of the unborn to receive the protections accorded to other human beings, of varying sizes, in the law. But before he reached that point, he declared the judgment of the Court that "*Roe* and [*Planned Parenthood v.*] *Casey* must be overruled." And they were to be overruled precisely along the lines that were now long settled in the orthodoxy of conservative jurisprudence. "The Constitution makes no reference to abortion," Alito wrote, "and no such right is implicitly protected by any constitutional provision, including the one on which the defenders of *Roe* and *Casey* now chiefly rely—the Due Process Clause of the Fourteenth Amendment."[8] The right to abortion did not fall within the narrow class of rights protected under the Due Process Clause, rights that were "long rooted in the tradition" of our law. Whether they were substantively true or justified as rights was another question, put to the side; for the accent was on rights readily recognized because they have long been familiar to us.

Alito did not address the critical matter of "viability" until midway through his opinion, well after he had run through a lengthy list of statutes and holdings in common law dating back to the thirteenth century. The record revealed that the law had punished abortion as at least a grave misdemeanor, even before "quickening," when the movement of the child could be felt. "Viability" was taken by the Court in *Roe* as the critical marker: roughly, the point of development sufficiently advanced that the child could be sustained outside the womb. Viability was now the line that needed to be dissolved and refuted here, and Alito set to work.

In the first place, the whole notion of dividing a pregnancy into trimesters was, as Alito said, "the Court's own brainchild." Neither litigant in *Roe* had put that idea forward.[9] The point had been made for years that the line of "viability" was shifting and deeply unclear. As Justice O'Connor had observed long ago, the onset of viability keeps getting pushed back with advances in technology. At the time of *Roe*, viability was estimated at about twenty-eight weeks, but it has now advanced to about twenty-three to twenty-four weeks. But how could the definition of a human life deserving of the protection of the law depend on the current state of the art in incubators?

Viability depends also, as Alito noted, on a "'number of variables,' including 'gestational age,' 'fetal weight,' a woman's 'general health and nutrition,' and the 'quality of the available medical facilities.'"[10] But just why is any of this relevant to the standing of the child as a human being who can claim the legal protection that would flow to any other human being when marked for a lethal act? Alito brought the matter into focus in this way: "If, as *Roe* held, a State's interest in protecting prenatal life is compelling 'after viability,'...why isn't that interest 'equally compelling before viability'?"[11] Alito was drawing here on the stirring dissent of Justice Byron White in the 1986 *Thornburgh* case:

> The governmental interest at issue is in protecting those who will be citizens if their lives are not ended in the womb. The substantiality of this interest is in no way dependent on the probability that the fetus may be capable of surviving outside the womb at any given point in its development, as the possibility of fetal survival is contingent on the state of medical practice and technology, factors that are in essence morally and constitutionally irrelevant. The State's interest is in the fetus as an entity in itself, and the character of this entity

does not change at the point of viability under conventional
medical wisdom. Accordingly, the State's interest, if compelling after viability, is equally compelling before viability.[12]

This moving passage made perfect sense—if one took as the
grounding predicate the one supplied by the lawyers from Texas in
Roe: that the child in the womb has been nothing other than human
from its first moments, that it receives its nourishment from its
mother but is a separate organism, with a genetic definition of its
own, and has never been merely part of the mother's body. From that
perspective, the point of viability was just another phase in the development of the same human being, living and growing.

But the justices who were willing to sustain a right to abortion
over the years were willing to hold to that line of viability precisely
because they wished to avoid that persistent, awkward truth: that the
child has never been a part of the mother, and never anything but
the same human being at any stage of the pregnancy. Even when it
came to the later stages of pregnancy, the child was referred to persistently as mere "potential life." For the sake of staying faithful to
those earlier concessions of the Court, Justice Alito was content to
keep using that phrase, even though he surely knew that it made no
sense: The embryo or fetus in the womb can never have been merely
"potential life." A pregnancy test announces the presence of a living,
growing entity. If that were not the case, an abortion would be no
more "indicated" than cosmetic surgery. And if there is a living being
in the womb, it cannot be an orange or a bird; it can be only a human
being. But as the opinion went on, it seemed evident that Alito was
still reluctant to say those magic words that the lawyers from Texas
had spoken in their briefs half a century earlier, even though their
point, about the human standing of the unborn child from its first
moments, was not only sound but inescapably true. I do not think

that Alito's caution here sprang from a puzzlement over filling in the ellipses or connecting the dots. It seems to me that his reticence, or his circumspection, had something do with the theory of conservative jurisprudence that was forming the cast of his opinion. That may explain why he held back, on the matter of viability, from the answer that was truly telling and decisive, the answer that Natural Law would have given to the ordinary Man on the Street: Why would any person lose his standing as human being because he was weak and dependent on the care of others? Do patients in intensive care lose their standing as rights-bearing beings? To a person of any ordinary sensibility, a human being in need of care would seem to engage the solicitude of others to offer that care. When stripped to its core, the argument over viability reduces to nothing other than the classic Rule of the Strong, or Might Makes Right. The very weakness of the child in the womb, its need for the protection and nourishment of others, was taken as the ground for its erasure as a rights-bearing being. That this meaning of "viability" has somehow gone unnoticed by people with college educations may be a measure of the mental screening that had to be absorbed as people settled in comfortably with a right to abortion, without—shall we say?—a demanding reflection.

The long settled position among conservatives was that the Court in *Roe* had taken out of the hands of citizens at the local level the question of whether small human beings in the womb were covered under their laws on homicide. As Alito put it, "the Court usurped the power to address a question of profound moral and social importance that the Constitution unequivocally leaves to the people."[13] When the majority in *Roe* lifted this issue of abortion to the level of a constitutional right under federal law, they made this issue the business of the national government. With that move, confirmations for the Supreme Court would be attended by fierce and escalating libels and a poisoning of our political life. The conservative position through all of this was that the poisoning would cease when abortion ceased to be the business of the national government.

Curiously, it seemed to go unnoticed that when the Supreme Court made abortion the business of the national government, it made this subject the business of the other parts of the national government, and not solely the courts. As we have seen, the national government had many reasons for dealing with abortion well before *Roe v. Wade*. There was the matter of abortion in the medical facilities of the federal government, in the territories, and in the District of Columbia. Inevitably the question would have to arise as to whether medical care supported by the government was permitted, or even required, to pay for abortions with federal funds. And would abortion be permitted in medical schools, hospitals, and clinics receiving federal aid? If so, it would fall to Congress to consider the protection of "conscience" for doctors and nurses who did not wish to be conscripted to perform abortions. The executive branch would also wield discretion of its own here: Would the National Institutes of Health use fetal tissue in research? Would American diplomats resist schemes to promote abortion in international organizations? One way or another, decisions would have to be made, and the powers of the federal government would come into play, even with a light touch, in marking the limits to "the right to abortion."

Or that, at least, is what some of us sought to bring about in advancing the most modest first step in legislating on abortion: a proposal to protect the lives of those babies, born alive, who had *survived* abortions. Here was the chance to establish a limit to the freedom to have an abortion that might possibly be supported by people on both sides of the controversy. One federal judge had already held that there was no obligation to preserve the life of a child who had survived an abortion and lingered for twenty-one days. He referred to the born child as a "fetus," and remarked that this fetus "was not a person whose life state law could legally protect."[14] The Supreme Court quietly vacated that judgment but neglected to say anything emphatic about what was wrong with it. Still less did the Court take time to affirm that the right to abortion in *Roe v. Wade* must have some limit—and that limit must surely be at least when a child is born alive. If the Court had indeed vacated that judgment on the child born alive, apparently that judgment did not make it out into the country.[15] For the survivors of abortion were being killed in numbers even larger than we had imagined at the time. That fact became brutally clear several years ago with the discovery of Dr. Kermit Gosnell's abattoir in Philadelphia. Botched late-term abortions brought the need to snip the necks of those babies who had inconveniently survived. The police got wind of the fact that rather grisly things were taking place in Gosnell's filthy clinic, but they knew that it would be better for them to avert their eyes. Whatever was going on in those clinics, they had the sense that it was somehow taking place on the outer edges of a constitutional right.[16]

To counter that sense, some of us thought it would still be worth it to mark a limit to abortion at the point of live birth. The bill was called, in awful legislative language, the "Born-Alive Infants Protection Act" (2002). Since I had some hand in making the case for that bill in public writing and in walking the halls of Congress, I was given the privilege of leading the testimony on the bill in the Judiciary Committee of the House.[17] I recall that moment now in order to make again a point that has still not broken through the fog on this issue: Once the federal judiciary made the "right to abortion" the business of the federal government, there was no way to exclude the Congress and the executive branch from the authority to deal with abortion at a burgeoning number of points, all of which would require judgments to be made. The decision to return abortion to the political arena in the states cannot possibly perform the trick, then, of removing this issue from the vast field covered by the national government.

As we sought to explain this point and engage the powers of Congress, we reached back to a classic opinion of Chief Justice Marshall in *Cohens v. Virginia* (1821). Marshall argued there that "the judicial power of every well constituted government must be *co-extensive* with the legislative, and must be capable of deciding every judicial question which grows out of the Constitution and laws" [emphasis added].[18] And yet, even jurists are persistently taken by surprise by the corollary of that axiom: that the legislative power must be coextensive with the judicial power. Any issue that comes within the competence of the federal judiciary must come, presumptively at least, within the reach of the federal legislature and federal executive as well. For how could it be possible that the federal courts are competent to address abortion in all of its dimensions, while the doctors of the law ponder deeply over the question of whether Congress may legislate on the same subject?

And so we proposed, as part of the premises of the bill, this "finding" to restate the very logic of the separation of powers:

> If the Court can articulate new rights under the 14th Amendment, whether civil rights or a 'right' to abortion, the legislative branch must be empowered to vindicate those same rights, on the same clause in the Constitution where the judges claimed to find it, and in filling out those rights, marking their limits. The one thing that should not be tenable under this Constitution is that the Court can articulate new rights and *then assign to itself a monopoly of the legislative power in shaping those rights.* [Emphasis added.]

To deny that proposition is to remove the Supreme Court from the web of restraints that mark the character and logic of the separation of powers. But Justice Alito's opinion in *Dobbs* reflected the understanding, long settled in conservative circles, that the power over abortion would lie mainly with the "police powers" of the states. And that line of argument, quickly picked up by Republican candidates to Congress, now casts a pall of doubt on any attempt to legislate on abortion at the national level, even to mark the limits of abortion at the child born alive. The insistent theme of conservative jurisprudence has been that the matter of abortion belongs entirely in the states because there is no consensus and no clear truths that bear on the question of taking fetal life. That this teaching has taken hold even in the most respected and authoritative organs of conservative opinion was registered with a bracing clarity by the editors of the *Wall Street Journal* on the afternoon after *Roe v. Wade* was overturned:

> Some in the pro-life movement want Congress to ban abortion nationwide. But that will strike many Americans as hypocritical after decades of Republican claims that repealing *Roe* would return the issue to the states.
>
> A national ban may also be an unconstitutional intrusion on state police powers and federalism. Imposing the abortion values of Mississippi or Texas on all 50 states could prove to be as unpopular as New York or California trying to do the same for abortion rights.[19]

The editorial staff of the *Journal* could write in this way precisely because the conservative majority on the Court had held firmly to the conservative mantra that the national government had no tenable truths to put in place on the human standing of the child in the womb. For truths of that kind would justify the Congress in drawing on many of its levers of power to offer some protection to unborn children, even in the states having virtually no restrictions on abortion. To avoid that result, Justice Alito had to preserve a preternatural restraint, holding back from those simple but telling words: that the offspring in the womb has been nothing other than a human being from its first moments and never merely a part of the body of its mother. If Alito had put that anchoring point in place, it would have laid the groundwork for invoking the powers of Congress under the Fourteenth Amendment: if the unborn child was recognized unequivocally as a human being, the Fourteenth Amendment gives the Congress the power to act when a state withdraws the protections of the law from a whole class or subset of the inhabitants of the state.

That is what made Justice Breyer and his colleagues in dissent sound rather like messengers coming in, out of season, from another galaxy. The dissenters charged the Court with saying "that from the very moment of fertilization, a woman has no rights to speak of. A State can force her to bring a pregnancy to term, even at the steepest personal and familial costs."[20] And yet that is what Justice Alito and his colleagues had carefully avoided saying. In fact, as Alito made clear, "Our opinion is not based on any view about if and when prenatal life is entitled to any of the rights enjoyed after birth."[21] The issue of abortion would be returned to the states, and the Court would offer no directions as to how and when a legislature might choose to protect the child in the womb.

The indelicate truth that could not speak its name was that, in the conservative jurisprudence at work in this opinion, the child in the womb *did not supply the ground of the constitutional argument* or *the object of official concern.* The dissenters actually nailed this point: "the state interest in protecting fetal life," they wrote, "plays no part in the majority's analysis. To the contrary, the majority takes pride in not expressing a view 'about the status of the fetus.'"[22] The center of the problem for the conservative judges was a theory about the rightful and wrongful reach of the judges, quite apart from the moral substance of the case.

For their own part, the dissenters readily took it as a given that the only "persons" with serious interests at stake here were the women who see their lives and prospects diminished if they are deprived of the chance to order an abortion at a timely moment. What was notably erased from the scene was any recognition of that small creature in the womb as one who might have the standing of a human being, and whose injuries would also "count."

And as the dissenters well recognized, the conservative majority in *Dobbs* had done nothing to refute that assumption. It had not moved to put in place the rival understanding that the child is indeed a human being with a claim to be protected by the law from its first moments. That was the case even as Justice Alito was quite crisp in pointing out that the test of "viability" made little sense. He came very close—closer than any other justice—to suggesting that the child in the womb might rightly command the protection of the law even at its earliest moment: the legitimate interests of the State in regulating abortion could tenably encompass, he said, a "respect for and preservation of prenatal life at all stages of development." But he evidently felt constrained from saying what James Wilson said in the first days of the Constitution. As I recalled in the opening pages of this book, Wilson, one of the premier minds among the American Founders, drew us to the question: If we have natural rights, when do they begin? And his answer was: They begin as soon as we begin to be: "In the contemplation of law, life begins when the infant is first able to stir in the womb. By the law, life is protected not only from immediate destruction, but from every degree of actual violence, and, in some cases, from every degree of danger."[23]

It is a measure of our current jurisprudence that none of the conservative justices has felt free to speak words of that kind. Against that I set down, in the journal *First Things*, what I regarded as the clear alternative, which would accord with a Natural Law perspective.[24] The

dominant conservative view of the problem had been set forth most
sharply by the man regarded as the leading conservative jurist, and
for me, a beloved friend. The issue of abortion should be returned to
the states, wrote Justice Scalia, so that the voters could make their own
"value judgment[s]" on the matter: "The whole argument of abortion
opponents is that what the Court calls the fetus and what others call
the unborn child *is a human life....* There is of course no way to determine that as a legal matter; it is in fact a value judgment. Some societ-
ies have considered newborn children not yet human, or the incom-
petent elderly no longer so."[25]

    "Value judgment" is a term that came into play with Nietzsche
and Max Weber, as people began to lose confidence in speaking of
"moral truths." They would speak instead of those things that were
important insofar as people "valued" them. This mode of thought
has long been settled in the social sciences, and it has made its way
even to conservative lawyers and judges through the language of legal
positivism. And so, whether the child in the womb will be regarded
as a human being will depend entirely on how most people in the
states "value" the unborn child as a human being—and how strenuous they think the law should be in casting protections over that
child.

    Lincoln famously said, of the gravest issue of his day, that the
question was "whether the black man is not or is a man." If he is a
man, then he, too must have the right to be governed only with his
own consent. And he will have the same claim to have his freedom
and safety protected by the law. The late Harry Jaffa remarked tellingly that the standing of the black man as a man could not be a
"value judgment." As Roger Wertheimer has reminded us, even some
rather educated and decent men in the middle of the nineteenth
century were inclined to regard the black slave as "some sort of
demi-person," not yet a full or "real" human being as measured by

the scale of evolution.[26] So I tried to offer a gentle plea to my old friend on the Court: that it would be quite as unthinkable to invite people in our own day to offer their earnest "value judgments" on when that life in the womb becomes fully human.

The alternative is strikingly simple and needs no new "theory" to explain it. The Court could easily move along the lines taken by the lawyers from Texas in *Roe:* The laws against abortion would be binding even on those who would feel aggrieved if the right to elect that surgery were denied them, and so the task of the legislators is to show why it is "justified" to cast the protection of the laws around small beings in the womb, even if that judgment does not accord with the heartfelt convictions of others. To say such a thing—that a law finds its justification in protecting human life—should cause no tremors in the circles of conservative jurisprudence. It offers nothing that does not flow from the very rationale and character of law, nothing that would be strange or ill-fitting in a courtroom or coming from a panel of judges.

And yet speaking in this way would have made a profound difference to the way in which the matter was returned to the states. Consider what a difference it would have made if the justices had not only upheld the Mississippi law but also said something like the following:

> The case has been amply made by now, in the settled findings of embryology, that the child in the womb has been human from its first moments, a distinct life, not merely a part of the mother's body. The legislature in Mississippi is amply justified in extending the protections of the law over this small human being, residing for a long period in her mother's womb. It falls to the states to weigh the question of when it would be justified to take this human life, with

the same standards of judgment that enter into gauging
the justification for the taking of any other human life. And
so this matter should be returned to the domain in which
citizens and their legislatures are free to deliberate again
on the question of how the taking of life in abortion will
be treated in their laws on homicide.

That reasoning is straightforward and simple. It would have been a
notably different thing from sending the matter of regulating abortion
back to the states with an opinion that drew on the words of conservative justices, present and past, and giving essentially this guidance:

The question of when human life begins, or what is to be
regarded as a human life in any stage, has been a controversial matter, heatedly debated, eluding consensus, and
inflaming our politics. The judges who form this Court
have no clearer answer to those questions than the answers
that may be supplied by the first nine names in any telephone directory. And as the locale shifts to cities and states,
so too will the temper and values borne by those first nine
names. We therefore send this matter back for people in
the states to deliberate upon again—to make their own
value judgments on when human life begins, and on when
that developing life commands the obligation of the law to
protect it.

Surely, these divergent approaches make the most striking contrast. The first approach would have invited the American people to
deliberate seriously again on the question of what justifies the taking
of an undeniably human life. The latter stylishly steers around any
serious deliberation, for it is framed on the premise that there is no

truth by which to gauge our judgments. As C. S. Lewis once alerted us, it makes no sense to enter any serious conversation, or any moral argument, on those terms. It would seem the most natural thing, then, to ask for that serious conversation, instead of the sounding of "value judgments," which begin by pretending that there is no ground of truth for any answer. For the justices to speak in the most natural way, with the assumption that there are right and wrong answers out there, would have required no striking departure from the way our better jurists have always spoken. To take a line from Lincoln, "The change it contemplates would come gently as the dews of heaven, not rending or wrecking anything."[27]

The draft of the opinion in the *Dobbs* case had indicated where the Court would be moving. But the finished opinion confirmed beyond peradventure the path of argument that was chosen by the Court—and the path firmly foreclosed. The Court carefully avoided those words that would have laid the ground for the involvement of the Congress and the federal government in limiting abortion: that the offspring in the womb cannot be anything but a human being from its first moments, and not merely a part of the mother's body. That sentence would have supplied the ground of justification for the states in casting the protections of law on the unborn child. But without that anchoring truth supplying the ground, the matter would simply be returned to the states for people to offer their "value judgments" or their "beliefs" on when the offspring in the womb becomes a human life and should come within the protections of the law.

And so Justice Alito could unfold his impressive scholarly record of the common law running back to the medieval treatise long attributed to Henry de Bracton and carrying the story from that point to laws passed in the states in the middle of the nineteenth century.[28] At the time the Fourteenth Amendment was ratified, as Alito noted, twenty-eight of the thirty-seven states had made abortion a crime even when it was performed before "quickening," when the movement of the child could be felt.[29]

But that historical record was given radically different meanings by the dissenters as well as by the members of the conservative majority. For the conservative majority the historical record fitted the conservative argument over "substantive due process": that the judges may act to create dramatic new rights under the Due Process Clause only when there is a record of a right "long recognized in our tradition." What the historical record established for the conservatives was summed up by Justice Alito: that "we are aware of no common law case or authority...that suggests a positive *right* to procure an abortion at any stage of pregnancy" [emphasis in original].[30] And so it was wrong for the Supreme Court to have intervened and snatched this matter from the states.

But for the defenders of abortion, and the dissenters in *Dobbs*, the historical record revealed something notably different: There had already been a disposition long settled on the liberal side to reduce moral arguments on abortion to "religious belief." From that perspective the laws restricting abortion in the past could be portrayed as merely the raw imposition of outmoded religious beliefs on those who do not share them. When matters were viewed in that way, it would of course color the reading of the whole historical record. And that was precisely the line taken by the dissenters in *Dobbs*. For Alito, the long history of laws on abortion revealed and confirmed an understanding long settled. But the dissenters saw no moral implications to be drawn from that historical record. For them it made no difference at all that, at the time the Fourteenth Amendment was adopted, there had been an ongoing surge in the states, led by the medical profession, to firm up the laws barring abortion. For the dissenters that outpouring of legislation could be dismissed as simply a reflection of what the medical profession *believed* about the embryo in the womb, or how little a profession composed massively of males held any regard for the interests at stake for women in these surgeries. The dissenters asked, What rights did the framers and ratifiers of the Fourteenth Amendment have in mind? But they also pointed out that it was not the people who had ratified the Fourteenth Amendment: "Men did," they said. "So it is perhaps not so surprising that the ratifiers were not perfectly attuned to the importance of reproductive rights for women's liberty, or for their capacity to participate as equal members of our Nation. Indeed, the ratifiers—both in 1868 and when the original Constitution was approved in 1788—did not understand women as full members of the community embraced by the phrase 'We the People.'"[31] Seen through this lens of "gender identity," the legal issue could be nicely separated from the substance of the bloody things going on in these surgeries. And the victims could be screened completely from the picture.

When it comes to viewing the historical record, there comes into play a version of the central question in Plato's *Euthyphro*: Is something good because the gods love it, or do the gods love it because it is good? In this case, is something good because it is old, or has it become old because we have judged something about it to be enduringly good? Those laws on abortion passed widely in our states by the 1860s and 1870s—do we credit them with authority because they were soundly grounded in the evidence of embryology woven with principled reasoning? Or do we accord them the authority to bind us simply because they are old? Once again, just a few words on that head in the *Dobbs* opinion could have done the work: to wit, that we respect those enactments in the nineteenth century because they were based on a growing body of evidence, *which makes the argument as true in our time as it was in theirs*. Those were words that the conservative justices curiously held back from speaking because of a constitutional theory that commanded their reticence.

The telling confirmation on this point came from Justice Kavanaugh, in his concurrence, when he observed that many women have come to regard the choice of abortion as critical to their professional and personal lives, while on the other side, "many pro-life advocates forcefully argue that a fetus is a human life."[32] Justice Kavanaugh could not have set down those words if the conservative majority had understood the historical record to mark the recognition of an unfolding objective truth about the child in the womb.

But when the matter was detached in this way from that anchoring *truth* about the human entity in the womb, the situation was reduced to a contest between two groups animated by clashing beliefs, each trying to use the powers of law to impose their beliefs on other people. That was a gross reading, and yet thanks to the premises put in place by the Court, it was not an inapt reading. For if the matter is painted by the Court as a matter of the local majority coming to a "value judgment" and enacting a policy, what do we have in hand but a prettied-over, stripped-down, and unalloyed positivism? It should be no surprise that the people who care deeply about a right to abortion are not consoled or satisfied by the report that abortion will be widely available to anyone living in, or near, a blue state. And even the people in those blue states have shown a resentment not readily stilled. They were led to believe that a woman has a right to an abortion, and now they are told that she may not have it if 51 percent of the people around her are strongly unwilling to let her have it. The conservative account has been that when the matter is returned to the states, as the Court says in *Dobbs*, this grave moral question is put properly in the hands of a self-governing people to determine who is protected under their laws on homicide. *But when detached from the moral ground that would justify those laws*, the laws on abortion are naturally seen by their opponents—as they see virtually any other law that forbids their desires—as the flexing of brute power alone.

Ironically, there was one place where the dissenters did indeed discover, as James Madison said, "that veneration which time bestows on every thing."[33] The dissenters affected to stand in misty awe of a decision whose leading virtue is that it endured for forty-nine years. But of course that was precisely the argument that had been put to the Court by the legendary John W. Davis when he sought to defend the policy of racial segregation in schools in *Brown v. Board of Education*. Davis raised a precedent thought to have grown venerable with age, the decision of the Court in *Plessy v. Ferguson*. That decision had been left largely undisturbed for fifty-eight years, and Davis argued now that "somewhere, sometime, to every principle comes a moment of repose when the decision has been so often announced, so confidently relied upon, so long continued, that it passes the limits of judicial discretion and disturbance."[34] Justice Alito suffered not a moment of doubt that the dissenters in *Dobbs* would have long ago favored the overruling of this precedent on racial segregation, even though it had lasted longer than *Roe v. Wade*.

Justice Alito crystallized what was so novel and implausible in the theory of precedent being offered by the dissenters: "The dissent's foundational contention," he wrote, "is that the Court should never (or perhaps almost never) overrule an egregiously wrong constitutional precedent unless the Court can 'poin[t] to major legal or factual changes undermining [the] decision's original basis.'... The unmistakable implication of this argument is that only the passage of time and new developments justified those decisions [being overruled]."[35] The settled view of Alito and the majority was that, like *Plessy*, "*Roe* was egregiously wrong from the start."[36] Was it even imaginable that the dissenters would hold "that overruling *Plessy* was not justified until the country had experienced more than a half-century of state-sanctioned segregation and generations of Black school children had suffered all its effects"?[37] Would the dissenters not have judged that *Plessy* had been wrong even on the day it was handed down? Then they could hardly fault the majority for concluding in the same way that no more decades needed to pass before time would reveal what was wrong with *Roe v. Wade.*

And yet, in what did the wrongness of *Roe* lie? Nowhere in this carefully crafted opinion of the Court, both comprehensive and fine-grained, did the conservative majority pronounce any words on the *wrongness* of abortion. That judgment of rightness or wrongness would be left, again, to the value judgments of the people in the states. In *Roe v. Wade* the Court had drawn the right to abortion from the Due Process Clause of the Fourteenth Amendment, and now the conservative majority held to the argument that nothing in the Constitution or the Due Process Clause could plausibly entail this utter novelty of a right to abortion. Conservatives still clung to the notion that substantive due process was an oxymoron, that there was something immanently suspect about drawing substantive rights from that clause. And yet, Thomas Cooley, in his famous *Constitutional Limitations* (1871), recognized that the Due Process Clause could carry all of the deep principles bound up with a regime of law, even if the drafters of the Constitution had neglected to mention them: "When the government, through its established agencies, interferes with the title to one's property, or his independent enjoyment of it... we are to test its validity by those principles of civil liberty and constitutional protection which have become established in our system of law, and not generally by rules that pertain to forms of procedure merely."[38]

In other words, the taking of private property for public use without compensation would be deeply wrong in a constitutional order even if there had been no mention of such a right in the Fifth Amendment. The same sense of things was engaged when Justice

George Sutherland overturned the conviction of "the Scottsboro boys" in Alabama in 1933. These were black youngsters tried for rape in a hostile setting, with less than star legal counsel, a situation so wanting in the rudiments of any fair process of judgment that Sutherland found it at odds with any plausible understanding of due process. But the deep lesson taught by Sutherland—and so widely unnoticed—was that the conviction in this case would have been wrong *even if there were no Sixth Amendment* to mandate the "Assistance of Counsel for...defense."[39] Stuart Banner, offering his commentary on Cooley, observed that "when natural law was no longer available as a barrier to class legislation and property rights, due process took its place."[40]

In the famous *Palko* case of 1937,[41] Justice Cardozo had offered two paths for discovering the rights embedded in the due process of law, but for some reason, one of the paths has been forgotten. The test cited most often is an appeal to history, to a "principle of justice so rooted in the traditions and conscience of our people as to be ranked as fundamental." But that is actually the second of the two paths Cardozo laid out. The other, the first path, involves the consideration of whether the rights in question are "of the very essence of a scheme of ordered liberty"—and whether "a fair and enlightened system of justice would be impossible without them."[42] That first path involved arrangements so bound up with a regime of law that it is inconceivable that any justice could be rendered in their absence. We understand that in the very logic of a regime of law, "condemnation shall be rendered only after trial," that no trial shall be held without a hearing of the evidence, and the hearing "must be a real one, not a sham or a pretense." Looking back to Justice Sutherland in the Scottsboro case, Cardozo made the point that "due process" was denied where "ignorant defendants in a capital case were held to have been condemned unlawfully when in truth, though not in form, they were refused the aid of counsel."[43]

In contrast, the privilege of avoiding "self-incrimination" had become long familiar, and there was no doubt, as Cardozo said, of a need "to give protection against torture, physical or mental." But "justice...would not perish," as he said, "if the accused were subject to a duty to respond to orderly inquiry."[44] It might indeed be legitimate to draw adverse inferences when a man holds back evidence of a serious crime of which he has direct knowledge—as in the case offered by the late Judge Henry Friendly, when a person in custody could reveal whether the victim of a kidnapping was still alive and still in the country.

That right to avoid self-incrimination did not arise from the very logic of the regime of law. It stood rather among those things long rooted, or at least long known, in our tradition. As Cardozo pointed out, that right had long been incorporated in the law of continental Europe as well, running back to the Roman law. Still, it was a matter of tracing the historical lineage. In striking comparison, the first path invited judges to draw out the implications that spring from the very logic of law. (As in that first principle of moral and legal judgment articulated by Thomas Reid and embraced by James Wilson: that we don't hold people blameworthy or responsible for acts they were powerless to effect.) That is an exercise in thinking back to the "first principles of justice." It has the inescapable whiff of moral philosophy. The second path, focused on history, avoided moral judgments altogether: the judges would merely consult the record and see, for example, if this right to abortion was one known long in our tradition of law. On that cardinal point Justice Alito established quite clearly, through his long, exhaustive survey, that no right of that kind had even been hinted in the history of our law. The findings ran rather in the other direction, to condemning and punishing. That is the path of argument now long fixed and settled in conservative jurisprudence.

It was as predictable as the night following the day that Justice Alito's opinion would trigger fierce reactions—and overreactions. The opposition sounded the alarm that the overturning of *Roe* would call into question a long string of precedents that had led up to the new right created in *Roe*. Justice Alito sought to make clear that the decision to overrule *Roe* would unsettle nothing in that earlier chain of newly discovered rights. Nothing here would change the judgments on the wrong of barring contraception to married couples in *Griswold v. Connecticut*,[45] the wrong of imposing compulsory sterilization (later and clumsily described as a "right to procreation") in *Skinner v. Oklahoma*,[46] or the wrong of barring marriage across racial lines in *Loving v. Virginia*.[47] Alito tried to draw a clear line: "What sharply distinguishes the abortion right from the rights recognized in the cases on which *Roe* and *Casey* [*v. Planned Parenthood*] rely is something that both of those decisions acknowledged: Abortion destroys what those decisions call 'potential' life and what the law at issue in this case regards as the life of an 'unborn human being.'"[48]

Those earlier cases did not involve a right to do something lethal to another human being. "None of the other decisions cited by *Roe* and *Casey* involved," as Alito said, "the critical moral question posed by abortion. They are therefore inapposite. They do not support the right to obtain an abortion."[49] But then again, the Court would not confirm the key point here that a human life *was* being taken. The opinion declared only that abortion destroys "what those decisions call 'potential life,'" or "what the law at issue [in *Dobbs*] regards as the life of an 'unborn human being.'" The Court was merely reporting the view of the matter stated in those earlier cases—it was not presuming to pronounce its own emphatic view on whether these offspring in human wombs were in fact "unborn human beings." The Court was studiously holding back from pronouncing a judgment on the most decisive point at all.

For their own part, the defenders of abortion did not see such a sharp dividing line. Alito had left up in the air the question of whether this right to abortion involved the killing of something that truly counted as a human being or simply of something others happened to believe is a "potential" human life. With that dividing line fading, it should have been no surprise that the people who were worried about the survival of those other rights would now demand that the Court be held *to its own account* of the ground on which those earlier rights stood. If the test involved rights "long rooted in our tradition," that was certainly not the case when the Court in *Griswold* announced the arrival of the new constitutional right to contraception in 1965. There were still laws restricting access to contraception, especially for teenagers, on the books at the time. Nor was it the case in 1942 when the Court in *Skinner* insisted on a new right not to be subjected to compulsory sterilization. That was especially the case as the justices in *Skinner* took care to frame an argument that would not challenge Justice Holmes's classic opinion, in *Buck v. Bell*, making a swashbuckling case in favor of compulsory sterilization.[50] As for interracial marriage, Lyman Trumbull of Illinois had managed the Fourteenth Amendment in its passage through the Senate, and he assured his colleagues that nothing in this new amendment would challenge the laws, in Illinois as well as Virginia, that barred marriage across racial lines.[51] If we have changed our minds on that matter since then, it cannot be because of anything in the "original understanding" of the men who framed and voted for the amendment or because of anything in the text of the Constitution. If we changed, it is because the justices had drawn upon moral reasoning to explain a meaning of "equal protection" or "due process of the law" that had not been fully understood at the time the Fourteenth Amendment was adopted.

Thus the difference between *Roe* and the other cases simply came down to this: the justices had come to judge those other "rights" as justified and truly rightful, but no longer regarded it as unarguably rightful to kill small human beings in wombs. Once again, as ever, the matter would turn on whether one set of rights was justified while this other supposed "right" was not. And yet that was conspicuously *not* the argument that the Court was making here; it was in fact the argument that it was carefully working *not* to make.

Professor Richard Epstein made the same point, but from another direction.[52] In sending the matter of abortion back to the States, the Court suggested that it would be giving a wide latitude to the legislatures. If any laws made on abortion were challenged, the Court would engage the so-called "rational basis" standard—that is, the law would pass muster if there were any plausible connection to a passably reasonable end. In that vein, Justice Alito continued in the path marked out by conservatives such as Rehnquist and Scalia in supporting the jurisprudence of the New Deal: he would applaud the overturning of those now-scorned precedents that took from the hands of the people the authority to pass laws mandating maximum hours for workers (*Lochner v. New York*)[53] or a minimum wage for women (*Adkins v. Children's Hospital*).[54] Justice Alito was reminding lawyers and the public that the Court had indeed struck down a long line of important precedents in the past.

But as Professor Epstein pointed out, the "rational basis" standard could have sustained the legislation in *Plessy v. Ferguson*. As Justice Henry Billings Brown made clear in *Plessy*, he and his colleagues had already sustained laws that *barred* the separation of races on railway cars.[55] But they were willing to sustain the law in *Plessy*, in the same way, for they did not see how the Fourteenth Amendment, as understood by its framers, foreclosed either one of these policies. They also noted that conventions of segregation were accepted by jurists in the North as well as the South: racial segregation in the schools of Boston had been sustained by Chief Justice Shaw in Massachusetts, and more recently the separation of the races in public conveyances had been upheld by the courts in Pennsylvania, Michigan, and Illinois. The justices also knew that the framers of the Fourteenth Amendment saw no challenge in that amendment to the laws that barred inter-racial marriage. And nothing in the amendment had impelled them to desegregate the public schools in the District of Columbia. And so the test of "rational basis," as it has been understood in our own time, could have worked readily to uphold that decision, so highly decried, in *Plessy*.[56]

Professor Epstein was lifting the curtain now: if "rational basis" would have been enough to sustain those earlier laws on maximum hours and minimum wages, struck down in the New Deal, why would it not have worked quite as well to sustain the other laws that the Court had struck down in the landmark cases leading up to *Roe v. Wade*? In his concurrence in *Griswold*, Justice White thought that the statute was meant to discourage "all forms of promiscuous or illicit sexual relationships, be they premarital or extramarital"— and he found that purpose to be "permissible and legitimate." (Still, he didn't think that purpose supplied a rational basis for forbidding contraceptives to married couples.)[57] But what could have been more telling here than the dissent voiced by that leading figure in New Deal jurisprudence, Justice Hugo Black, Franklin Roosevelt's first appoint-ment to the Supreme Court? Black professed to find the law in Connecticut on contraceptives "every bit as offensive to me as it is to my Brethren of the majority."[58] But he saw in the Court's decision something having the whiff of "natural law," some claim to finding high principles of law that could challenge the laws put in place by elected legislators. And so he insisted again, as he had been insisting for almost thirty years, that "there is no provision of the Constitution which either expressly or impliedly vests power in this Court to sit as a supervisory agency over acts of duly constituted legislative bodies and set aside their laws because of the Court's belief that the legislative policies adopted are unreasonable, unwise, arbitrary, capricious or irrational."[59]

Black was offering here the ringing orthodoxy of the New Deal: legislatures should be given a wide berth, in what would later be called the "rational basis" test. But if this were to be the guiding test for the Court, Professor Epstein delivered the unwelcome news: those precedents leading to *Roe* are indeed open to serious challenge. The simple but hard point, made again by Epstein, is that the most decisive explanation for overturning *Roe* while keeping those earlier precedents unchallenged is that there is something justified in those freedoms for contraception and marriage, but emphatically not so justified in the killing of nascent lives in utero.[60] That remains, in my judgment, the most tenable ground for this critical distinction. But it was the ground, or the reasoning, that the conservative majority was steeling its collective loins *not* to offer.

Justice Holmes, a man ever more clever than wise, knew that he was being stylishly provocative when he published his prayer that "every word of moral significance could be banished from the law altogether." But the power of sly provocation is that the message it conveys may be widely absorbed as a truth with little awareness of what we have come to absorb. How else might we explain Justice Kavanaugh in his concurring opinion in *Dobbs*: "The issue before this Court," he wrote, "is not the policy or morality of abortion. The issue before this Court is what the Constitution says about abortion. The Constitution does not take sides on the issue of abortion. The text of the Constitution does not refer to or encompass abortion."[61] The Constitution is also silent on the matter of whether people may be held responsible for acts they were powerless to commit, and whether defendants should be presumed innocent until proven guilty. Are we to suppose, then, that the Constitution is utterly empty of moral premises and suppositions, including most notably the anchoring moral premise, never mentioned in the Constitution, that human beings may rightly be ruled only with their consent in a regime structured by law? It can only be through reasoning of that kind that Justice Kavanaugh could reach his most telling line, that "the Constitution is neutral" on abortion. It is "neither pro-life nor pro-choice....[It] leaves the issue for the people and their elected representatives to resolve through the democratic process." The issue was fully open because, as he wrote in that critical line cited earlier, "many pro-life advocates forcefully argue that a fetus is a human life"—as though there was no settled truth on this matter, long confirmed in embryology.[62]

On this construction, a "conservative jurisprudence" on abortion must earnestly begin with the axiom that there is no truth to be known on the human standing of that child in the womb. But if so, it is a jurisprudence that accepts, as a grounding premise, a radical falsehood. Whatever else it is, it cannot be a coherent jurisprudence.

Justice Kavanaugh is a thoughtful man, at the beginning of what promises to be distinguished tenure on the Court, and so some of us hope that he may be willing take a sober second look at what he has put in place here. For he may discover that in his discourse on the neutrality of the Constitution he has stepped back into a question at the center of the classic debate between Abraham Lincoln and Stephen Douglas. Douglas insisted that the Constitution was utterly neutral or, we might say, pro-choice, on slavery. Douglas professed not to "care" whether slavery was voted up or down in the territories as long as it was done in a properly democratic way with the vote of a majority. Lincoln recognized that the framers of the Constitution had to make a prudential accommodation with slavery. But the underlying principles were still at work withholding any endorsement or approval of slavery and putting limits on the expansion of slavery. Lincoln recalled that, in one of their encounters, Douglas argued for his principle on the ground that "God made man and placed good and evil before him, allowing him to choose for himself." Lincoln remarked that "at the time I thought this was merely playful," but as Douglas persisted, Lincoln finally came back to him to say, "God did not place good and evil before man, telling him to make his choice. On the contrary, he did tell him there was one tree, the fruit of which he should not eat."[63] God was not exactly "pro-choice" on evil. For Lincoln this was the degradation of the democratic dogma: that the regime was entirely one of "process" but no substance; that we were free to choose anything at all—say, slavery or genocide—as long as we did it in a democratic way, through the vote of a majority.[64] But would we really say that the Constitution was "neutral" on genocide or the taking of innocent life? Does a regime of law not begin by taking seriously the difference between innocence and guilt, that we visit punishment on people only after we show that they are guilty of wrongdoing and deserving of punishment? And the "unalienable right" to "life" did not mean a right to life everlasting; it meant rather the right of any ordinary person, innocent of wrongdoing, to be protected from a lawless, unjustified assault on his life. How could anyone understand those moral premises underlying this regime and think they could possibly be "neutral" or indifferent on the question of whether the Constitution would license a regime of killing small, innocent human beings? And yet the Constitution may indeed be typically read in that way by those who have tutored themselves to see the Constitution as one of the most striking artifacts and accomplishments of Positive Law, majestically detached from those moral grounds from which it sprung.

In one of his reviews, the legendary Broadway critic Brooks Atkinson remarked, "I've knocked everything in this show except the chorus girls' legs, but there nature anticipated me." I have not sought to be so severe as I have offered this close and critical reading of the governing opinion in the *Dobbs* case. And I would not want this critique, as sharp as it may be, to distract anyone from the massive good that the Court has done for the law—and the country—with this decision. It delivered us from a web of inversions and glib stories that people had come to absorb as they talked themselves into a skein of untruths: that medical science does not know when the child in the womb becomes a human being, that the weakness or dependence of the unborn child is a predicate for withdrawing medical care and the protection of the law, and that it is possible to remove a whole class of human beings from the circle of rights-bearing beings simply by shifting a label. In *Huckleberry Finn*, Huck tells Aunt Sally that his boat has been delayed because "we blowed out a cylinder-head."

"Good gracious!" she exclaims, "anybody hurt?"

Huck says, "N'om. Killed a nigger."

Aunt Sally, much relieved, says, "Well, it's lucky; because sometimes real people do get hurt." In our own day, minds may be eased by hearing that it's only a fetus who has been killed, not any real person.

The issue of abortion has been returned to the public arena, where citizens can deliberate now, with practical effect, on just who should be covered by their laws on homicide. But it makes a profound difference whether the people in the states are invited to deliberate in a Nietzschean framework in which moral truths have been displaced by "value judgments," with no fixed measure of "truth." Those accomplished justices who shaped the opinion in *Dobbs* will not be astonished or jarred if their writing stirs some searching critiques even on the part of their friends. If I am right in those missteps I've seen in the argument, those steps portend serious strains of coherence, as courts and legislatures, in future cases, draw out the implications that they see springing from this opinion.

The experience with *Brown v. Board of Education* offers an enduring lesson here. That decision was regarded in almost all quarters as magnificently right, and yet even the professors and judges who welcomed that opinion were candid in confessing that they had trouble fixing on the ground of principle that justified the decision. As I have sought to show in these pages, that original confusion begat in turn other serious confusions, which gave us an enduring scheme of "racial preferences" quite sharply at odds with the principle that explains the wrong of racial discrimination. In short, we have learned that "getting the right outcome" may not be enough.

Still, those accomplished justices in the majority may have "wrought better than they knew." And indeed, they may have wrought better than *I* know. For the reasons unfolded in these pages, I fear that the decision in *Dobbs* will beget a rocky future with many upsetting, and perhaps demoralizing, surprises. On the other hand, it may produce results wondrous beyond anything that any of us has expected. When Lincoln sprung the Emancipation Proclamation, it was instantly derided for having all of the moral force of a "bill of lading."[65] For Lincoln did not have the authority to divest, from their rights of property, all owners of slaves in the land. He could invoke his executive power only as a war measure: he could emancipate only those slaves held in the states at war with the federal government, the slaves whose labor was freeing up whites for service on the battlefield against the United States. And yet, even with all of its legal constraints, the proclamation bore a meaning that was soon and widely grasped. It was an anti-slavery manifesto, meant to impart an anti-slavery dynamic. In the same way, the decision in *Dobbs*, as excruciatingly circumscribed as it is, will be seen as animated by an affirmation of the sacred value of life.

Samuel Alito, a gifted and wise man, seasoned in the art and statecraft of judging, and steeled with the nerve to judge, has often shown the deft hand of a teacher: In opening and framing the problem, he set down clues that act as hints. He said enough to lure his readers into reasoning on their own the rest of the way to the conclusion. He has, for the first time, set down in the official pages of the Court some of the telling markers along the way as a cluster of cells turns itself into the child who can be seen on a sonogram. He has also put in place the reasoning that shows why the sliding scale of "viability" offers no principled ground for marking any point at which a non–human being turns into a human being who comes within the protection of the law. He has supplied, in short, the rudiments of a principled argument on abortion, and sending them aloft in the world, they may awaken again the powers to think anew, even in the blue states.

Even beyond that, we may be taken by surprise by another turn in "the cunning of history": The laws in the pro-life states will surely be challenged, as they seek to protect the nascent being in the womb at its earliest moments. It will fall to conservative judges to explain why those laws may be rightly sustained even as they protect the embryonic life at five or six weeks, or even earlier. And on that question, there is no more accessible strand of reasoning to grasp than Justice Alito's telling line in *Dobbs*: "If, as Roe held, a State's interest in protecting prenatal life is compelling 'after viability,' ... why isn't that interest 'equally compelling before viability'?"[66] In other words, as the lawyers for Texas sought to explain in *Roe v. Wade*, that child in the womb has never been anything other than human *at every stage of its existence.* Of course, some judges may respond with the simple vulgarity that the majority in *Dobbs* was willing to settle in with: that there is no truth on this matter for judges to declare, and so we simply respect the laws that the people in the states have enacted for themselves, almost regardless of what they are. Which is to say: the law is the decree of those with the power to make it. But other judges may take seriously the obligation to gauge the reasoning that is offered to justify the imposition of these laws on people who disagree. And if the judges reach back to Justice Alito as they seek to explain their judgments, we will have come full circle: even conservative judges may find it natural to speak now the words that the dissenters in *Roe* were never moved to speak, in explaining why it was *justified* for the laws to protect small humans in wombs in Texas.

One way or another, we will see the results play out, and we will be able to judge. But judging implies that there are indeed standards of judgment, giving us right or wrong answers, or what some of us call the *truth*. If judging were merely a matter of subjective feelings, with no testing truths, Thomas Reid's rejoinder would apply again: a judge would be ill-named—"he ought to be called a feeler."[67] But if there are truths to be known, they will come to us in the manner, as Aristotle said, most distinctively natural for human beings. They will come in the course of giving reasons. And those reasons will lead us back then, with Thomas Reid, to the anchoring axioms in the "laws of reason."[68] Which is to say we will be back, as we will ever be, with the Natural Law.

Notes

Epigraphs

1. Montesquieu, *The Spirit of the Laws*, ed. David Wallace Carrithers, trans. Thomas Nugent (Berkeley and Los Angeles, California: University of California Press, 1977), 99. Nugent's translation of the first French edition (Geneva: Barillot, 1748) was first published in 1750 in London by Nourse.
2. Deuteronomy 30:11–14, New American Bible Revised Edition, United States Conference of Catholic Bishops, https://bible.usccb.org/bible/deuteronomy/30.

Acknowledgments

1. Barack Obama, *The Audacity of Hope: Thoughts on Reclaiming the American Dream* (New York: Three Rivers Press, 2006), 93–96.

Chapter 1: *The Natural Law Challenge*

1. Tom Stoppard, *Jumpers* (New York: Grove Press, 1972), 87.
2. Cicero, *On the Republic* 3.7, in *The Political Works of Marcus Tullius Cicero*, trans. Francis Barham (London: Edmund Spettigue, Chancery Lane, 1841).
3. "From Thomas Jefferson to Roger Chew Weightman, 24 June 1826," Founders Online, https://founders.archives.gov/documents/Jefferson/98-01-02-6179.
4. Abraham Lincoln, speech in Peoria, Illinois, October 16, 1854, in *The Collected Works of Abraham Lincoln*, vol. 2, ed. Roy P. Basler (New Brunswick: Rutgers University Press, 1953), 266.
5. James Wilson, "On the Natural Rights of Individuals" (originally published in 1804), in *The Works of James Wilson*, vol. 2, ed. R. G. McCloskey (Cambridge, Massachusetts: Harvard University Press, 1967), 589. The essay can also be found in a more recent and perhaps more widely accessible edition: *The Collected Works of James Wilson*, vol. 2, ed. Kermit L. Hall and Mark David Hall (Indianapolis: Liberty Fund, 2007), 1057–58.
6. Baruch de Spinoza, *A Theologico-Political Treatise and A Political Treatise*, trans. R. H. M. Elwes (New York: Dover Publications, 2004), 200. From chapter 16 of the *Theologico-Political Treatise*.
7. Oscar Hammerstein II (lyrics) and Jerome Kern (music), "Can't Help Lovin' Dat Man," from *Show Boat* (1927).

8. Francisco de Vitoria, *De Indis Et De Jure Bells Reflectiones*, ed. Ernest Nys (Washington, D.C.: Carnegie Institution, 1917), 248. The *Reflections* were originally published in 1696, from a lecture delivered at the University of Salamanca in 1539.

9. Wilson, "On the Natural Rights of Individuals," 597; see page 1068 in the Liberty Fund edition.

10. United States v. Windsor, 570 U.S. 744 (2013), at 26 of Scalia's dissent. Where possible, throughout the book, I cite the official final printed version of Supreme Court and other court cases. Where only the slip opinion is available, I quote from it, but for the reader's convenience I supply the standard citation to the not-yet-printed version of the decision.

11. Obergefell v. Hodges, 576 U.S 644 (2015), at 2 of Scalia's dissent.

12. Bostock v. Clayton County, Georgia, 590 U.S. ___ (2020).

13. See "Brief of Scholars of Philosophy, Theology, Law, Politics, History, Literature, and the Sciences as *Amici Curiae* in Support of Petitioner" in the case of R. G. & G. R. Harris Funeral Homes, Inc. v. Equal Employment Opportunity Commission, 590 U.S. __ (2020). David S. Crawford, Michael Hanby, and Margaret Harper McCarthy were the principal authors.

14. See Michael Hanby and David Crawford (with an assist from Margaret Harper McCarthy), "The Abolition of Man and Woman," *Wall Street Journal*, June 24, 2020.

15. "Kagan: 'We Are All Originalists,'" The BLT: The Blog of LegalTimes, June 29, 2010, https://legaltimes.typepad.com/blt/2010/06/kagan-we-are-all-originalists. html. Kagan was responding to a question from Senator Leahy of Vermont and speaking of the framers who had written the Constitution: "Sometimes they laid down very specific rules. Sometimes they laid down broad principles. Either way, we apply what they tried to do.... In that way, we are all originalists."

16. Jonathan Gienapp, *The Second Creation: Fixing the American Constitution in the Founding Era* (Cambridge, Massachusetts: Harvard University Press, 2018), 21–22, 112.

17. See Max Farrand, ed., *The Records of the Federal Convention of 1787*, rev. ed., vol 2 (New Haven: Yale University Press, 1966), 376; quoted in Hadley Arkes, *Beyond the Constitution* (Princeton, New Jersey: Princeton University Press, 1990), 61.

18. See Arkes, *Beyond the Constitution*, especially chapters 5–7.

19. The Natural Law was fitted distinctly to those creatures with the gift of reason, and so, against the "law of a dog" or of sheep, the "law of a man, which...is allotted to him according to his proper natural condition is that he should act

in accordance with reason." Thomas Aquinas, *Summa Theologica* I-II 91.6, *Basic Writings of Saint Thomas Aquinas*, vol. 2, ed. Anton C. Pegis (New York: Random House, 1945), 756. "[T]he divine law seems to be more akin to the eternal law…than the natural law, according as the revelation of grace is of a higher order than natural knowledge. But natural law is one for all men." Ibid., I-II 91.5, 754. But as ever, the first and most telling thing to be cited is from St. Paul in Romans 2:14: "For when the Gentiles, who have not the law, do by nature those things that are of the law; these having not the law are a law to themselves." The Holy Bible, Douay-Rheims Version.

Chapter 2: *The Path of Vignettes*

1. Roe v. Wade, 410 U.S. 113 (1973), at 159.
2. Neil Gorsuch, *A Republic, If You Can Keep It* (New York: Forum Crown Books, 2019), 112.
3. Philosophy Overdose, "4: Reid on Causation and Active Powers—Reid's Critique of Hume (Dan Robinson)," YouTube, June 19, 2021, at 14–15, but especially 24ff, https://www.youtube.com/watch?v=I7i-lJ-awH0; Philosophy Overdose, "2: Reid & Common Sense Realism—Reid's Critique of Hume (Dan Robinson)," YouTube, June 19, 2021, at 18–20, 25–30, but especially 47–50, https://www.youtube.com/watch?v=oRBak-E9xCo.
4. Thomas Reid, *Essays on the Active Powers of the Human Mind* (Cambridge, Massachusetts: MIT Press, 1969), 249. Originally published in 1788.
5. Philosophy Overdose, "6: Reid on Personal Identity: Reid's Critique of Hume (Dan Robinson)," YouTube, June 19, 2021, at 44–49, https://www.youtube.com/watch?v=LfLZoRhaX34.
6. Thomas Reid, *An Inquiry into the Human Mind on the Principles of Common Sense*, ed. Derek R. Brookes (Pennsylvania Station: Pennsylvania State University Press, 1997), 16–17, originally published in 1764.
7. Quoted in Thomas West, *Vindicating the Founders* (Oxford: Rowman & Littlefield, 1997), 7.
8. Thomas Reid, *Essays on the Intellectual Powers of Man* (Cambridge, Massachusetts: MIT Press, 1969), 654, originally published in 1814–15.
9. This is my version of Reid's principle: "What is done from unavoidable necessity…cannot be the object either of blame or moral approbation." Reid, *Essays on the Active Powers*, 361.
10. "As a rational being, and consequently as belonging to the intelligible world, man can never conceive of the causality of his own will except under the idea of freedom; for to be independent of determinism by causes in the sensible

world (and this is what reason must always attribute to itself) is to be free." Immanuel Kant, *Groundwork for the Metaphysics of Morals*, trans. H. J. Paton (New York: Harper & Row, 1948), 120, originally published in 1785. See chapter 4 note 3 below.

11. Immanuel Kant, *Fundamental Principles of the Metaphysics of Morals*, trans. Thomas K. Abbott (Indianapolis: Bobbs-Merrill, 1949), 42 and 58, originally published in 1785.

12. There may be no better compendium of the strands of Holmes's writing and thought that denied any moral ground of justification for the law than that found in Albert Alschuler's book *Law without Values: The Life and Work and Legacy of Justice Holmes* (Cambridge, Massachusetts: Harvard University Press, 2000), especially 88–89.

13. C. S. Lewis, *Mere Christianity* (New York: Macmillan Publishing Co., 1977), 17–18, originally published in 1943.

14. Ibid.

15. Reid, *Essays on the Intellectual Powers of Man*, 464–65, note 4. Cited in Hadley Arkes, *First Things* (Princeton, New Jersey: Princeton University Press, 1986), 23.

16. Ibid., 474.

17. See G. E. Moore, "The Objectivity of Moral Judgment" in *Ethics* (1912), chapter 3. From Moore's rather extended working of the problem, we may as well extract these lines as any: "It may be held that whenever any man asserts an action to be right or wrong, what he is asserting is merely that he *himself* has some particular feeling towards the action in question. Each of us, according to this view, is merely making an assertion about *his own* feelings: when *I* assert that an action is right, the *whole* of what I mean is merely that *I* have some particular feeling towards the action; and when *you* make the same assertion, the *whole* of what you mean is merely that *you* have the feeling in question towards the action."

18. Aristotle, *Politics*, 1253a.

19. Jean-Jacques Rousseau, *The Social Contract, I*, book 4, chapter 6, n. 5, in *Social Contract*, ed. Sir Ernest Barker (London: Oxford University Press, 1960), 203, originally published in 1762.

20. Oliver Wendell Holmes Jr., "The Path of the Law," in *Collected Legal Papers* (New York: Harcourt Brace and Company, 1920), 179.

21. Alschuler, *Law without Values*, 88–89.

22. Newman in *Roe v. Maher*, 408 F. Supp., 663, note 3, quoted by Justice Powell in *Maher v. Roe*, 432 U.S. 464 (1977), 468. Justice Powell had been part of the

majority in *Roe v. Wade*, and so it is quite interesting that only four years later, Powell was willing to write an opinion that rejected this opinion by Judge Newman in the District Court in Connecticut. At that time Powell and most of his colleagues were willing to hold that abortion and childbirth were indeed not on the same moral plane, and that a state may legitimately tilt its policies to favor childbirth over abortion.

23. Quoted in Alschuler, *Law without Values*, 80, note 10.

24. Philosophy Overdose, "2: Reid & Common Sense Realism."

Chapter 3: The Ploughman and the Professor

1. Gibbons v. Ogden, 22 U.S. 1 (1824), at 222 and 278.

2. Alexander Hamilton, *Federalist* no. 31, in *The Federalist* (New York: Random House), 188.

3. Bertrand Russell, *The Problems of Philosophy* (Oxford: Oxford University Press, 1959), 89, originally published in 1912.

4. Thomas Jefferson, letter to Peter Carr, August 10, 1787, in *Writings of Thomas Jefferson*, ed. Paul Leicester Ford (New York and London: G. P. Putnam's Sons, 1899), 902, cited in Carroll William Westfall, *Architecture, Liberty and Civic Order: Architectural Theories from Vitruvius to Jefferson and Beyond* (Farnham, Surrey, UK: Ashgate, 2015), 120.

5. Abraham Lincoln, *The Collected Works of Abraham Lincoln*, vol. 2, ed. Roy P. Basler (New Brunswick, New Jersey: Rutgers University Press, 1953), 222.

6. J. Budziszewski, *What We Can't Not Know* (Dallas, Texas: Spence Publishing, 2003).

7. Abraham Lincoln, speech in Chicago, July 10, 1858, in *The Collected Works of Abraham Lincoln*, vol. 2, ed. Roy P. Basler (New Brunswick, New Jersey: Rutgers University Press, 1953), 499, note 5.

8. James Wilson, "Of the Law of Nature," in *The Works of James Wilson*, ed. Robert Green McCloskey (Cambridge, Massachusetts: Cambridge University Press, 1967), 126, originally published in 1804.

9. See Thomas Reid, *Essays on the Active Powers of the Human Mind* (Cambridge, Massachusetts: MIT Press, 1969), 48, originally published in 1788.

10. Nyquist v. Mauclet, 432 U.S. 1, at 17–18 (1977). The case involved access to a subsidized higher education in New York. The privilege would be available only to students who were American citizens, but New York was willing to extend the privilege to resident aliens if they filed an intention to become a citizen. With that provision in place, Rehnquist was not prepared to set aside as

untenable a policy of reserving some privileges for citizens. He wrote here in dissent.

11. John Stuart Mill, *Utilitarianism* (Indianapolis: Bobbs-Merrill, 1957), 61, originally published in 1861.

12. See, for example, Hadley Arkes, *The Return of George Sutherland* (Princeton, New Jersey: Princeton University Press, 1994), 80–81, for analysis of Sutherland's reasoning in Patton v. United States, 281 U.S. 276 (1930). And see also 263, 268, and 272 on how that reasoning may affect the reading of other cases.

13. See Judge Brown's powerful concurring opinion in Hettinga v. United States, 677 F.3d 471 (2012). Judge Brown adverted to the sharp dissent of Justice MacReynolds in Nebbia v. New York, 291 U.S. 502 (1934), in an opinion that has long been filtered out of our histories and case books.

14. See *Nebbia v. New York.*

15. Janice Rogers Brown, *Hein Hettinga* concurrence, note 13.

16. See Adkins v. Children's Hospital; same v. Willie Lyons, 261 U.S. 525 (1923).

17. Lochner v. New York, 98 U.S. 45 (1905). Quite recently Chief Justice Roberts was willing to join the flash mob of jurists ever ready to denounce *Lochner* as an embarrassment for the Court. And in the same sweep he commended West Coast Hotel Company v. Parrish, et ux., 300 U.S. 379 (1937), the case in which the Supreme Court, turning now to sustaining the New Deal, overruled Sutherland's classic opinion in the *Adkins* case. See Roberts's dissent in Obergefell v. Hodges, 576 U.S. 644 (2015).

18. *Adkins*, at 557, note 16.

19. Ibid., at 558.

20. Edwards v. California, 314 U.S. 160 (1941), at 176, 184–85.

21. Bowen v. American Hospital Assn., 476 U.S. 610 (1986). For a more detailed examination of this case, see Hadley Arkes, *Beyond the Constitution* (Princeton, New Jersey: Princeton University Press, 1990), chapter 9, especially 232–44.

22. See United States v. University Hospital, 729 F.2d 144 (1984), at 162.

23. Ibid.

24. See Arkes, *Beyond the Constitution.*

25. See Arkes, "Antijural Jurisprudence," in *Natural Rights & the Right to Choose* (Cambridge: Cambridge University Press, 2002), 112–46.

26. Gilbert Ryle, *The Concept of Mind* (Chicago: University of Chicago Press, 2002), originally published in London and New York, 1949.

Chapter 4: On Aquinas and That Other First Principle of Moral Judgment

1. Thomas Reid, *Essays on the Active Powers of the Human Mind* (Cambridge, Massachusetts: MIT Press, 1969), 48, originally published in 1788. And later: "If the obedience be impossible; if the transgression be necessary; it is self-evident that there can be no moral obligation to what is impossible, that there can be no crime in yielding to necessity; and that there can be no justice in punishing a person for what it was not in his power to avoid. These are first principles in morals, and to every unprejudiced mind, as self-evident as the axioms of mathematics. The whole of moral science must stand or fall with them" (296).

2. Thomas Aquinas, *Summa Theologica*, I-II 94.2, in *The Writings of Saint Thomas Aquinas*, vol. 2, ed. Anton C. Pegis (New York: Random House, 1945), 774–75.

3. "In contradistinction to natural laws, these laws of freedom are called moral laws." Immanuel Kant, *The Metaphysical Elements of Justice* (Indianapolis: Bobbs-Merrill, 1965), 42, originally published in 1797. In the *Groundwork for the Metaphysics of Morals* Kant says that "the question, 'How is a categorical imperative possible?'... can be answered so far as we can supply the sole presupposition under which it is possible—namely the Idea of freedom." Immanuel Kant, *Groundwork for the Metaphysics of Morals*, trans. H. J. Paton (New York: Harper & Row, 1964), 129, originally published in 1785.

   In that vein Kant wrote of those "two standpoints" from which we may view ourselves: From one standpoint, we are in the "sensible world," the world governed by the laws of nature—if we fall, we fall down; if we are struck in the face, we feel pain; if we eat something monstrous, we get a gastrointestinal reaction. But from the other standpoint, we are not in the world of "determinism" but of "freedom," the freedom to exert our own will and make our own choices. And that, he said, was the "intelligible world," where we have access to reasons in forming our judgments. Kant expressed the matter in this way: "Man can consider himself first—so far as he belongs to the sensible world—to be under the laws of nature (heteronomy); and secondly—so far as he belongs to the intelligible world—to be under laws which, being independent of nature, are not empirical but have their ground in reason alone.

   "As a rational being, and consequently as belonging to the intelligible world, man can never conceive of the causality of his own will except under the idea of freedom; for to be independent of determinism by causes in the sensible world (and this is what reason must always attribute to itself) is to be free." Ibid., 120.

In short, moral judgment arises only in the domain of freedom, where people have the power to will their own acts and access to the laws of reason in judging those acts.

4. Reid, *Essays on the Active Powers*, 361, note 1.

5. Aristotle: "Every polis is a species of association, and...all associations are constituted for the purpose of attaining some good, for all men do all of their acts for the purpose of attaining some good." *Politics* 1252a.

   And Aquinas: "In those things which clearly act for an end we declare the act to be that towards which the movement of the agent tends.... This may be seen in the physician who aims at health, and in a man who runs towards an appointed goal. Nor does it matter, as to this whether that which tends to an end be endowed with knowledge or not; for just as the target is the end of the archer, so is it the end of the arrow's flight. Now the movement of every agent tends to something determinate since it is not from any force that any action proceeds, but heating proceeds from heat and cooling from cold; and therefore actions are differentiated by their active principles." *Summa Contra Gentiles*, book 3, chapter 2.

6. John Stuart Mill, *Utilitarianism*, chapter 5.

7. Hearings before the Subcommittee on the Constitution, Committee on the Judiciary, United States Senate, 99th Congress, Sess. 1 (Medical Evidence Concerning Fetal Pain), May 21, 1985, p. 38.

8. Ibid.

9. Abraham Lincoln, debate with Stephen Douglas in Quincy, Illinois, October 13, 1858, in *Collected Works of Abraham Lincoln*, vol. 3, ed. Roy P. Basler (New Brunswick, New Jersey: Rutgers University Press, 1953), 256–57.

10. From Douglas's speech in his last debate with Lincoln:

> You will find in a recent speech delivered by that able and eloquent statesman, Hon. Jefferson Davis, at Bangor, Maine, that he took the same view of this subject that I did in my Freeport speech. He there said:
>
> If the inhabitants of any territory should refuse to enact such laws and police regulations as would give security to their property or to his, it would be rendered more or less valueless in proportion to the difficulties of holding it without such protection. In the case of property in the labor of man, or what is usually called slave property, the insecurity would be so great that the owner could not ordinarily retain it. Therefore, though the right would remain,

the remedy being withheld, it would follow that the owner would be practically debarred, by the circumstances of the case, from taking slave property into a territory where the sense of the inhabitants was opposed to its introduction. So much for the oft repeated fallacy of forcing slavery upon any community.

Stephen Douglas, debate with Abraham Lincoln in Alton, Illinois, October 15, 1858, in *Collected Works of Abraham Lincoln*, vol. 3, ed. Roy P. Basler (New Brunswick, New Jersey: Rutgers University Press, 1953), 296.

11. Abraham Lincoln, debate with Stephen Douglas in Alton, Illinois, October 15, 1858, in *Collected Works of Abraham Lincoln*, vol. 3, ed. Roy P. Basler (New Brunswick, New Jersey: Rutgers University Press, 1953), 317.

12. Ibid., 318.

13. Abraham Lincoln, speeches in Columbus and Cincinnati, Ohio, September 16 and 17, 1859, in *Collected Works of Abraham Lincoln*, vol. 3, ed. Roy P. Basler (New Brunswick, New Jersey: Rutgers University Press, 1953), 430–31.

14. Obergefell v. Hodges, 576 U.S. 644 (2015); Hurley v. Irish-American Gay, Lesbian and Bisexual Group of Boston, Etc., 515 U.S. 557 (1995).

15. *Obergefell v. Hodges*; West Virginia State Board of Education v. Barnette, 319 U.S. 624 (1943).

16. See Scalia's concurrence in Barnes v. Glen Theatre, Inc., 501 U.S. 560 (1991), at 576, drawing on an earlier case in which "nude sunbathers challenging public indecency law claimed their 'message' was that nudity is not indecent."

17. Katzenbach v. McClung, 379 U.S. 294 (1965).

18. Loving v. Virginia, 388 U.S. 1 (1967).

19. Abraham Lincoln, speech at Cooper Institute, New York, February 27, 1860, in *Collected Works of Abraham Lincoln*, vol. 3, ed. Roy P. Basler (New Brunswick, New Jersey: Rutgers University Press, 1953), 547–48, note 9.

20. "Let's take a case a little bit more like ours, and—and it doesn't involve words, but just a cake. It is Red Cross, and the baker serves someone who wants a red cross to celebrate the anniversary of a great humanitarian organization. Next person comes in and wants the same red cross to celebrate the KKK. Does the baker have to sell to the second customer? And if not, why not?" Neil Gorsuch, oral argument in Masterpiece Cakeshop, Ltd., et al., Petitioners v. Colorado Civil Rights Commission, et al., 584 U.S. ___ (2018), December 5, 2017, 84.

21. "If someone came in and said, I want a cake...to celebrate our wedding anniversary, and I want it to say November 9, the best day in history, okay, sells them a cake. Somebody else comes in, wants exactly the same words on the cake, he says: Oh, is this your anniversary? He says: No, we're going to have a

party to celebrate Kristallnacht. He would have to do that?" Samuel Alito, oral argument in *Masterpiece Cakeshop v. Colorado Civil Rights Commission*, December 5, 2017, 68.

22. Lincoln, speech at Cooper Institute, 549, note 9.
23. Ibid., 547–48.

Chapter 5: Are There Natural Rights?

1. As Wilson put it, the object was not to "acquire new rights by a human establishment," but rather "to acquire a new security for the possession or the recovery of those rights, to the enjoyment or acquisition of which we were previously entitled by the immediate gift, or by the unerring law, of our all-wise and all beneficent Creator." James Wilson, "Of the Natural Rights of Individuals," in *The Works of James Wilson*, ed. Robert Green McCloskey (Cambridge, Massachusetts: Harvard University Press, 1967), no. 2, 585, originally published in 1804.
2. Cited in ibid., 587.
3. Ibid.
4. Abraham Lincoln, sixth debate with Stephen Douglas, at Quincy, Illinois, October 13, 1858, in *The Collected Works of Abraham Lincoln*, vol. 3, ed. Roy P. Basler (New Brunswick, New Jersey: Rutgers University Press, 1953), 245, 257.
5. Alexander Hamilton, *Federalist* no. 84.
6. I gave this argument a chance to breathe in Hadley Arkes, *Beyond the Constitution* (Princeton, New Jersey: Princeton University Press, 1990), chapter 4: "On the Dangers of a Bill of Rights: Restating the Federalist Argument."
7. See Sedgwick's telling remarks in *Annals of Congress*, 1st Congress, vol. 1 (August 15, 1789), 731.
8. Abraham Lincoln, fragment, in *The Collected Works of Abraham Lincoln*, vol. 4, ed. Roy P. Basler (New Brunswick, New Jersey: Rutgers University Press), 169, note 4. This was a fragment that Lincoln wrote for himself on the Constitution, the Union, and the Declaration in January 1861, before he was inaugurated.
9. Abraham Lincoln, speech at Cooper Institute, New York, February 27, 1860, in *The Collected Works of Abraham Lincoln*, vol. 3, ed. Roy P. Basler (New Brunswick, New Jersey: Rutgers University Press, 1953), 547–48, 541.
10. Immanuel Kant, *Lectures in Ethics*, trans. Louis Infield (New York: Harper & Row, 1963), 228.
11. See my own treatment of this issue, cast in the larger context of the properties of categorical moral truths: Hadley Arkes, *First Things: An Inquiry into the First*

Principles of Morals and Justice (Princeton, New Jersey: Princeton University Press, 1986), 103–15.

12. See John Marshall, Address on the Constitutionality of the Alien and Sedition Acts, December 1798, in *The Political Thought of American Statesmen*, ed. Richard G. Frisch and Morton J. Stevens (Itasca, Illinois: Peacock Publishers, 1973), 99–116.

13. See Anontin Scalia in District of Columbia v. Heller, 554 U.S. 570 (2008): "Like most rights, the right secured by the Second Amendment is not unlimited. From Blackstone through the 19th-century cases, commentators and courts routinely explained that the right was not a right to keep and carry any weapon whatsoever in any manner whatsoever and for whatever purpose. See, e.g., *Sheldon*, in 5 Blume 346; Rawle 123; Pomeroy 152–153; Abbott 333. For example, the majority of the 19th-century courts to consider the question held that prohibitions on carrying concealed weapons were lawful under the Second Amendment or state analogues. See, e.g., *State* v. *Chandler*, 5 La. Ann., at 489–490; *Nunn* v. *State*, 1 Ga., at 251; see generally 2 Kent *340, n. 2; *The American Students' Blackstone* 84, n. 11 (G. Chase ed. 1884). Although we do not undertake an exhaustive historical analysis today of the full scope of the Second Amendment, nothing in our opinion should be taken to cast doubt on longstanding prohibitions on the possession of firearms by felons and the mentally ill, or laws forbidding the carrying of firearms in sensitive places such as schools and government buildings, or laws imposing conditions and qualifications on the commercial sale of arms."

14. See Daniel Robinson, *Toward a Science of Human Nature: Essay on the Psychologies of Mill, Hegel, Wundt, and James* (New York: Columbia University Press, 1982), 93.

15. See Arkes, *First Things*, 165, note 11 and passim.

16. William Blackstone, *Commentaries on the Laws of England* (Chicago: University of Chicago Press, 1979), book 4, chapter 5, 66–67, originally published in 1769.

17. Abraham Lincoln, in last debate with Stephen Douglas in Alton, Illinois, October 15, 1858, in *The Collected Works of Abraham Lincoln*, vol. 3, ed. Roy P. Basler (New Brunswick, New Jersey: Rutgers University Press, 1953), 301, note 4.

18. See John Locke, *Second Treatise on Civil Government*, chapter 4 ("Slavery") and chapter 5 ("Property"), paragraphs 22–5l.

Chapter 6: On Civil Rights: Theories in Search of a Principle

1. This argument on the wrong in principle of racial discrimination was first adumbrated in my essay "Civility and the Restriction of Speech: Rediscovering the Defamation of Groups" in *Supreme Court Review 1974*, ed. Philip B. Kurland (Chicago: University of Chicago Press, 1974). But the argument was drawn out more fully in my *The Philosopher in the City* (Princeton, New Jersey: Princeton University Press, 1981), 47–50, and it has since threaded through my other works—most notably in *First Things: An Inquiry into the First Principles of Morals and Justice* (Princeton, New Jersey: Princeton University Press, 1986), 97–99.

2. Beauharnais v. Illinois, 343 U.S. 250 (1952).

3. Quoted in Arkes, "Civility and the Restriction of Speech," 253.

4. Quoted in *Beauharnais v. Illinois*, 300–301. Jackson also offered a review of the laws on criminal libel, still holding on in the states and still supported (though with eroding conviction in the Supreme Court) with Jackson's rationale: Local governments are closer to the scene of the damages done to reputations and to the injuries wrought by inciting racial hatreds. Those local governments have the first responsibility in dealing with the damage and meting out punishments. Jackson argued that the federal courts should cede a large measure of deference to the authorities who are, as we might say today, the "first responders." In this vein, see Jackson's dissent in Terminiello v. City of Chicago, 337 U.S. 1 (1949), at 34–35.

5. Brown v. Board of Education, 347 U.S. 483 (1954).

6. "To separate [children in grade schools and high schools, children of] similar age and qualifications solely because of their race generates a feeling of inferiority as to their status in the community that may affect their hearts and minds in a way unlikely ever to be undone. The effect of this separation on their educational opportunities was well stated by a finding in the Kansas case by a court which nevertheless felt compelled to rule against the Negro plaintiffs: 'Segregation of white and colored children in public schools has a detrimental effect upon the colored children. The impact is greater when it has the sanction of the law, for the policy of separating the races is usually interpreted as denoting the inferiority of the negro group. A sense of inferiority affects the motivation of a child to learn. Segregation with the sanction of law, therefore, has a tendency to [retard] the educational and mental development of negro children and to deprive them of some of the benefits they would receive in a racial[ly] integrated school system.'" *Brown v. Board of Education*, at 494.

7. Clark's study was cited, along with other studies, in footnote 11 to the Court's opinion in the *Brown* case. Kenneth Clark, "Effect of Prejudice and Discrimination on Personality Development," Mid-Century White House Conference on Children and Youth, 1950. For a treatment of the flaws and contradictions in this study, see Hadley Arkes, "The Problem of Kenneth Clark," in *Commentary*, November 1974, 37–46. For a fuller, more rounded analysis of the reasoning in *Brown*, see Richard Morgan, "Coming Clean about Brown," *City Journal*, Fall 1996. Michael Uhlmann offered his own skillful account of the difficulties encountered by the justices as they sought to work through the rationales that could finally explain and justify the judgment they were about to reach. See his "The Road Not Taken: Why the Court Should Have Listened to Robert Jackson," *Claremont Review of Books*, Summer 2004.

8. Palmer v. Thompson, 403 U.S. 217 (1971).

9. Loving v. Virginia, 388 U.S. 1 (1967), at 2.

10. See Arkes, *First Things*, 344–45.

11. See my treatment of this issue as part of the puzzle of "privacy" in the law in ibid., chapter 15, "Privacy and the Reach of the Law."

12. *Loving v. Virginia.*

13. See Justice Stewart's concurring opinion in Zablocki v. Redhail, 434 U.S. 374 (1978), at 392.

14. United States v. Windsor, 570 U.S. 744 (2013), holding invalid the Defense of Marriage Act of 1996, and Obergefell v. Hodges, 576 U.S. 644 (2015), holding invalid then the laws of marriage that confine marriage to one man and one woman.

15. Plessy v. Ferguson, 163 U.S. 537 (1896).

16. *Loving v. Virginia*, at 11, note 8.

17. *Plessy v. Ferguson*, at 559.

18. Ibid., 560.

19. Ibid., 561.

20. See Akhil Amar, *America's Unwritten Constitution* (New York: Basic Books, 2012), 213. See also Hadley Arkes, *Constitutional Illusions & Anchoring Truths* (Cambridge, Massachusetts: Cambridge University Press, 2010), chapter 7, "And Yet... a Good Word on Behalf of the Legal Positivists," on the case of Bob Jones University.

21. As a notable case in point, see McLaurin v. Oklahoma State Regents, 339 U.S. 637 (1950).

22. Katzenbach v. McClung, 379 U.S. 294 (1964).

23. Ibid.

24. Missouri ex rel. Gaines v. Canada, 305 U.S. 337 (1938).

25. From the interview of Cecil Partee, in Milton Rakove, *We Don't Want Nobody Nobody Sent* (Bloomington, Indiana: Indiana University Press), 156.

26. See *Plessy v. Ferguson,* at 549, note 15.

27. Here I steal from myself, and with thanks from friends at Cambridge University Press borrow from my book *Constitutional Illusions and Anchoring Truths: The Touchstone of Natural Law* (2010), 65–68.

28. Regents of the University of California v. Bakke, 438 U.S. 265 (1978).

29. Ibid., notes 6 and 7 in Powell's opinion.

30. Ibid., at 296–97.

31. "Race Relations," Gallup, https://news.gallup.com/poll/1687/race-relations.aspx; see also Karlyn Bowman and Eleanor O'Neil, "Public Opinion on Affirmative Action," American Enterprise Institute, June 23, 2016, https://www.aei.org/research-products/report/public-opinion-on-affirmative-action/; for an older piece, see Stuart Taylor, "Do African-Americans Really Want Affirmative Action?" *The Atlantic*, December 2002. Taylor reported on a survey sponsored by the *Washington Post*, the Kaiser Family Foundation, and Harvard University in the spring of 2001. The question was whether "race or ethnicity should be a factor when deciding who is hired, promoted, or admitted to college, or that hiring, promotions, and college admissions should be based strictly on merit and qualifications other than race or ethnicity?" Overall, only 5 percent of the sample expressed the view that "race or ethnicity should be a factor." The surprising finding was that, of the 323 African Americans in the sample, only 12 percent said that "race or ethnicity should be a factor," and 86 percent held to the view that admissions and hiring should be based strictly on merit and qualifications other than race or ethnicity. As Taylor summed it up, "By a ratio of 7-to-1, black respondents in this poll rejected racial preferences. The ratio was 12-to-1 among both Hispanic and Asian respondents."

32. Abraham Lincoln, a fragment written around August 1858, in *The Collected Works of Abraham Lincoln*, vol. 2, ed. Roy P. Basler (New Brunswick, New Jersey: Rutgers University Press, 1953), 532.

33. See Parents Involved in Community Schools v. Seattle School District, 426 F.3d 1162 (2005), at 1222. And for the Supreme Court, see Parents Involved in Community Schools v. Seattle School District No. 1; Meredith v. Jefferson County Board of Education, 551 U.S. 701 (2007). Roberts offered a version of Judge Bea's concluding line with only the slightest changes: "The way to stop discrimination on the basis of race is to stop discriminating on the basis of race."

Chapter 7: Speech and the Erosion of Relativism

1. FCC v. Fox Television Stations, Inc., 567 U.S. 239 (2012).
2. Ibid., at 2314.
3. Chaplinsky v. New Hampshire, 315 U.S. 568 (1942).
4. Cohen v. California, 403 U.S. 15 (1971).
5. Rosenfeld v. New Jersey, 408 U.S. 901 (1972).
6. See Burger's opinion in Paris Adult Theatre v. Slaton, 413 U.S. 49 (1973), at 67. Burger offered the possibility of a "'live' performance of a man and woman locked in a sexual embrace at high noon in Times Square," and remarked that the performance would not be "protected by the Constitution [even if the two people] simultaneously engage in a valid political dialogue."
7. *Chaplinsky*, at 569.
8. *Cohen*, at 25.
9. Ibid., at 24.
10. See G. E. Moore, "The Objectivity of Moral Judgment," chapter 3 in *Ethics* (Ulan Press, 2012), originally published in 1912. See Thomas Reid, *Essays on the Active Powers of the Human Mind* (Cambridge, Massachusetts: MIT Press, 1969), 442, originally published in 1788. And see chapter 2, note 15 above.
11. *Cohen*, at 18.
12. Aristotle, *Politics*, 1253a.
13. Thomas Aquinas, *Summa Theologica*, I-II 96.2, *Basic Writings of Saint Thomas Aquinas*, vol. 2, ed. Anton C. Pegis (New York: Random House, 1945) 792–93.
14. See Hill et al. v. Colorado et al., 530 U.S. 703 (2000).
15. See the incomparable Judge Sprizzo in United States v. Lynch, 952 F. Supp. 167 (1997).
16. Matal v. Tam, 528 U.S. ____ (2017), at 1.
17. Leo Strauss, *Natural Right and History* (Chicago: University of Chicago Press, 1953), 2.
18. Terminiello v. Chicago, 337 U.S. 1 (1949).
19. Ibid., at 2.
20. Ibid., at 3–4.
21. Ibid., at 6.
22. R.A.V. v. City of St. Paul, Minnesota, 505 U.S. 377 (1992).
23. *Terminiello*, at 16.
24. Ibid.
25. Ibid., at 17–18, 20.
26. Ibid., at 22.
27. Ibid., at 23–24.

28. Ibid., at 26.
29. Gitlow v. New York, 268 U.S. 652 (1925).
30. Schenck v. United States, 249 U.S. 47 (1919).
31. See Jackson's adoption of this argument in his dissent in *Terminiello*, at 26.
32. *Terminiello*, at 15.
33. *R.A.V. v. City of St. Paul*, at 379.
34. Ibid., at 380.
35. Ibid., at 393.
36. Ibid., at 385.
37. Ibid., at 396.
38. Ibid., at 391.
39. Ibid., at 422.
40. Ibid., at 415.
41. Justice White explained: "Our fighting words cases have made clear, however, that such generalized reactions are not sufficient to strip expression of its constitutional protection. The mere fact that expressive activity causes hurt feelings, offense, or resentment does not render the expression unprotected." Ibid., at 414.
42. *Chaplinsky*, at 572.
43. Among other choice items were these: "Don't Pray for the USA," "Thank God for IEDs," "Pope in Hell," "Priests Rape Boys," "God Hates Fags," "You're Going to Hell," and "God Hates You." See Snyder v. Phelps, 562 U.S. 443 (2011). Eight of the nine justices were content to fold these outbursts into the class of speech protected by the First Amendment. But see Justice Alito's argument, holding on alone in dissent.

Chapter 8: The Conservatives and the Lure of Defensive Relativism: Spiraling Down

1. Matal v. Tam, 582 U.S. ___ (2017).
2. Ibid., at 1.
3. Snyder v. Phelps, 562 U.S. 443 (2011).
4. Ibid., at 1.
5. See Hadley Arkes, "Marching through Skokie," *National Review*, May 12, 1978, 588ff.
6. Abraham Lincoln, Letter to Henry Peirce and Others, April 6, 1859, in *The Collected Works of Abraham Lincoln*, vol. 3, ed. Roy P. Basler (Newark, New Jersey: Rutgers University Press, 1953), 376.

7. Masterpiece Cakeshop, Ltd., v. Colorado Civil Rights Commission, 584 U.S. ___ (2018), concurring opinion by Justice Gorsuch joined by Justice Alito, 7.
8. Iancu v. Brunetti, 588 U.S ___ (2019).
9. Chisholm v. Georgia, 2 U.S. 419 (1793).
10. Thomas Reid, *Essays on the Active Powers of the Human Mind* (Cambridge, Massachusetts: MIT Press, 1969), 4–5, originally published in 1813–1815. Immanuel Kant pointed out that the concept of number is one of those things grasped a priori by any functional person, wherever that person may be found. I once suggested the example of a British ship landing at a South Sea Island in the eighteenth century, with three sailors going ashore to encounter men from a culture they never knew. Without knowing anything about the conventions of that local culture, do we think that the natives would understand the difference between one strange man standing there as opposed to *three*? Would we not suppose, as Kant would say, that the ordinary human creature would grasp the distinctions of one, many, and all—singularity, plurality, totality?
11. *Iancu*, at 1, 6, and 10.
12. Ibid., at 3.
13. Ibid, at 7.
14. Ibid., at 5–6.
15. Ibid., at 6.
16. Ibid., at 1.
17. Ibid., at 7–8.
18. See John Finnis, *Natural Law and Natural Rights* (Oxford: Clarendon Press, 1980), 74. The line was set down by John Finnis, but it was later sung by Robert George.

Chapter 9: Recasting Religious Freedom
1. See Eisenstadt v. Baird, 405 U.S. 438 (1972).
2. See Burwell v. Hobby Lobby Stores, Inc., 573 U.S. 682 (2014).
3. Bishop William Lori, "Our First, Most Cherished Liberty: A Statement on Religious Liberty by the United States Conference of Catholic Bishops Ad Hoc Committee for Religious Liberty," March 2012. Bishop Lori's argument took on special force in these passages:
   "It is a sobering thing to contemplate our government enacting an unjust law. An unjust law cannot be obeyed. In the face of an unjust law, *an accommodation is not to be sought*, especially by resorting to equivocal words and deceptive practices. If we face today the prospect of unjust laws, then Catholics in America, in solidarity with our fellow citizens, must have the courage not to obey them.

No American desires this. No Catholic welcomes it. But if it should fall upon us, we must discharge it as a duty of citizenship and an obligation of faith....

"An unjust law is 'no law at all.' It cannot be obeyed, and therefore one does not seek relief from it, but rather its repeal.

"The Christian church *does not ask for special treatment*, simply the rights of religious freedom for all citizens. Rev. King also explained that the church is neither the master nor the servant of the state, but its conscience, guide, and critic [emphasis added]."

I would record a special thanks to Thomas Sarrouf, my devoted and indefatigable aide in research, who managed to find these papers containing the passages I remembered, even as they continued to elude me.

4. John Paul II, *Veritatis Splendor*, Vatican, August 6, 1993, section 32.
5. John Courtney Murray, *We Hold These Truths* (Lanham, Maryland: Rowman and Littlefield, 2005), 63–64, originally published in 1960 by Sheed and Ward.
6. The Judiciary Committee of the Senate, in 1985, offered a survey of the leading texts on embryology and gynecology, and years later Ryan Anderson of the Witherspoon Institute would do an updating containing items of this kind:

    > Fertilization is a sequence of events that begins with the contact of a *sperm* (spermatozoon) with a *secondary oocyte* (ovum) and ends with the fusion of their *pronuclei* (the haploid nuclei of the sperm and ovum) and the mingling of their chromosomes to form a new cell. This fertilized ovum, known as a *zygote*, is a large diploid cell that is the beginning, or *primordium, of a human being*. Keith L. Moore, *Essentials of Human Embryology*....
    >
    > The development of a human being begins with fertilization, a process by which two highly specialized cells, the *spermatozoon* from the male and the oocyte from the female, unite to give rise to a new organism, the *zygote*. Jan Langman, *Medical Embryology*, 3rd edition....
    >
    > Zygote. This cell, formed by the union of an ovum and a sperm...represents the *beginning of a human being*. The common expression "fertilized ovum" refers to the zygote. Keith L. Moore and T. V. N. Persaud, *Before We Are Born: Essentials of Embryology and Birth Defects*, 4th edition.

    [Emphasis in the original.] Ryan Anderson, "Life Begins at Fertilization," Princeton University, https://www.princeton.edu/~prolife/articles/embryoquotes2.html.

7. See, for example, Reynolds v. United States, 98 U.S. 145 (1878), at 163, quoting James Madison, "Memorial and Remonstrance against Religious Assessments," 1785.

8. Brackets in the original. See Hadley Arkes, *First Things: An Inquiry into the First Principles of Morals and Justice* (Princeton, New Jersey: Princeton University Press, 1986), 193.

9. Welsh v. United States, 398 U.S. 333 (1970); Arkes, *First Things,* 194n7.

10. Utah was admitted to the Union in 1896, and by 1904 the Church of Jesus Christ of Latter-day Saints barred new polygamous marriages. In a policy of civic prudence, the plural marriages then in place would not be disturbed. The partners in those marriages would gradually be taken away with time.

11. See Justin Dyer, "Reason, Revelation, and the Law of Nature in James Wilson's Lectures on Law," *American Political Thought* 9, no. 2 (Spring 2020): 26484.

12. John Paul II, *Encyclical Letter: Fides et Ratio of the Supreme Pontiff John Paul II to the Bishops of the Catholic Church on the Relationship between Faith and Reason,* Vatican, September 14, 1998.

13. Ibid., chapter 4, section 36.

14. Ibid.

15. Ibid., chapter 4, section 38.

16. Ibid., chapter 4, section 48.

17. Ibid., chapter 5, section 53.

18. Ibid., chapter 6, section 76.

19. Michael Novak, *On Two Wings: Humble Faith and Common Sense at the American Founding* (San Francisco: Encounter Books, 2002).

20. Ellis Sandoz, ed., *Political Sermons of the American Founding Era, 1730–1805,* rev. ed., vol. 1 (Indianapolis: Liberty Fund, 1998), 628–56, at 637.

21. *Fides et Ratio,* chapter 3, section 35.

22. James V. Schall, *At the Limits of Political Philosophy: From "Brilliant Errors" to Things of Uncommon Importance* (Washington, D.C.: Catholic University of America Press, 1996), 191.

23. Genesis 18:25, in *The Five Books of Moses: A Translation with Commentary,* trans. Robert Alter (New York: W. W. Norton, 2008), 89.

24. Masterpiece Cakeshop, Ltd. v. Colorado Civil Rights Commission, 584 U.S. _____ (2018), concurring opinion by Justice Gorsuch, joined by Justice Alito, at 7.

25. See Abraham Lincoln, in the majestic Message to Congress in Special Session on July 4, 1861, in *The Collected Works of Abraham Lincoln,* vol. 4, ed. Roy P. Basler (New Brunswick, New Jersey: Rutgers University Press, 1953), 434–35.

26. Madison, "Memorial and Remonstrance."

27. Harry V. Jaffa, "The Decline and Fall of the American Idea," in *The Rediscovery of America: Essays by Harry Jaffa on the New Birth of Politics*, ed. Edward J. Erler and Ken Masugi (Lanham, Maryland: Rowman and Littlefield, 2019), 233.

28. See Richard Garnett, letter to *First Things*, October 2019, 3–4, and my response, 5–7.

29. Jaffa, "Decline and Fall of the American Idea," 187.

30. Town of Greece v. Galloway, 572 U.S. 565 (2014).

31. Gunnar Gundersen, "God and Conscience: Is There an Objective Limit to Religious Freedom?" (summer fellowship faculty lecture and notes, James Wilson Institute for Natural Rights & the American Founding, Washington, D.C., August 3, 2018).

32. Winston Churchill caught this sense of the matter, as only a practiced political man could, in a commentary on Edmund Burke:

    "A Statesman in contact with the moving current of events and anxious to keep the ship on an even keel and steer a steady course may lean all his weight now on one side and now on the other. His arguments in each case when contrasted can be shown to be not only very different in character, but contradictory in spirit and opposite in direction: yet his object will throughout have remained the same; his resolves, his wishes, his outlook may have been unchanged; his methods may be verbally irreconcilable. We cannot call this inconsistency. In fact it may be claimed to be the truest consistency. The only way a man can remain consistent amid changing circumstances is to change with them while preserving the same dominating purpose."

    Winston Churchill, "Consistency in Politics," in *Thoughts and Adventures* (London: Butterworth, 1932), 39, cited by Harry Jaffa in his magisterial *A New Birth of Freedom: Abraham Lincoln and the Coming of the Civil War* (Oxford: Rowman and Littlefield, 2000), 125.

33. Fred Smith, "US Principles at Stake as Economy Keeps on Growing," *Financial Times*, May 17, 2012, https://www.ft.com/content/017c512e-9f62-11e1-a455-00144feabdco.

34. Obergefell v. Hodges, et al., 576 U.S. 644 (2015), brief of *amicus curiae* of Dr. Paul R. McHugh, et al., brief of *amicus curiae*, with Professor Gerard Bradley as Counsel of Record, April 3, 2015. McHugh relied here on the findings in Lisa Diamond, "Female Bisexuality from Adolescence to Adulthood Results from a 10-year Longitudinal Study," *Development Psychology* 44, no. 1 (February 2008): 5–14.

35. For one of the earliest statements on this point, see Justice Samuel Chase in Calder v. Bull, 3 U.S. 386 (1798), at 388.

36. Hepburn v. Griswold, 75 U.S. 603 (1869), 624.

37. Gilardi v. U.S. Department of Health and Human Services (HHS), No. 13-5069 (D.C. Cir. 2013), at 17–18.

38. Ibid., at 26.

39. Cyril Korte v. Sebelius, No. 12-3841 (7th Cir., 2013); Grote v. Sebelius, 708 F.3d 850 (7th Cir., 2013), at 63.

40. Michaiah Bilger, "Poll Shows Majority Support Banning Abortions When Unborn Baby's Heart Starts Beating," LifeNews, August 16, 2021, https://www.lifenews.com/2021/08/16/poll-shows-majority-support-banning-abortions-when-an-unborn-babys-heart-starts-beating/.

41. Leo XIII, *Libertas: Encyclical of Pope Leo XIII on the Nature of Human Liberty*, Vatican, June 20, 1888, https://www.vatican.va/content/leo-xiii/en/encyclicals/documents/hf_l-xiii_enc_20061888_libertas.html.

42. "It is not impossible, in the sense of self-contradictory, that we should see cows fasting from grass every Friday or going on their knees as in the old legend about Christmas Eve." See G. K. Chesterton, *The Everlasting Man* (1925), available at http://www.gkc.org.uk/gkc/books/everlasting_man.pdf. I want to thank my indispensable aide in research, Sean Tehan, who has cultivated an interest in Chesterton even as an undergraduate. He was able to track down the source long after I had forgotten just where, in G.K.C.'s vast and rollicking work, I had first read it.

43. We are living, as she wrote, "off the religious capital of a previous generation," and "that capital is being perilously depleted." Gertrude Himmelfarb, *One Nation, Two Cultures: A Searching Examination of American Society in the Aftermath of our Cultural Revolution* (New York: Alfred Knopf, 1999), 146. In an earlier lecture at the American Enterprise Institute, in 1995, she offered this reflection as an historian: "In retrospect, one might say that Victorian England was living off the moral capital of religion, and that post-Victorian England, well into the twentieth century, was living off the capital of a secularized morality. Perhaps what we are now witnessing is the moral bankruptcy that comes with the depletion of both the religious and the secular capital." Gertrude Himmelfarb, "From Victorian Virtues to Modern Values," American Enterprise Institute, February 13, 1995, https://www.aei.org/events/from-victorian-virtues-to-modern-values/.

44. Himmelfarb recalled that "when Darwin was asked what he himself believed to be the implications of his theory for religion and morality, he said that the idea of God was 'beyond the scope of man's intellect,' but that man's moral obligation remained what it had always been: to 'do his duty.'" She went on to say that "Leslie Stephen, after abandoning the effort to derive an ethic from Darwinism, finally confessed: 'I now believe in nothing, but I do not the less

believe in morality....I mean to live and die like a gentleman if possible.' Frederick Harrison, the archpriest of English Positivism and agnosticism, when asked by his son what a man should do if he fell in love and could not marry, replied indignantly: 'Do! Do what every gentleman does in such circumstances.' And when his son persisted in wanting to know why love was proper only in marriage, Harrison could barely contain himself: 'A loose man is a foul man. He is anti-social. He is a beast.... It is not a subject that decent men do discuss." Ellipses in original. Gertrude Himmelfarb, "The Victorian Ethos before and after Victoria," in *Victorian Minds* (Chicago: Ivan Dee, 1999), 290–91, originally published in 1952.

45. Abraham Lincoln, speech in Lewistown, Illinois, on August 17, 1858, in *The Collected Works of Abraham Lincoln*, vol. 2, ed. Roy P. Basler (New Brunswick, New Jersey: Rutgers University Press, 1953), 546.

46. Dred Scott v. Sandford, 60 U.S. 393 (1856), 550.

47. Hadley Arkes, *Natural Rights and the Right to Choose* (New York and Cambridge: Cambridge University Press, 2002), 1.

48. Locke v. Davey, 540 U.S. 712 (2004).

49. Ibid, at 2; see also ibid., at 6.

50. Trinity Lutheran Church of Columbia, Inc. v. Comer, 582 U.S. ____ (2017).

51. Ibid., John Roberts's opinion for the Court, at 11, 15.

52. At the time of this writing the Supreme Court has just extended the same rule in Carson v. Makin, 596 US. ____ (2022). The state of Maine made grants available to parents in school districts so small that they cannot sustain a high school of their own or readily contract with the high school of another district. Parents would be reimbursed in part as they sent their children to private schools. But because of the constitution of Maine, those grants would not be available to schools with a religious character. Chief Justice Roberts, writing for the Court, affirmed the reasoning that had finally taken hold in the case of *Trinity Lutheran Church v. Comer,* and he seemed to confirm a principle now becoming settled. But this time the liberal wing would not join. Justices Breyer and Kagan moved into dissent, along with Justice Sotomayor.

53. There has been a recent, encouraging move in another direction with Fulton v. City of Philadelphia, 593 U.S. ____ (2020). The Court took at least a first step in rescuing Catholic Social Services in Philadelphia, which was being denied a license and closed down in the enduring and sacred mission of finding parents for children because it would not place children with same-sex couples. The authorities preferred to shut down this valuable adoption service rather than

accept a policy that signaled an unwillingness to extend moral acceptance to the homosexual life.

54. Ronald Knox, "Reunion All Around" in *Essays in Satire* (New York: Kennikat Press, 1968), 75–76, originally published in 1928.

55. Ibid., 76.

Chapter 10: The Moral Turn in Jurisprudence

1. The Holy Bible, King James Version, 2 Samuel 12:1–7.

2. See Nixon v. Administrator of General Services, 433 U.S. 425 (1977), at 472 (Brennan), 491 (Blackmun), 493 (Powell), and 486 (Stevens).

3. John Locke, *Second Treatise on Civil Government: An Essay Concerning the True Original, Extent, and End of Civil Government*, section 143, in *Social Contract* (New York: Oxford University Press, 1962), 85.

4. For a fuller account of this connection, see Hadley Arkes, *Constitutional Illusions and Anchoring Truths: The Touchstone of the Natural Law* (Cambridge: Cambridge University Press, 2010), 18–19.

5. Montesquieu, *The Spirit of the Laws* (Berkeley, California: University of California Press, 1977), preface, originally published in 1748.

6. Jean-Jacques Rousseau, *The Social Contract*, ed. Sir Ernest Barker (London: Oxford University Press, 1960), book 2, chapter 6, 172–73, originally published in 1762.

7. Samuel Johnson, "Essay on Milton," in *Lives of the Poets*, originally published 1779–81.

8. See Wilson in Chisholm v. Georgia, 2 U.S. 419 (1793), at 458.

9. Paul Ramsey, "Reference Points in Deciding on Abortion," in *The Morality of Abortion*, ed. John Noonan (Cambridge, Massachusetts: Harvard University Press, 1970), 72–73.

10. Ibid., 67.

11. Roe v. Wade, 410 U.S. 113 (1973), Brief for the State of Texas, October 19, 1971, at 18 and passim.

12. See Robert P. George and Christopher Tollefsen, *Embryo: A Defense of Human Life* (New York: Doubleday, 2008), chapter 2, especially 38 and 50.

13. *Roe v. Wade*, Brief for the State of Texas, 19–20.

14. Kelly v. Gregory, 282 App. Div. 542, 125 N.Y.S. 2d 696, at 697. Quoted in ibid. This and other rich material can be found in that remarkable brief prepared by the lawyers defending the laws in Texas in *Roe v. Wade*. It is even more worth seeing now than it was then.

15. *Roe v. Wade*, Rehnquist's dissent at 173.

16. Doe v. Bolton, 410 U.S. 179 (1973), White's dissent at 221–22.
17. Ibid., at 222.
18. Ibid.
19. Ibid., at 221.
20. *Roe v. Wade*, at 174, quoting Justice Cardozo in Snyder v. Massachusetts, 291 U.S. 97 (1934), at 105, with a line Cardozo would accent again three years later in Palko v. Connecticut, 302 U.S. 319 (1937).
21. Oliver Wendell Holmes, "Montesquieu," in *Collected Legal Papers,* 258, cited by Walter Berns, *The First Amendment and the Future of American Democracy* (New York: Basic Books, 1976), 164.
22. Oliver Wendell Holmes to Harold Laski, March 4, 1920, in *Holmes-Laski Letters,* vol. 1, 249, cited in ibid., 167.
23. And marked by a "history" of abortion not only exposed later as quite fraudulent, but recognized as fraudulent at the time by one of the lawyers working to challenge the law in Texas. Young David Tunderman was a student at Yale Law School working with the legal team challenging the laws on abortion in Texas. He had become aware that there was something deeply flawed, to put it mildly, in the history of abortion in America served up by Cyril Means. In a memo to his team, he struck a style that would become familiar, accepting of the suppression of evidence that might get in the way of the hallowed cause:

> Where the important thing to do is to win the case no matter how, however, I suppose I agree with Means's technique: begin with a scholarly attempt at historical research; if it doesn't work out, fudge it as necessary; write a piece so long that others will read only your introduction and conclusion; then keep citing it until the courts begin picking it up. This preserves the guise of impartial scholarship while advancing the proper ideological goals.

    "Memo from David Tunderman to Roy Lucas...5 August 1971," cited by Justin Buckley Dyer in *Slavery, Abortion, and the Politics of Constitutional Meaning* (Cambridge: Cambridge University Press, 2013), 67.
24. I was not present at the dinner, but I have heard more than one account of the conversation from persons in—shall we say—the best position to recall what was said.
25. United States v. Vuitch, 402 U.S. 62 (1971).

Chapter 11: *After the Overruling of Roe: The Natural Law Moment*

1. Dobbs v. Women's Health Organization, 597 U.S. _____ (2022).

2. "Abortion," Gallup, January 9, 2022, https://perma.cc/DJ6A-M77K.

3. Micaiah Bilger, "Poll Shows 55% of Americans Support Heartbeat Bills Banning Abortions on Babies with Beating Hearts," LifeNews, May 15, 2019, https://www.lifenews.com/2019/05/15/poll-shows-55-of-americans-support-heartbeat-bills-banning-abortions-on-babies-with-beating-hearts/.

4. *Dobbs*, Justice Alito, opinion of the Court, at 3, quoting Justice White's dissent in Roe v. Wade, 410 U.S. 113 (1973), at 222.

5. *Dobbs*, Justice Alito, opinion of the Court, at 7.

6. Ibid., at 6–7.

7. Ibid., at 8.

8. Ibid., at 5.

9. Ibid, at 47.

10. Ibid., at 53.

11. Ibid., at 50. Here Alito was quoting from the plurality opinion in the famous *Webster* case, in 1989, when the Court seemed to be on the verge of overturning *Roe* and returning the issue of abortion to the political arena. See Webster v. Reproductive Health Services, 492 U.S. 490 (1989), at 519.

12. See Thornburgh v. American College of Obstetricians and Gynecologists, 476 U.S. 747 (1986), at 795.

13. *Dobbs*, Justice Alito, opinion of the Court, at 44.

14. Judge Clement Haynsworth in Floyd v. Anders, 440 F. Supp. 535, at 439 (D.S.C. 1977).

15. See Anders v. Floyd, 440 U.S. 445 (1979).

16. See Ann McElhinney and Phelim McAleer, *Gosnell: The Untold Story of America's Most Prolific Serial Killer* (Washington, D.C.,: Regnery Publishing, 2017), especially chapter 7.

17. The fuller story of the reasoning behind the bill and the steering of that bill through Congress is told in part as a memoir in my book, *Natural Rights and the Right to Choose* (New York and Cambridge: Cambridge University Press, 2002).

18. Cohens v. Virginia, 19 U.S. 264 (1821), at 384.

19. "Abortion, Roe v. Wade, and the Supreme Court: The Big Picture," *Wall Street Journal*, June 24, 2022.

20. See *Dobbs*, Justices Breyer, Sotomayor, and Kagan, dissenting, at 2.

21. *Dobbs*, Jutice Alito, opinion of the Court, at 38.

22. *Dobbs*, Justices Breyer, Sotomayor, and Kagan, dissenting, at 26.

23. See James Wilson, "Of the Natural Right of Individuals," in *The Works of James Wilson*, vol. 2 (Cambridge, Massachusetts: Harvard University Press, 1967), 585–91, originally published in 1804.

24. See Hadley Arkes, "On Overruling Roe," *First Things* (March 2022), 35–40.

25. Planned Parenthood of Southeastern Pennsylvania v. Casey, 505 U.S. 833 (1992), 982.

26. Roger Wertheimer, "Understanding the Abortion Argument," *Philosophy and Public Affairs* 1, no. 1 (Autumn 1971): 67–95, at 84.

27. Abraham Lincoln, Appeal to the Border States: Proclamation Revoking General Hunter's Order of Military Emancipation of May 9, 1862, in *The Collected Works of Abraham Lincoln*, vol. 5, ed. Roy P. Basler (New Brunswick, New Jersey: Rutgers University Press, 1953), 223.

28. *Dobbs*, Justice Alito, opinion of the Court, at 16–20.

29. Ibid., at 23–25.

30. Ibid., at 28.

31. *Dobbs*, Justices Breyer, Sotomayor, and Kagan, dissenting, at 14–15.

32. *Dobbs*, Justice Kavanaugh, concurring, at 1.

33. James Madison, *The Federalist*, no. 49.

34. John W. Davis, "Argument on Behalf of the Appellees in *Briggs v. Elliott*," DC State Library, December 7, 1953, https://dc.statelibrary.sc.gov/bitstream/handle/10827/32143/FED_SC_Argument_on_Behalf_BvE_1953.pdf?sequence=1&isAllowed=y, 17–18. *Briggs v. Elliott* was one of the companion cases brought together under *Brown v. Board of Education*.

35. First two brackets in original, third bracket mine. *Dobbs*, Justice Alito, opinion of the Court, at 69.

36. Ibid., at 6.

37. Ibid., at 70.

38. Thomas Cooley, *A Treatise on the Constitutional Limitations*, 2nd ed. (Boston: Little, Brown, 1871), 356–57, quoted in Stuart Banner, *The Decline of Natural Law: How America's Lawyers Once Used Natural Law and Why They Stopped* (New York: Oxford University Press, 2021), 206–7.

39. For a fuller account, see Hadley Arkes, *The Return of George Sutherland: Restoring a Jurisprudence of Natural Rights* (Princeton, New Jersey: Princeton University Press, 1994), 262–73. The case was Powell v. Alabama, 287 U.S. 45 (1933).

40. Stuart Banner, *The Decline of Natural Law* (Oxford: Oxford University Press, 2021), 206 and passim.

41. Palko v. Connecticut, 302 U.S. 319 (1937).

42. Ibid., at 325.

43. Ibid., at 327.

44. Ibid., at 326.

45. Griswold v. Connecticut, 381 U.S. 479 (1965).

46. Skinner v. Oklahoma ex. rel. Williamson, 316 U.S. 535 (1942).

47. Loving v. Virginia, 388 U.S. 1 (1967).

48. *Dobbs*, Justice Alito, opinion of the Court, at 32.

49. Ibid.

50. See *Skinner v. Oklahoma*.

51. *Congressional Globe: Containing the Debates and Proceedings of the First Session of the Thirty-Ninth Congress* (Washington, D.C.: Congressional Globe Office, 1866), part 1, at 322.

52. Richard Epstein, "Roe's Awkward Departure," Hoover Institution, May 9, 2022, https://www.hoover.org/research/roes-awkward-departure.

53. Joseph Lochner, Plaintiff in Error v. People of the State of New York, 198 U.S. 45 (1905).

54. Adkins v. Children's Hospital of D.C., 261 U.S. 525 (1923).

55. See Justice Brown in Plessy v. Ferguson, 163 U.S. 537 (1896), at 545–46.

56. Ibid., at 548.

57. *Griswold*, at 505.

58. Ibid, at 507. "There is no single one of the graphic and eloquent strictures and criticisms fired at the policy of this Connecticut law either by the Court's opinion or by those of my concurring Brethren to which I cannot subscribe— except their conclusion that the evil qualities they see in the law make it unconstitutional."

59. Ibid., at 520–25.

60. Epstein, "Roe's Awkward Departure."

61. *Dobbs*, Justice Kavanaugh, dissenting, at 2.

62. Ibid., at 1–2.

63. Abraham Lincoln, Speech at Peoria, Illinois, on October 16, 1854, in *The Collected Works of Abraham Lincoln*, vol. 2, ed. Roy P. Basler (New Brunswick, New Jersey: Rutgers University Press, 1953), 278.

64. See Harry V. Jaffa in his classic *Crisis of the House Divided: An Interpretation of the Issues in the Lincoln-Douglas Debates* (Garden City, New York: Doubleday, 1959), 348.

65. See Richard Hofstadter, *The American Political Tradition and the Men Who Made It* (New York: Vintage Books, 1955), 132, cited in Harry Jaffa, "The

Emancipation Proclamation," *Equality and Liberty* (Claremont, California: Claremont Institute, 1999), 141, originally published 1964.

66. *Dobbs*, Justice Alito, opinion of the Court, at 50.
67. Thomas Reid, *Essays on the Active Powers of the Human Mind* (Cambridge, Massachusetts: MIT Press, 1969), 474, originally published in 1788.
68. Ibid., 442.

Index